W9-AWI-429

Garden State, pp. 18-19, 149-151

Potato Champion Fries, pp. 9-10

Liba Falafel Sandwiches (& Fries), p. 147

High Noon Quesadillas, p. 241

MAXimus/MiniMUS, p. 161

MikeyD's Cheesesteak Sandwiches, p. 155

Fried Green Tomato Salad, p. 140

East Side King, p. 126

The
TRUCK FOOD
Cookbook

The TRUCK FOOD Cookbook

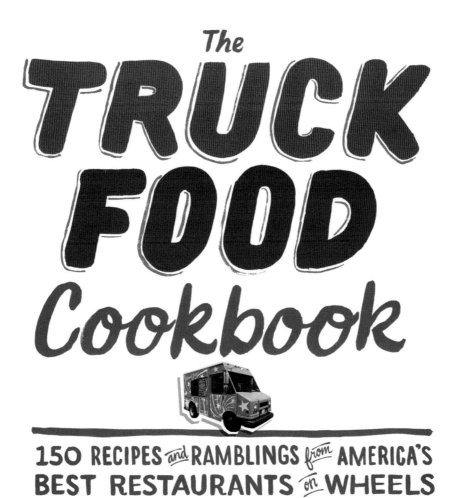

150 RECIPES *and* RAMBLINGS *from* AMERICA'S BEST RESTAURANTS *on* WHEELS

John T. Edge

RECIPES *and* PHOTOGRAPHS BY ANGIE MOSIER

WORKMAN PUBLISHING · NEW YORK

Library of Congress Cataloging-in-
Publication Data is available.

ISBN 978-0-7611-5616-1

Cover lettering illustrations and art
direction by Jean-Marc Troadec
Book design by Lisa Hollander
Front cover and spine photos by Mike Vago
Back cover picture frames by magann/
fotolia.

Additional photography by: age fotostock:
Jesus Sierra p.1, kord.com p.202,
Superstock p.226; fotolia: Heather Hood
p.16, Sportstock p.54, Charles Amundson
p.78, Paul Hill p.118, Henryk Sadura p.132,
HD Fanatic p.152; K.L.Kohn p.162, Paul
Moore p.188, Geophis p.268, Museum of
the City of New York: Hot Dog Stand 1939
Berenice Abbott p.182; Melissa Lucier
p. viii; Rachel Styer p.30.

Portions of the articles on pages 95, 188–89,
208–09 originally appeared in a different
form in *The New York Times,* and are used
with permission.

Workman books are available at special
discounts when purchased in bulk for
premiums and sales promotions as well
as for fund-raising or educational use.
Special editions or book excerpts can also
be created to specification. For details,
contact the Special Sales Director at the
address below, or send an e-mail to
specialmarkets@workman.com.

Workman Publishing
Company, Inc.
225 Varick Street
New York, NY 10014-4381
www.workman.com

Printed in China

First printing April 2012
10 9 8 7 6 5 4 3 2 1

"We cook food that hits
our customers like a bong hit."

—ROY CHOI, LOS ANGELES

"My sense of taste
is at full strength only when
I'm standing up."

—CALVIN TRILLIN, NEW YORK CITY

ACKNOWLEDGMENTS

The cast of characters behind *The Truck Food Cookbook* was large and generous:

DEDICATION:

FOR MY WIFE, BLAIR, WHO ALWAYS WELCOMED ME HOME WITH SALADS...

Angie Mosier shot the photographs, wrangled the recipes, and smiled, even in a hostage situation (see page 88). Judith Winfrey and Natalie Jordi helped her.

Deep thanks to Peter Workman and Bob Miller for their ink-stained vision. At Workman, Suzanne Rafer drove the truck, abetted on the editorial and design side by Jean-Marc Troadec, Lisa Hollander, Erin Klabunde, Barbara Mateer, David Schiller, and Peggy Gannon. Over in publicity, sales, and marketing, the crew of engaged and enthusiastic collaborators included Selina Meere, Page Edmunds, Walter Weinz, Jessica Wiener, Jenny Mandel and the special sales team, Marilyn Barnett and the folks in gift sales, and the digital crew headed by Andrea Fleck-Nisbit.

As usual, my agent, David Black, kicked butt.

Rob Long drove me about Los Angeles. Warren Hansen, the cart maven of Madison, Wisconsin, shared freely. Jane Thompson, Christian Krogstad, Kelly Rodgers, and Gretchen Barron unveiled Portland. Robb Walsh and Allison Cook showed me the greasy side of Houston. Mark Estes, Claudia Alarcon, and Virginia Wood shared Austin tips. With Ruth Lafler, I walked Fruitvale. Andrea Weigl drove me in Durham. Rick Nelson talked me through Minneapolis.

Brad Parsons shepherded me about Seattle. Jonathan Kauffman introduced me to taco buses. Peter McKee indulged me a cream cheese dog. Leslie Kelly and Nancy Leson drank and talked with me. Kirsten Hines kept an eye out in San Francisco. With Caleb Zigas, I strolled the Mission. Ed Levine and Zack Brooks tramped through Manhattan with me. With Gary Nabhan and Janos Wilder, I ate Sonoran hot dogs.

In addition to Angie's photographs, we turned to a few other good folks, including Jessi Langsen, who shot Koo's Grill, Matthew Bufford, who shot Bike Basket Pies, and Marshall Wright, who shot El Naranjo. Kate Medley captured Durham. Lou Weinert trained his lens for my author portrait. The Museum of the City of New York shared the Berenice Abbott photo on page 182.

I wrote the great majority of this book while on a fellowship at Escape to Create, in Seaside, Florida. Malayne Demars, Marsha Dowler, Linda Cook, Lynne Nesmith, and Karen Holland were marvels. Joyce Wilson, sage of the Gulf Coast, made me feel welcome. So did Robert Davis, street food advocate and new urbanism pioneer.

Small portions of this book appeared, in decidedly different forms, in the *Oxford American, Gourmet, Garden & Gun, The New York Times,* and *Men's Health.*

In honor of the work done by the Street Vendor Project in New York City, and La Cocina in San Francisco, the author and Workman Publishing have made donations to each concern.

CONTENTS

STREET ECONOMICS:
What It Costs

IT TAKES $900,000 to open a Chipotle Mexican Grill. A SUBWAY will set you back as much as $200,000. The startup cost for a wheeled restaurant, on the other hand, is often a fraction of what's needed to open a sit-down restaurant.

A standard-issue street food truck, purchased new, will set you back $100,000 or more. But eBay is chockablock with ads for used food trucks that can be had for $10,000 and used food carts that can be had for $2,000. (Back in 2002, along with a friend, I bought a hot dog–shaped cart for $3,000, but that's a long story, one you can read about on page 2.)

Then there's the matte of permits. New York City, for example, allots just thre thousand or so food vendor licenses each year. As you might expect, they're trade by way of a robust black market, fetching anywhere from $5,000 to $20,000. A city like Austin is more hospitable to vendors; ther approximately one thousan licensed vendors pay $200 so for their permits.

STREET EATS ETHICS

I was in Saigon, Vietnam, in 2007, eating curbside bánh xèo and bun cha, when I read that the Supreme Court of India had decided to ban street sellers from cooking dishes on the sidewalks of New Delhi. The move was understood to be part of an effort to sweep clean India's capital in advance of the 2010 Commonwealth Games.

Cooks at the curb in Vietnam are well-equipped.

That decision was met with derision. Such a change would be unmanageable. Such an edict would be unenforceable in a city where, by some estimates, 100,000 food vendors work the city streets, selling paneers and kachoris and samosas. Street food, as citizens of New Delhi had known it for generations, was to be transformed. City officials planned a licensing system for hawkers. They spoke of food courts of the sort found in Singapore and other Southeast Asian cities.

They revealed that under the new system curbside vendors would begin paying taxes.

Sitting on that curb in Saigon, I thought of home. Back in the States, after a long break, a nascent street food movement was gathering steam. Cities were loosening regulations—not tightening them—in an effort to make city streetscapes more vital, more appealing. Young chefs were chucking fine-dining aspirations and opting, instead, to dish the culinary equivalent of the Great American Novel from retrofitted taco trucks.

Recent Mexican immigrants were winning Anglo audiences for Sonoran-style hot dogs, stippled with jalapeño sauce.

In Vietnam, I saw a country with a vital street food scene, a place where local food and street food were one, where economic necessities dictated a dependence on local farmers and artisans that, back in the States, would appear a mere pipe dream. In many ways, Vietnam looked like the promised land of curb cuisine. And yet, it was in Vietnam that I got a glimpse,

INSPIRED, CURIOUS, AND HUNGRY, I BEGAN PLOTTING THE BOOK YOU NOW HOLD IN YOUR HANDS.

through developments in India, at just how precarious life for a street cook can be, and by extension, just how fragile the street food ecosystem is.

Travels in Vietnam did not constitute the sum total of my street food experience. I had, through the years, eaten my fair share of cilantro and onion-capped *tacos al pastor* and nori-wrapped planks of Spam *musubi*. And I had walked the streets of Oaxaca, Mexico, eating *tlayudas* from a late-night stall, perched at the gates of the cathedral.

More important, I had worked the other side of the aisle, too. Over the course of three nights in New Orleans, a stint that ended early in the morning on a New Year's Day, I had worked a wienie-shaped Lucky Dogs cart in the French Quarter, selling hot dogs to the late-night throngs.

Lucky Dog vendors feed the street parade.

That experience, an account of which closes this book, presaged this project, too.

Introducing Dunce Dogs

A FEW YEARS passed between my time on the streets in New Orleans and the summer afternoon when I bought my own wienie-shaped hot dog cart, and installed it on the square in my hometown of Oxford, Mississippi. Along with a couple friends, including Andy Harper, I launched Dunce Dogs. Andy, who has a doctorate in environmental history, handled logistical and technical matters. My wife, Blair, a poet, painter, and college lecturer, coined our motto, "Think Genius, Eat Dunce." I wrote an operations manual to help employees understand the brand.

I was full of myself, full of the possibilities for the project, which is why the manual included lines like this: "Dunce Dogs references the hot dog shape of dachshund dogs and tells consumers that, although we take our hot dogs seriously, we don't take ourselves too seriously." We bought a

The perfect slogan: Think Genius, Eat Dunce.

business license. The county health department inspected our so-called physical plant. We established two locations. The county clerk let us set up on the courthouse lawn during the day. For night shifts, a friendly lawyer with an office near the college bars agreed to trade wienies for access to his front yard.

We approached the business with idealistic motives. Our plan was to offer Oxford honest $3 lunches. We sold all-beef natural casing dogs, not cereal-stuffed tube steaks. We were determined to be different. To be better. We concocted a buttermilk slaw and a pimiento cheese spread, both of which we slathered on dogs. And we bought holster-mounted blow torches to meet requests for melted pimiento cheese.

It all fell apart, of course. And quickly. I couldn't hack the hours while simultaneously writing and working my university job. (Also, at the time we opened the stand both Andy and I had full-time jobs, full-time wives, and brand-new toddlers.)

On a trial Dunce Dogs run.

Six months after we bought the cart, we sold it to a fellow named Jamo, who sold it to a fellow named Louie, who sold it to a fellow named Jamie. As far as I know, someone still works the cart, at least when school is in session, selling late-night dogs to drunks emptying out of Oxford bars. But our commitment to democratic ideals and natural casing dogs has been kicked to the curb.

The Dunce Dog Stand is no longer mine. But, after spending a year on the road, crisscrossing the country, documenting the evolution of modern American street food, my belief in its possibilities is stronger than ever. Recent years have been epochal for American street food. Over the course of my traveling year, as I made my research rounds, street food rolled out of the gutter. It went mainstream. It bridged race and class gaps. Street food as served in New York City even became, Lord help us all, the focus of a proposed TV show, starring Courteney Cox of *Friends* and *Cougar Town* fame.

America Comes of Age

A NUMBER OF FACTORS made street food the hip culinary phenomenon of the moment: The economy, for one. All of a sudden, cheap deliverables for the consumer were in vogue. And so were cheap start-up costs for producers who lacked the money for the build-out of new restaurants but who were able—in a grand creative tradition shared by filmmakers and other dreamers—to max out their credit cards to rehab a linen services truck or a carny wagon.

But there were other reasons, too. America has long been a mobile society, attuned to eating on the go. That once meant a bite-and-bolt burger, eaten between gear shifts on the highway. Of late, however, we've begun to fuse our demand for quick-access food with a demand for honest and delicious food. Dana Cowin of *Food & Wine* magazine calls this a trend toward "luxocratic" foods, indulgences that are both luxurious and democratic, foods that rely on haute technique but bas delivery. That, in a nutshell, describes the best street food.

More important, perhaps, than such current developments was the cumulative effect of Hispanic immigration. Across the country taco trucks were no longer considered exceptional. For a New Wave of chef-entrepreneurs, they were now inspirational.

I realized this while standing in the parking lot of a low-rise office building on the south side of San Francisco, waiting for the arrival of Julia Yoon's Seoul On Wheels truck. Wal-Mart was the tenant of the building. Fresh-faced men and women were buzzing around in khaki pants and khaki skirts, talking into or pecking at iPhones. When the truck arrived—to sell kimchi-topped burgers and Korean burritos called korritos—a rush of middle managers and data programmers piled out of those buildings. They made for the truck in much the same way that roofers and framers and masons have long poured out of construction sites lured by the promise of taco truck-peddled carne asada-stuffed tacos and chorizo-girded tortas.

IT'S A SHOWCASE FOR STREET THEATER, AN OPPORTUNITY TO BROADCAST BOTH ETHIC AND AESTHETIC.

Harried, without time for a sitdown meal, they arrived with cash. And they ordered big.

Much of the street food I document here is outsider food, immigrant food, the food of the underclass. Accept this sort of street food on its own terms and it serves as an entrée to people and place, a passkey to understanding customs and mores. (Dismiss it and you run the same risk that all closed-minded eaters do: Your worldview atrophies,

Food for flea market treasure-seekers.

your lunch and dinner possibilities narrow.)

For eaters, traditional street food is among the most primal of bites, nutrition reduced to its most elemental form, a source of unalloyed pleasure. For cooks, such food offers an entrepreneurial path toward self-reliance. It's a showcase for street theater, an opportunity to broadcast both ethic and aesthetic.

Old and New Ground

I PAY HOMAGE to a wide range of traditional vendors, from *elotes* vendors peddling mayonnaise-slathered and cayenne-strafed cobs of corn at weekend flea markets in Texas, to the rice and lamb vendors of Manhattan, fighting for a patch of pavement and the promise of a $100 daily net. I pay homage to the New Guard of vendors, too. I'm talking about the insurgent band of young cooks who now stand at the helm of stepside vans, retrofitted Airstreams, and reimagined fiberglass carts,

Are you on the bus?

griddling grass-fed beef and tucking burgers inside focaccia buns.

They're the sort of cooks who refuse to bide their time and sock away money in the hopes of saving enough to open a brick-and-mortar palace of a restaurant, swagged in chintz, outfitted with damask and crystal and attitude. Their work is informed, in equal measure, by the farm-to-fork movement, classical culinary matriculation, hard knocks education, punk rock gestalt,

and a universal impatience, characteristic of cooks in their twenties and thirties.

The pages that follow include profiles of both the old guard and the new. Truth be told, there are probably more of the new within than the old. That composition does not communicate some sort of value judgment. (To my mind and palate, the best new guard vendors take their inspiration from traditional cart food folk.) It merely reflects the present and projects the future.

A Note on Methods and Scope

CONSIDER THIS a street food snapshot taken just as the revolution revved up. I focused my attention on two types of cities. Primary were places like Portland, Oregon, where the street food scene is a well-integrated part of daily life. Secondary were cities like Minneapolis, where street food shows promise. I studied scenes like Austin, Texas, where a wide variety of dishes are sold. And I focused on cities like Tucson, Arizona, where a single dish defines the gestalt.

Street food is, by its very nature, ephemeral. By the time you hold this book in your hands a number of these vendors will have closed. Others will have moved. Others still will have traded their carts in for brick-and-mortar restaurants. That's why, instead of naming a definitive address for a cart or truck, I often note the corner, the parking lot, the stretch of road where a truck or cart last parked to do business.

The recipes that follow were adapted, in large part, from street food vendor instructions collected by my colleague Angie Mosier. (She also shot most of the photographs.) When Angie couldn't secure a recipe from a vendor, especially when the dish in question was rooted in long-standing tradition, Angie developed a recipe to reflect the ingredients and methods typically applied.

One more thing to know: my definition of street food. As showcased in this book, it's not food sold for consumption on the street by vendors doing business from kiosks or walk-up windows cut into kitchens. Street food, as defined here, is food sold by vendors who have the possibility of mobility. In other words, if the kitchen has wheels and can move, then I care. If it can't, I don't.

Left to Right:
Top Row: The Carribean in Portland. Cartoon cart art.
Middle Row: Austin food truck trailer park. Side door view of Liba's in San Francisco.
Bottom Row: Bay area coffee on wheels. Doug Quint of New York's Big Gay Ice Cream Truck.

A late night nosh in Portland at Potato Champion.

Back alley trucks East Side Kings, Austin.

Meat patty, with jerk chicken and rice, Jamerica, Madison.

Window service at Garden State, Portland.

The pairing of fries and pies appears,

at first glance, to serve no cause but rhyme. Truth is, in the American South, where I was born and raised, those words get combined often. We have long fried pies in cast-iron skillets roiling with lard. A quick dip in burbling fat bestows texture. Witness the empanada. Behold the french fry. What's more, that quick dip cooks a pie—or a potato or almost anything else—more quickly than does baking or roasting. And, lest you think we're sedentary folk, always reclining on the veranda or some such, we have long tucked those pies in brown paper bags and hit the road or hit the street.

That quick transformation is what street food cooks prize. Long cook times are the bane of vendors the world over, from Hanoi, Vietnam, where curb vendors sell vermicelli-threaded *cha gio,* to Tucson, Arizona, where Tohono O'odham tribe members fry bread in pots of boiling oil and top them with beans and meats to fashion Native American tacos. In the recipes that follow, if you keep the grease hot and the portion size small, you can be in and out of the kitchen, stall, cart, or truck in the time it takes to refuel the propane tank.

POTATO CHAMPION FRIES

POTATO CHAMPION'S DOUBLE-FRY TECHNIQUE, which I interpret here, yields potatoes that are cottony on the inside and crisp on the out. Texture, as any good fry obsessive knows, is as important as taste. If you want to dunk your fries in the Tarragon and Anchovy Mayonnaise, keep in mind the mayonnaise needs to sit for at least one hour before using.

A bouquet of fries meant to be eaten hot from the fryer.

Note the table full of ketchups and other embellishments.

SERVES 4 TO 6

2 pounds large russet potatoes, peeled

Peanut or canola oil

Kosher salt

Tarragon and Anchovy Mayonnaise (optional, recipe follows), for serving

1 Cut the potatoes lengthwise into ½ inch–thick slices. Stack 2 to 3 slices on top of each other and cut them lengthwise into ½ inch–wide strips. Place the sliced potatoes in a large bowl of cold water for 10 minutes to remove the starch. Drain the potatoes and pat them dry with paper towels.

2 Line a rimmed baking sheet with parchment paper. Add enough oil to a large heavy pot to reach a depth of 4 inches. Attach a deep fry thermometer to the side of the pot and heat the oil over medium-high heat until the thermometer registers 325°F. Working in batches and being careful not to overcrowd the pot, carefully add the potatoes to the hot oil and cook them until tender, 4 to 5 minutes per batch, stirring them occasionally with a slotted spoon. Using the slotted spoon, transfer the potatoes to the parchment-lined baking sheet and let cool for 30 minutes. Do not discard the oil.

3 When ready to serve, reheat the reserved oil over high heat to 375°F. Working in batches, return the potatoes to the hot oil and cook them until golden and crisp, stirring

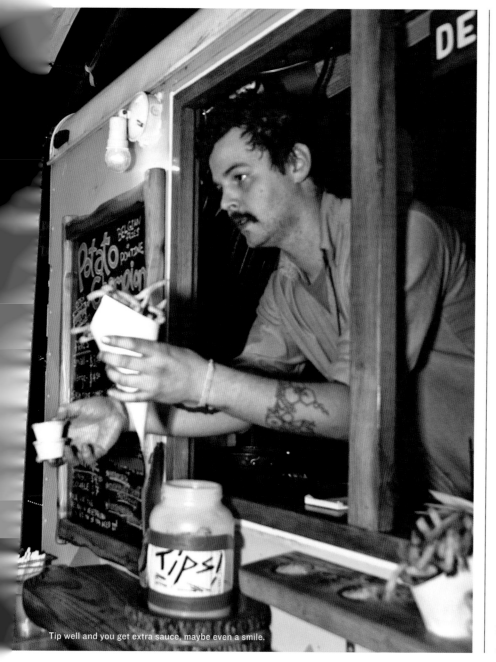

Tip well and you get extra sauce, maybe even a smile.

occasionally, 4 to 5 minutes. With the slotted spoon, transfer the fries to paper towels to drain. Sprinkle the fries with coarse salt and serve immediately with the Tarragon and Anchovy Mayonnaise, if desired.

Tarragon and Anchovy Mayonnaise

I DON'T LIKE THE SACCHARINE sweetness of ketchup. Not on my burgers. More important, not on my fries. Which is why I like this stuff so much. In Belgium, where fries may have originated, *friteries* serve a wide range of sauces, many of which are mayonnaise based. This recipe from Potato Champion relies on mayo as a mere binder for more pungent flavors.

MAKES ABOUT I CUP

I cup mayonnaise

2 tablespoons coarsely chopped fresh tarragon

2 tablespoons coarsely chopped fresh dill

2 anchovy fillets, coarsely chopped

Combine the mayonnaise, tarragon, dill, and anchovies in a food processor or blender and pulse until the herbs are finely chopped. Transfer the mayonnaise to a bowl, cover, and refrigerate for at least 1 hour. The mayonnaise can be refrigerated, covered, for up to 2 days.

PORTLAND POUTINE

THE QUEBECOIS ARE CRAZY for this stuff. So are their snowbird kin down in Florida. Think mashed potatoes and gravy. But with texture. And with cheese. The texture comes when you substitute fried potatoes for mashed potatoes. The cheesy savor comes from curds, the solids formed when milk coagulates, those same solids that, following pressing and aging, become say, cheddar. Inspired by Mike McKinnon's Potato Champion *poutine*, which he engineered to satisfy Portland's drinking class, this is great at two in the morning or two in the afternoon.

LAST SEEN: Hawthorne Boulevard and SE 12th Avenue, Portland, Oregon

POTATO CHAMPION

ALONG WITH WHIFFIES FRIED PIES (see page 274) and a clutch of other vendors, including a graffiti-tagged camper van dishing pastas under the name Yarp?!, Potato Champion works a late-night pod in southeastern Portland. The trailer is greenish in color. A cartoon lumberman, who looks like he's fond of playing dress-up pirate, covers the door.

Mike McKinnon, a drummer in the Portland band Reporter, fell for Belgian-style frites when traveling, well, through Belgium. At the back left corner of the truck is a massive pile of oil-poached frites waiting to hit deep oil for the second time.

Mike serves straight potatoes in paper cones, with horseradish ketchup, rosemary truffle ketchup, and tarragon-anchovy mayonnaise on the side. And, although the Belgians would sneer, he serves that supremely trashy Canadian specialty *poutine* in pasteboard coffins, piled high with goo and gravy.

SERVES 4 TO 6

2 tablespoons ($^{1}/4$ stick) butter

2 tablespoons all-purpose flour

2 cups beef stock

1 teaspoon salt

$^{1}/2$ teaspoon freshly ground black pepper

Potato Champion Fries (page 9)

$^{1}/2$ pound fresh cheese curds (see Note)

1 Melt the butter in a saucepan over medium heat and stir in the flour. Cook the butter and flour, stirring constantly, until deep brown in color, about 10 minutes. Stir in the beef stock, salt, and pepper. Let the liquid come to a boil, then reduce the heat to low and cook until it is the consistency of thick gravy, about 15 minutes. Remove the gravy from the heat and keep it warm if not using immediately.

2 Pile up 4 to 6 batches of fries, crumble the cheese curds over each serving, and pour the gravy on top. Serve the *poutine* before those splinters of potato turn soggy.

N O T E : If you can't find cheese curds locally, try coarsely shredded cheddar or American.

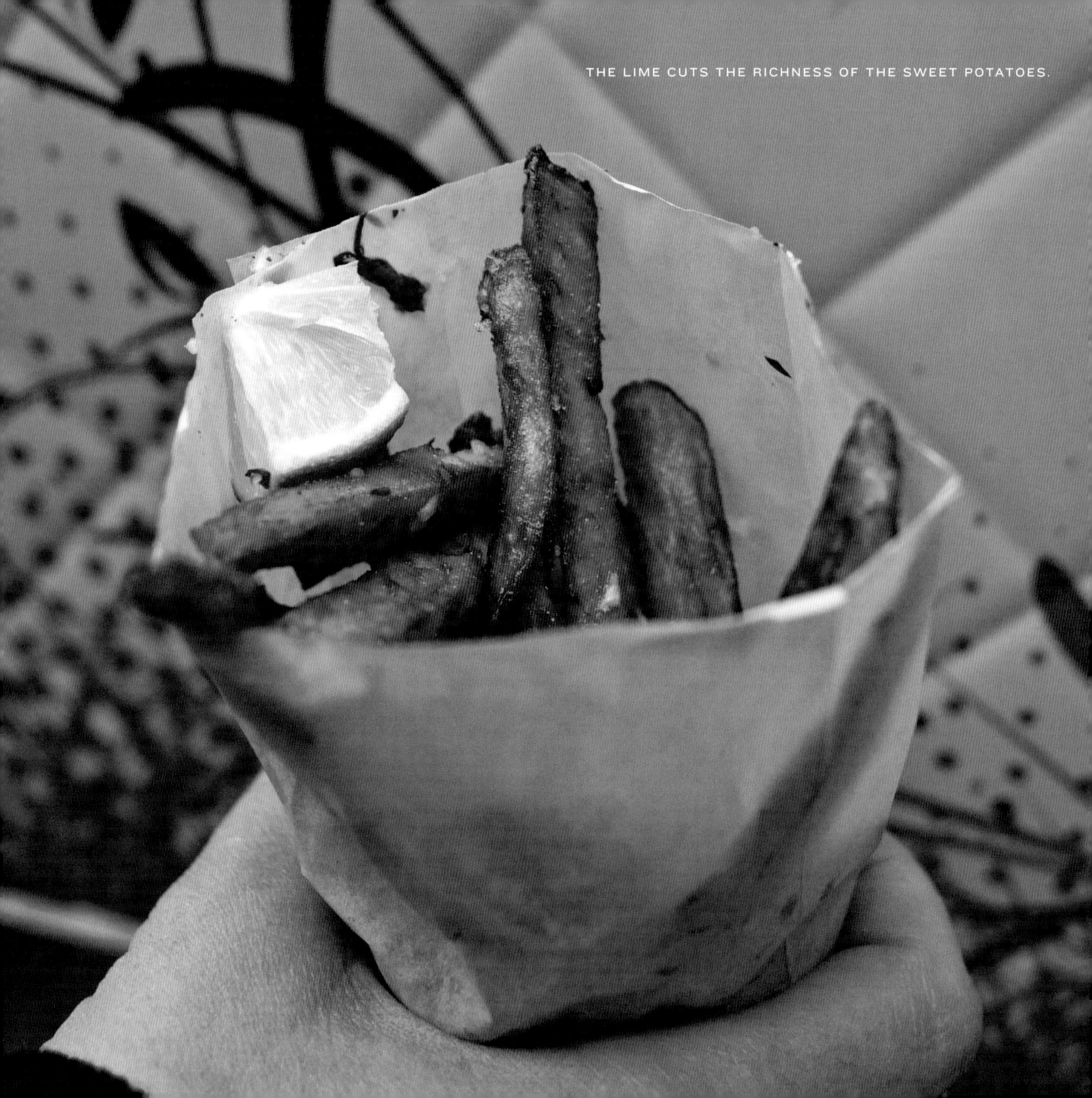
THE LIME CUTS THE RICHNESS OF THE SWEET POTATOES.

SWEET POTATO FRIES
WITH CILANTRO, GARLIC, AND LIME

I LOVE THE IDEA of sweet potato fries. The reality of sweet potato fries is often another matter. They usually brown too quickly and taste acrid. These things, on the other hand, are brilliantly golden and sweet, thanks to Liba's key technique, a quick roll of the sweet potatoes in rice flour.

Gail Lillian, proprietor of Liba falafel truck, San Francisco.

A green machine brings freshness to the streets.

Read about the Liba truck on page 148.

SERVES 4

3 pounds sweet potatoes, peeled

2 cups rice flour

2 quarts canola oil

4 tablespoons minced garlic

1/4 cup chopped fresh cilantro

Salt

4 lime wedges, for serving

1 Cut the sweet potatoes lengthwise into 1/4-inch-thick slices. Stack 2 or 3 slices on top of each other and cut them lengthwise into 1/4-inch-wide strips.

2 Place the rice flour in a large shallow bowl. Working in batches, add the sweet potato strips and toss to coat. Transfer the floured sweet potatoes to a baking sheet.

3 Heat the oil in a deep fryer or Dutch oven over medium-high heat until a deep fry thermometer attached to the side of the pot registers 325°F. Make sure that you have at least 3 inches of space between the surface of the oil and the top of the pot, as the oil will bubble up when the sweet potatoes are added. Working in batches and being careful not to overcrowd the pot, carefully add the sweet potatoes to the hot oil and cook them until softened, about 3 minutes. Using a slotted spoon, transfer the sweet potatoes to paper towels to drain. Do not discard the oil.

4 When ready to serve, reheat the reserved oil over high heat to 350°F. Working in batches, return the sweet potatoes to the hot oil and cook them until crisp and slightly caramelized, 2 to 3 minutes. With the slotted spoon, transfer the sweet potato fries to paper towels to drain. Toss the fries with the garlic and cilantro and season them with salt to taste. Serve the sweet potato fries with the lime wedges.

FRIED YUCCA

THINK OF A POTATO with a little more character, a little more complex texture, and you've got yucca, a shrub native to South America and also known as manioc and cassava. (Grate the roots of that shrub and you have tapioca, of pudding fame.) Boil and then fry the root, as Pedro Vargas at Paladar Cubano stipulates, and you've got the perfect foil for dipping in garlic sauce.

A window into the Cuban world of Pedro Vargas.

SERVES 4 TO 6

6 pieces yucca (about 2 pounds total),
    peeled and cut into 3-inch chunks
    (see Note)
2 quarts vegetable oil
Salt
Garlic-Cilantro Sauce (recipe follows),
    for serving

1 Bring a large pot of salted water to a boil; the pot should be large enough to hold all of the yucca covered by at least 1 inch of water. Add the yucca to the pot and let boil for 10 minutes. Using a fork, pierce the yucca to test for doneness; it should feel like a potato that is half done, not too soft, not too hard (you know—Goldilocks texture). Remove the yucca from the heat and drain it in a colander. Let the yucca cool to room temperature, then refrigerate it for at least 2 hours, preferably overnight.

2 Once the yucca is cold to the touch, cut each piece lengthwise into fourths. Heat the vegetable oil in a deep fryer or Dutch oven over medium-high heat until a deep fry thermometer attached to the side of the pot registers 325°F. Working in batches and being careful not to overcrowd the pot, carefully add the yucca to the hot oil 4 to 6 pieces at a time and cook until golden brown, about 5 minutes. Using a slotted spoon, transfer the

That good and garlicky sauce packs a wallop.

fried yucca to a dish lined with paper towels to drain. Season the yucca with salt to taste. The yucca tastes best when cooked immediately prior to serving. Serve the yucca with the Garlic-Cilantro Sauce.

NOTE: Yucca is available at markets selling international foods and at some supermarkets.

Garlic-Cilantro Sauce

JEANETTE VARGAS, PEDRO'S WIFE, is a native of Wisconsin. They met in Seattle when Pedro was playing the conga and Jeanette was dancing. This garlic sauce recipe is her creation. I asked Pedro how the sauce came to be. "She likes garlic," said

First the yucca, then the dunk, then the Cubano sandwich (page 158).

Pedro. "A lot. She told me to put it in the blender. And so that's what I did."

MAKES ABOUT 2 CUPS

6 cloves garlic, peeled

1 bunch fresh cilantro

2 cups mayonnaise

Place the garlic and cilantro in a food processor and puree them. Add the mayonnaise and blend until smooth, 2 to 3 minutes. The sauce can be refrigerated, covered, for up to 1 week.

LAST SEEN: Aurora Avenue and North 90th Street, Seattle, Washington

PALADAR CUBANO

PEDRO VARGAS, who grew up in the town of Pinar del Río in western Cuba, is a conga player by vocation. His bona fides include stints with Barbarito Torres of Buena Vista Social Club fame. Outfitted with an adjacent wooden deck and set in a gravel lot on Seattle's multicultural thruway, Pedro's white truck, Paladar Cubano, doubles as a Cuban cultural center.

A boom box blasts *timba* and *casino,* Cuban riffs on salsa music. Plastered to the truck windows are posters for touring Cuban acts and a menu placard that reads "What is Mamey?" (It's a firm tree fruit with a taste comparable to sweet pumpkin; Paladar Cubano serves mamey shakes.)

Everyone in line seems to be ordering Cuban sandwiches, swabbed with lots of yellow mustard and toasted on a trouser press-like device. But I'm keen on Pedro's fried yucca chips, dipped into a pungent garlic sauce.

PORTLAND
AND THE DIY GESTALT

In Portland, Oregon, they call them pods, these groupings of carts that function like food courts, where multiple vendors work a spot of blacktop that's about the size of a generous parking space.

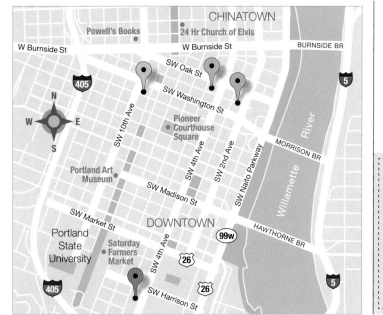

A s of this writing there are three primary weekday pods downtown and another in the college district. There are also pods in the leafy suburbs. And there's

WHERE THE PODS ARE:

⚲ SW 10th between SW Washington and SW Alder.

⚲ SW 5th between SW Oak and SW Stark.

⚲ SW 3rd at SW Oak.

⚲ SW 4th at Portland State U.

And check Foodcartsportland.com.

at least one late-night pod, where young drinkers on their way home from the bars scarf pocket pies and *poutine* and other deep-fried foods.

From the wrong angle, the clutch of carts at SW 5th Street between Oak and Stark looks like a gypsy camp, populated by the sons and daughters of traveling carnival folk. One downtown cart recalls the Child Catcher wagon from *Chitty Chitty Bang Bang*. Until recently, others were in service as camper vans.

From the right angle, however, another cart resembles an arts and crafts bungalow with brightly painted clapboard siding. And another is accessorized with a flower box, erupting with peonies, mounted beneath an order window. The Portland pod aesthetic is hand hewn and homegrown. It's a little funky. A little DIY. All of which is to say, it's representative of the broader Portland gestalt.

When street food advocates, no matter where they live, speak of American cities that serve as honest incubators of a street food scene, Portland is the name on the tip of everyone's tongue. Some cities try to legislate street food out of existence. Others see street vendors as the foes of brick-and-mortar businesses. The city of Portland grasps that pods are places where entrepreneurs with limited funds can take a chance on a new concept. Where operators who have brio but lack a flush bank account can make a go with their grandmother's recipe for chili con carne or their aunt's recipe for *pho*.

Portland has taken steps to support street life. In addition to maintaining city codes that are conducive to cart vendors, the city's bureau of planning commissioned *Food Cartology,* a study that found "food carts have a positive impact on street vitality and neighborhood life and advance public values, including community connectedness and distinctiveness, equity and access, and sustainability."

Portland is a hip and green town. No doubt about that. There are carts that vend soy curls, a straightforward term for fake pork rinds made with extruded soy. A vegan can find tempeh, lettuce, and tomato sandwiches aplenty. And, yes, an abiding eco-consciousness defines the mores of both street food vendors and their customers. (You'll notice that, rather than carry their food away in a foam container, a goodly number of Portland cart customers bring their own bowls and plates.)

But there's nothing faddish about Portland's eco-consciousness. And there's nothing faddish about the street food scene here. In Los Angeles, you get the impression that while taco trucks are there to stay, the spike in gourmet trucks may be short. In Portland, where nothing is gourmet, but so much of the food is sourced and prepared with integrity, the pod-based revolution appears to be permanent. And it appears to be sustainable.

- - - - - - - - - - - - - - - - - - -

Left to Right:

Top Row: The Little Blue Menu. The Swamp Shack—New Orleans, Portland style.

Middle Row: Hippy architecture. Garden State greeting.

Bottom Row: Lunchtime getaway. Two fried pies for the road.

CHICKPEA FRIES

THESE ARE, IN ESSENCE, rectangular chickpea fritters. This recipe, from Garden State, relies on many of the same techniques as its chickpea sandwich (you'll find that recipe on page 149). Reach for Lemon Aioli to go with the fritters, or maybe just a swab of mayonnaise and a squeeze of lemon juice.

All surfaces gleam at Garden State.

SERVES 4 TO 6

1¹/8 cups chickpea (garbanzo bean) flour (see Note)

Salt

¹/2 teaspoon freshly ground black pepper

¹/4 teaspoon ground cumin

¹/4 teaspoon cayenne pepper

2 cups water

¹/4 cup chopped fresh flat-leaf parsley

2 quarts vegetable oil, plus oil for the sheet pans

6 lemon wedges, for serving

Lemon Aioli (optional, page 151), for serving

Mayonnaise (optional), for serving

1 Place the chickpea flour, 1 teaspoon salt, and the black pepper, cumin, and cayenne pepper in a heavy pot over high heat and stir to mix. Gradually add the water while stirring with a flat-edged wooden spatula. You want to avoid lots of lumps of flour, but a few are okay. While stirring constantly, gradually lower the heat as the chickpea mixture thickens. The chickpea mixture is done once it pulls away from the side and bottom of the pot as you stir it, 10 to 15 minutes. When most of the water has been absorbed, add the parsley.

2 Lightly oil a rimmed baking sheet. Transfer the chickpea mixture to the baking sheet, spreading it out evenly so that it covers the pan completely. Oil the bottom of a second baking sheet. Place this pan on top of the chickpea mixture and press firmly to create a smooth, even surface, then remove the top pan. Let the chickpea mixture cool completely, then

Like fries, only fatter and better. Squeeze on the lemon.

cut it into sticks that are 1/4 inch wide and 2½ inches long.

3 Heat the oil in a deep fryer or Dutch oven over high heat until a deep fry thermometer attached to the side of the pot registers 350°F. Working in batches and being careful not to overcrowd the pot, carefully add the chickpea sticks to the hot oil and cook them until crisp and beginning to brown, about 4 minutes. Using a slotted spoon, transfer the chickpea fries to paper towels to drain. Lightly salt the fries and serve them with the lemon wedges and Lemon Aioli or mayonnaise, if desired.

NOTE: Chickpea (garbanzo bean) flour is available in health food stores and markets that specialize in Indian and African groceries.

A quilted metal beauty, shining in the sun.

LAST SEEN: 7875 SE 13th Avenue, in the Sellwood neighborhood of Portland, Oregon

GARDEN STATE

THE GARDEN IN QUESTION is not in Oregon, no matter how verdant the surrounding countryside might appear. No matter how fat the summer berries, how funky the fall mushrooms.

The Garden State is New Jersey, where Kevin Sandri lived before he came to the Portland neighborhood of Sellwood.

Kevin works in the Italian genre. That translates into meatballs stuffed into crusty loaves; and *arancini*, saffron risotto balls laced with fresh mozzarella; and chickpea fries that a Frenchman might recognize as *panisse*, all served from a quilted, stainless steel cart that gleams when the afternoon sun hits it.

TATER TOTS
WITH SUMAC

"SUMAC CUTS THE GREASE," was Michele Grant's rationale when I asked her why she sprinkles a comparatively exotic spice, associated with Persia, on mundane American Tater Tots. "Plus the lemony notes give the tots balance." She also offers smoked paprika "because my family is from Eastern Europe." At the time I visited The Grilled Cheese Truck, a lemon and garlic aioli was in development.

The Grilled Cheese Truck griddle is hot day and night.

SERVES 4 TO 6

l package frozen Tater Tots
Powdered sumac (see Note)

Prepare the Tater Tots according to the directions on the package. Sprinkle the Tater Tots with sumac to taste.

N O T E : Powdered sumac is a purple-colored, lemon-tinged spice used in the Middle East. It is available online at www.thespicehouse.com, www.williams-sonoma.com, and www.americanspice.com.

Read about The Grilled Cheese Truck on page 170.

A lowbrow side meets a highbrow spice for a symphony of trashy texture.

HAM CROQUETAS

STREET FOOD IS FRUGAL FOOD. A good street food cook wastes no scraps. Cook dinner and, no matter how good the food is, stray bites remain. That frugal instinct has birthed all manner of fritters, from *acarajé,* black-eyed pea fritters popular in West Africa, to this recipe for ham *croquetas* (croquettes), inspired by The Texas Cuban.

An only-in-Austin fusion.

MAKES 6 TO 8 CROQUETAS

2 tablespoons olive oil

I small onion, chopped

1/4 cup all-purpose flour

I cup milk

I teaspoon salt

1/2 teaspoon freshly ground black pepper

1/2 teaspoon paprika

1/2 cup finely diced cooked ham

2 large eggs

I1/2 cups plain, dried bread crumbs

2 quarts vegetable oil, for frying the croquetas

1 Heat the olive oil in a skillet over medium-high heat. Add the onion and cook until soft, about 3 minutes. Stir in the flour and cook, stirring, for about 4 minutes, then whisk in the milk and cook until thickened, 3 to 4 minutes, stirring the entire time.

Read about The Texas Cuban truck on page 159.

2 Remove the skillet from the heat and stir in the salt, pepper, paprika, and ham. Transfer the ham mixture to a bowl and refrigerate it, covered, for at least 1 hour.

3 Crack the eggs into a small bowl and beat them. Place the bread crumbs on a plate. Moisten your hands with water and pick up a golf ball–size portion of the ham mixture, forming it into a thick cigar shape. Dip the ham *croqueta* in the egg, then roll it in the bread crumbs. Repeat with the remaining ham mixture.

4 Heat the vegetable oil in a deep fryer or Dutch oven over high heat until a deep fry thermometer attached to the side of the pot registers 350°F. Working in batches and being careful not to overcrowd the pot, carefully add the *croquetas* to the hot oil and cook them until golden brown, 3 to 5 minutes. Using a slotted spoon, transfer the cooked *croquetas* to paper towels to drain.

Austin trucks and carts curate green space.

MOLOTES OAXAQUENOS

FORM THESE *MOLOTES* CORRECTLY, in close accordance with Iliana de la Vega's recipe, and zeppelin-shaped fritters emerge from the oil. Rather than providing mere decoration, lettuce leaves serve as handles with which you can grasp the hot bundles of corn and chorizo.

Clean design and clean flavors at El Naranjo.

MAKES 32 MOLOTES

6 tablespoons lard or vegetable oil

12 ounces good-quality fresh Mexican chorizo

10 ounces yellow flesh potatoes, preferably Yukon Gold, cooked until soft

Sea salt

2 pounds fresh white corn masa (see Note)

2 romaine lettuce hearts

2 cups vegetable oil, for frying

1 cup of Salsa Verde (page 216) or store-bought salsa verde of your choice

1 Heat 3 tablespoons of the lard or oil in a large skillet set over medium-high heat. Remove and discard the casings from the chorizo, crumble the sausage into the skillet, and cook until cooked through, about 10 minutes. Add the cooked potatoes and mash them into the chorizo, mixing them well. Season the chorizo mixture with salt to taste, then remove it from the heat and set it aside.

2 Place the masa in a large bowl and knead it, adding small amounts of warm water to moisten it if necessary, until the dough is soft and elastic. Knead in the remaining 3 tablespoons of lard or oil. The masa should feel like Play-Doh, soft but not sticky. Cover the masa with a damp kitchen towel and let it rest for 20 minutes.

3 Meanwhile, rinse the lettuce hearts under cold running water and pat them dry with paper towels. Cut the hearts crosswise into 3-inch-long pieces; you will need 32. Set the pieces of lettuce aside.

4 Form 32 golf ball–size balls of masa, each about 1 ounce. Keep the balls covered with a damp towel while making the *molotes*.

5 Place a ball of masa in the palm of your hand. Using your thumb, make an indentation in the center of the ball and fill it with 1 teaspoon of the chorizo mixture. Fold up the sides to enclose the filling, shaping the *molote* like a cigar. Repeat with the remaining balls of masa and filling. Place the *molotes* on a rimmed baking sheet, cover them loosely with plastic wrap or parchment paper, and refrigerate them for 15 minutes.

6 Heat the 2 cups of vegetable oil in a deep fryer or Dutch oven over medium-high heat until a deep fry thermometer attached to the

side of the pot registers 350°F. Working in batches and being careful not to overcrowd the pot, carefully add the *molotes* to the hot oil a few at a time and cook until golden and crisp, 3 to 5 minutes. Using a slotted spoon, transfer the *molotes* to paper towels to drain. Sprinkle the *molotes* with sea salt and arrange one on each piece of lettuce. Serve the *molotes* with dollops of *salsa verde.*

NOTE: If fresh masa is unavailable, substitute 3 cups of masa harina. To reconstitute it, follow the package directions.

A curbside menu consultation.

LAST SEEN: 85 Rainey Street, Austin, Texas

EL NARANJO

ILIANA DE LA VEGA is a native of Mexico City. She made her mark in Oaxaca, where along with her husband, architect Ernesto Torrealba, a native of Chile, she cooked in the 1990s at the restaurant El Naranjo. Iliana took chances with hypertraditional Oaxacan cookery, which is to say she fiddled with mole sauces and, in the process, confounded locals.

She embraces her role as rebel. That's what Iliana told me when we met. And that's what she told the *New York Times* back in 2002: "I find it very patronizing when people have this idea that to make Oaxacan cuisine you have to be a Zapotec woman with long braids and a serape working over a stone *comal.*"

In 2005, amid political unrest, she left Oaxaca, eventually settling in Austin. For the last couple of years she's been teaching classes at the Culinary Institute of America's campus in San Antonio. More recently still, she's been readying El Naranjo, her Oaxacan food cart. One taste of her miniature empanadas, perfumed with *huitlacoche,* and you'll know that the street food game in Austin changed for the better, and forever, in the early spring of 2010, when Iliana and Ernesto hit the street.

EMPANADAS DE HUITLACOCHE

ALSO KNOWN, RATHER INDELICATELY, as corn smut, *huitlacoche* is a fungus that infects corn. Think of it as the Mexican answer to Italian truffles and you're close to grasping the funk of the flavor. In Iliana de la Vega's recipe that funk is tempered by the sharp and resinous herb known as epazote.

Dispatching orders of haute Mexican food from the El Naranjo window.

MAKES ABOUT 30 EMPANADAS

FOR THE EMPANADA DOUGH

2 pounds fresh white corn masa (see Notes)

2 tablespoons lard or vegetable oil

Salt

FOR THE HUITLACOCHE FILLING

2 tablespoons vegetable oil

1/2 white onion, diced

2 serrano peppers, finely diced (do not remove the seeds)

2 large cloves garlic, minced

3 ripe plum tomatoes, finely diced

2 cans (7 ounces each) huitlacoche (see Notes), coarsely chopped

10 fresh epazote leaves (see Notes), chopped

Sea salt

2 quarts vegetable oil, for frying the empanadas

Salsa of your choice, for serving

1 Make the empanada dough: Place the masa in a large bowl and knead it, adding small amounts of warm water to moisten it if necessary, until the dough is soft and elastic. Knead in the lard or oil and salt to taste. The masa should feel like Play-Doh, soft but not sticky. Cover the dough with a damp kitchen towel and let it rest for 20 minutes.

2 Pull off small pieces of empanada dough and form them into balls by rolling them between your hands. You should have about 30 balls. Keep the balls covered with plastic wrap while making the filling and forming the empanadas.

3 Make the *huitlacoche* filling: Heat the 2 tablespoons oil in a large skillet over medium heat. Add the onion and serrano peppers and cook until the peppers are soft and the onion is translucent, about 5 minutes. Add the garlic and cook until the garlic is softened, about 1 minute. Add the tomatoes, reduce the heat, and let cook until the tomatoes are softened, 2 to 3 minutes. Add the *huitlacoche,* mix well, and continue cooking until the *huitlacoche* is heated through and the mixture is well blended, about 10 minutes. Add the epazote and season the *huitlacoche* filling with sea salt to taste. Set the filling aside to cool.

4 Place plastic storage bags over the top and the bottom plates of a tortilla press. Place a ball of dough in the center of the bottom of the tortilla press. Lower the top of the press to form a little tortilla. (If you don't own a press, roll out the tortillas with a rolling pin.) Transfer the tortilla to the palm of your hand and fill it with about 1½ teaspoons of the *huitlacoche* filling. Fold the empanada in half, as when making a turnover, pressing the edges together to seal them. Transfer the empanada to a baking sheet and cover it with a damp towel or plastic wrap. Repeat with the remaining balls of empanada dough and *huitlacoche* filling. Refrigerate the empanadas for 10 to 15 minutes.

5 Heat the 2 quarts oil in a deep fryer or Dutch oven over medium-high heat until a deep fry thermometer attached to the side of the pot registers 325°F. Working in batches and being careful not to overcrowd the pot, carefully add the empanadas to the hot oil and cook them until golden and crisp, 3 to 5 minutes. Using a slotted spoon, transfer the cooked empanadas to paper towels to drain. Serve the empanadas with salsa.

NOTES: If fresh masa is unavailable, substitute 3 cups of masa harina. To reconstitute it, follow the package directions.

Many of the ingredients and tools in this book—including, *huitlacoche,* epazote, and tortilla presses—are available at Mexican grocery stores. So are lots of other good things to eat and drink.

Read about the El Naranjo truck on page 23.

Empanadas—good as is or with crumbly Mexican cheese that has a texture comparable to feta.

A FREE-FORM PASTY IN ALL ITS GLORY.

CHICKEN CHEDDAR BACON PASTIES

THE DOUGH EMERGES from the oven looking rumpled and misshapen. The pasty sags in the middle from the sheer caloric heft of the ingredients. It oozes with puddles of creamy cheese and golden chicken. Initially conceived as a portable meal for laborers, LMN O'Pies' Madison iteration of the pasty requires a cardboard box for carriage and a fork for eating.

The pasty window is open, even when the snow envelopes Madison.

A little red wagon, straight out of Michigan.

MAKES 4 LARGE PASTIES OR 6 SMALL PASTIES

3 tablespoons butter

3 tablespoons all-purpose flour

1/2 teaspoon salt

1/2 teaspoon freshly ground black pepper

1 1/2 cups milk

1 cup grated cheddar cheese

LMN O'Pies Pasty Dough (recipe follows)

2 cups cooked and cubed boneless chicken

1/2 cup crumbled cooked bacon

1 egg, beaten

1 Preheat the oven to 375°F.

2 Melt the butter over low heat in a small saucepan. Stir in the flour, salt, and pepper. Gradually add the milk and cook, stirring until thickened, 5 to 7 minutes. Remove from the heat and stir in the cheddar cheese. Keep the cheddar sauce warm.

3 Remove the pasty dough from the refrigerator, divide it into 4 balls, and roll it out following the directions in the dough recipe. Fill each circle of dough with about 1/2 cup of the chicken, some of the crumbled bacon, and spoonfuls of the cheddar sauce to coat. Brush the edges of the dough with the beaten egg and then bring the sides of the dough together to meet in the middle. Pinch the edges together to make a good seal.

4 Place the pasties on a baking sheet and bake until golden brown, 10 to 15 minutes. Serve quick as a wink.

LAST SEEN: 100 block of Martin Luther King Jr. Boulevard, Madison, Wisconsin

LMN O'PIES

WHEN I ASKED PAUL, the counterman at LMN O'Pies, how to pronounce pasties, he said in reply, "Pah-sty is what I say. Pay-sties are for nipples." He also told me that the pasties of Michigan's Upper Peninsula are, as I suspected, the inspiration for this red hut on wheels, parked catercorner from The Dandelion. (The Upper Michigan pasties were more than likely inspired in turn by the pasties that migrant tin miners from Cornwall, England, once favored.)

The distance from Michigan to Wisconsin has afforded Lindsay Gehl, the baker behind LMN O'Pies, certain liberties. And she has taken those liberties, which is how I came to stand on Martin Luther King Jr. Boulevard, in the shadow of the state capitol building, and eat a chicken and bacon pasty, sauced with ranch dressing, and a brace of miniature cherry pasties.

LMN O'Pies Pasty Dough

TO MAKE A PASTY, you'll need a pasty dough recipe, like this one, inspired by the work of Lindsay Gehl at LMN O'Pies.

MAKES ENOUGH FOR 4 LARGE OR 6 SMALL PASTIES

3 cups all-purpose flour, plus flour for rolling out the dough

I teaspoon salt

3/4 cup (I1/2 sticks) cold butter or 3/4 cup lard, cut into 12 pieces

About 12 tablespoons ice water

1 Sift the flour and salt in a large bowl. Using a pastry cutter or 2 knives, work in the cold butter or lard until the mixture looks like course oatmeal. Add 6 tablespoons of the water and stir to combine until the dough starts to hold together. Add more water as needed to barely form a ball. Wrap the dough in plastic wrap and refrigerate it for at least 1 hour.

2 Remove the dough from the refrigerator and divide it into 4 large balls or 6 smaller balls. Lightly flour a work surface and, using a floured rolling pin, roll out each ball of dough into a circle about 1/4 inch thick. Add a little more flour if the dough is sticky, but don't overwork it. Now fill, bake, and eat.

SWEET POTATO AND SWISS CHARD PIES

THIS RECIPE FROM BIKE BASKET PIES finds inspiration in the farmers' market movement. Natalie Galatzer, who earned her undergraduate degree in molecular biology, is, like many folk in their twenties, a strong advocate of local food and local farmers. When we met, our rendezvous point was, appropriately, the farmers' market at the Ferry Plaza.

Natalie packs her panniers with pies.

MAKES 12 HAND-SIZE PIES

1 bunch rainbow, green, or Swiss chard

2 tablespoons olive oil

2 cloves garlic, crushed

1 tablespoon crushed red pepper flakes

2 pounds garnet sweet potatoes, peeled and cut into 1/2-inch cubes

3/4 cup unsweetened coconut milk

1/4 teaspoon ground cinnamon

1/8 teaspoon ground nutmeg

1 teaspoon salt, or more to taste

1 teaspoon freshly ground black pepper, or more to taste

Natalie's Pie Dough (recipe follows)

Flour, for rolling out the pie dough

1 Remove the coarse stems from the chard and chop them. Chop the chard leaves separately. Set the chard stems and leaves aside separately.

2 Heat the olive oil in a large skillet over medium heat. Add the garlic and red pepper flakes and cook until fragrant. Add the sweet potatoes and cook until beginning to soften, about 8 minutes, turning occasionally. Add the coconut milk, cinnamon, and nutmeg and stir to incorporate.

3 Add the chopped chard stems and the salt and black pepper to the sweet potato mixture and cook until the potatoes are almost fork-tender, about 15 minutes more. Add the chopped chard leaves and stir to combine. Taste for seasoning, adding more salt and/or pepper as necessary, keeping in mind that the coconut milk and the pie pastry will absorb some of the seasoning. Remove the sweet potato mixture from the heat and set it aside.

4 Preheat the oven to 425°F.

5 Divide each of the 2 disks of dough into 6 equal pieces. Using a floured rolling pin, roll out each round of dough on a lightly floured work surface to a thickness of 1/4 inch. Add a little flour if necessary to prevent the dough from sticking. Gently press the rounds of dough into the wells of one 12-cupcake, or two 6-cupcake, dark-surfaced cupcake tins. The dough rounds will extend up the side and over the edge of the wells. Place the cupcake tin in the refrigerator for 5 to 10 minutes for the dough to chill.

6 Spoon the sweet potato mixture into the wells of the cupcake tin, dividing it evenly among them. Place a cup of water close by to wet your fingers and fold the dough over the top of each pie, pinching the edges to prevent the dough from sinking into the filling. Wet your fingers frequently. Refrigerate the pies for about 15 minutes.

7 Bake the pies for 15 minutes, then lower the temperature to 350°F and bake the pies for 20 to 30 minutes longer. The pies are done when the sides of the crust are a deep golden brown.

8 Remove the pies from the oven and immediately slide a knife between the edges of the tin and the crusts and twist the pies to loosen them. Place the tin on a wire rack to cool for 5 minutes. Remove the pies from the tin and transfer them to parchment paper to cool completely. These pies are best eaten after they rest for 30 minutes or more.

Hand-size pies handcrafted by Natalie.

Natalie's Pie Dough

THIS PIE DOUGH recipe comes straight from Natalie.

MAKES ENOUGH DOUGH FOR 12 HAND-SIZE PIES

1 1/2 cups (3 sticks) cold unsalted butter

4 tablespoons cold nonhydrogenated shortening

1 1/2 cups all-purpose flour

4 teaspoons granulated sugar

1 1/2 teaspoons salt

2 tablespoons chilled apple cider vinegar

12 tablespoons ice water, or more as needed

1 Cut the butter and shortening into 1-inch cubes and put them in the freezer for a few minutes while you assemble the rest of the ingredients for the pie dough.

2 Place the flour, sugar, and salt in a large bowl and whisk to combine evenly. Using a pastry blender or 2 knives, cut the cold butter and shortening into the flour mixture until they are completely incorporated; the mixture should resemble coarse crumbs.

3 Mix the cider vinegar and ice water together and slowly add the liquid to the butter and flour mixture, working it in by hand quickly, until all the dough sticks together and is tacky but not too sticky. If the dough is too dry, add more ice water, a little bit at a time.

4 Divide the dough into 2 equal balls. Without working the dough too much, form each ball into a hockey puck-shaped disk. Wrap the disks of dough in plastic wrap and refrigerate them for at least 1 hour or freeze them. Remove the dough from the refrigerator about 15 minutes before you plan to roll it out. If the dough is frozen, transfer it from the freezer to the refrigerator to thaw 4 or 5 hours before you want to use it.

N O T E : At each stage, it is important to keep the dough cold.

LAST SEEN: On a bike and on Twitter in San Francisco, California

BIKE BASKET PIES

NATALIE GALATZER'S basket is bigger than most. Rectangular and crafted from heavy-duty wire, it holds a stack of diminutive pies, which the twenty-something insurgent baker prepares in her home kitchen and delivers on a bike route that wends from her Mission home through the streets of San Francisco and back again.

After college, Natalie worked in AmeriCorps. And then in South America. She has experimented over the past few years with a number of food strategies. She's tried freeganism, which relies in part on Dumpster diving. And she once pondered starting a supper club business in her apartment. But then she realized, "Hey, I can bake!"

When the gods prove munificent, Natalie Galatzer relies on windfall fruit. As in the fruit that grows on trees in her Mission neighborhood. When ripe, that fruit drops to the ground for the proverbial picking. (Sad to say, sweet potatoes don't grow on trees. Instead, Natalie gets her sweet potatoes for the pie featured here from a friendly farmer.)

JAMAICAN MEAT PATTIES

MOST OF THE JAMAICAN street food vendors I have encountered here in the United States serve prefab meat patties. Some, like O'Neill Reid of the Jamaican Dutchy cart on 51st Street in New York City—the one with the flat screen TV plastered across the bow—own up to the freezer box origins of their pale-yellow pastry pouches of curry-scented beef. Most don't. The following recipe is an homage to the flaky made-from-scratch renditions sold by Jamerica Restaurant.

Customers arrive on the mall by foot and bike alike.

MAKES ABOUT 12 PATTIES

FOR THE PASTRY

3 cups all-purpose flour, plus flour for rolling out the pastry

2 teaspoons baking powder

I teaspoon curry powder

I teaspoon salt

1/2 teaspoon freshly ground black pepper

3/4 cup lard or vegetable shortening

3/4 cup milk

FOR THE FILLING

I pound ground beef

I onion, diced

1/4 cup diced red bell pepper

I clove garlic, minced

I teaspoon dried thyme

2 teaspoons curry powder

I teaspoon salt

1/2 teaspoon freshly ground black pepper

I teaspoon Worcestershire sauce

1/4 cup beef broth

3 or 4 dashes of hot pepper sauce, preferably Pickapeppa, or more to taste

2 quarts vegetable oil, for frying the patties

1 Make the pastry: Combine the flour, baking powder, 1 teaspoon of curry powder, 1 teaspoon of salt, and 1/2 teaspoon of black pepper in a large mixing bowl. Add the lard or shortening, cutting the fat in with a pastry blender or fork until the mixture resembles coarse crumbs. Sprinkle the milk over the flour mixture, gently incorporating it with your hands until the dough comes together to form a ball. Divide the dough in half, wrap each half in plastic wrap, and refrigerate them for about 1 hour.

2 Make the filling: Place the beef and onion in a large skillet over medium-high heat and cook, breaking the meat up with a spoon, until browned, 2 to 3 minutes. Add the red bell pepper, garlic, thyme, 2 teaspoons of curry powder, 1 teaspoon of salt, 1/2 teaspoon of black pepper, and Worcestershire sauce and cook until the bell pepper begins to soften, about 5 minutes, then add the beef broth and hot pepper sauce. Bring to a boil, reduce the heat, and let the filling simmer until most of the liquid is absorbed, 20 to 30 minutes. Remove the filling from the heat and let it cool to room temperature.

3 Lightly flour a work surface and roll out one of the halves of dough to a thickness of about 1/4 inch. Using a small plate about 6 inches in diameter, trace circles on the dough with a knife and cut out 6 circles. Place about 1/4 cup of the filling in the center of one half of a circle of dough, wet the inside edge of the dough with a little water, and fold the other half of the dough over the filling to make a half-moon shape. Crimp the edge of the dough with a fork to seal the patty well. Repeat with the remaining dough and filling and then with the second dough half.

Patties are the burgers of Jamerica, ubiquitous and filling-heavy.

4 Heat the vegetable oil in a deep fryer or Dutch oven over high heat until a deep fry thermometer attached to the side of the pot registers 375°F. Working in batches and being careful not to overcrowd the pot, carefully add the patties to the hot oil and cook them until golden brown, about 5 minutes. Using a slotted spoon, transfer the cooked patties to paper towels to drain.

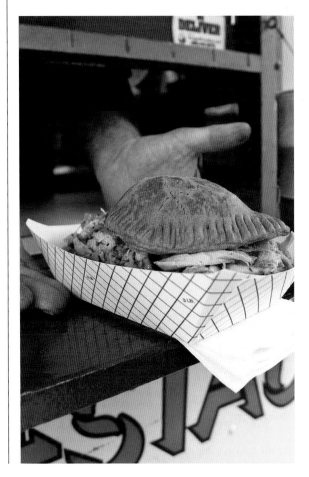

LAST SEEN: Library Mall, Madison, Wisconsin

JAMERICA RESTAURANT

ON THE DAY I VISITED Jamerica Restaurant, bottles of hot sauce lined the counter of this bright yellow hut. And rap, not reggae, blasted from the stereo. In other words, although proprietor Martin Deacon was raised in Port Antonio, Jamaica, he has now been flying the Jamaican flag in Madison for more than forty years. First came a grocery, which evolved into a restaurant, which birthed a weekday lunch cart. Assimilation led to the inclusion of jambalaya on Deacon's cart menu. Then came jerk tofu, which, as you might imagine, pales in comparison to the curried goat.

SALMON AND CHIPOTLE FRIED PIE

I'VE TALKED TO PEOPLE who call pies like these preacher pies, the reference being, I suppose, to the reward that follows a Sunday morning sermon. I've heard hunters talk of keeping a hot pie in the slash pocket of a tweed jacket on a cold morning. And at Whiffies Fried Pies, from which the recipe for these particular pies came, I've watched kids dance through the parking lot listening to hip-hop on their headphones while eating crescent-shaped salmon pies.

Handmade, hand-held, wrapped in tinfoil, and ready to go.

The muscled pie man fries late into the night.

MAKES ENOUGH FILLING FOR 12 SMALL FRIED PIES

Whiffies Fried Pie Pastry (page 274)

2 tablespoons blackening spice, preferably Chef Paul Prudhomme brand

8 ounces skinless wild salmon fillet

I tablespoon vegetable oil

1/2 cup sliced green bell pepper

1/2 cup sliced onion

I tablespoon freshly squeezed lemon juice

Chipotle Mayonnaise (recipe follows)

Flour, for rolling out the pie pastry dough

2 quarts vegetable oil, for frying the pies

1 Make the fried pie pastry dough and refrigerate it as described in Step 1 on page 274.

2 Heat the oil in a large skillet over medium-high heat. Sprinkle the blackening spice all over the salmon fillet. Cook the salmon until done to medium, 3 to 5 minutes per side. Transfer the salmon to a mixing bowl and set it aside. Do not wipe out the skillet.

3 Add the bell pepper and onion to the skillet and cook over medium-high heat until they begin to caramelize, about 5 minutes. Transfer the bell pepper and onion to a separate bowl. Add the lemon juice to the skillet and cook briefly, scraping up the browned bits from the

bottom of the skillet. Add these to the bell pepper and onion mixture.

4 Break up the salmon with a fork, then add the bell pepper and onion mixture and stir to combine. Add 2 tablespoons of the Chipotle Mayonnaise to bind the salmon filling and continue adding more of the mayonnaise until the filling is not as dense as a paste but not runny.

5 Roll out one piece of the pie pastry dough on a lightly floured work surface to a thickness of 1/4 inch. Using a small plate or saucer about 4 to 5 inches in diameter, trace circles on the dough with a knife and cut out the circles. Repeat with the second piece of dough.

6 Place about 2 tablespoons of salmon filling in the center of one half of a circle of dough. Wet the inside edge of the dough with a little water and fold the other half of the dough over the filling to make a half-moon shape. Crimp the edge of the dough with a fork to seal it well. Repeat with the remaining circles of dough and filling, and then repeat with the second dough half.

7 Heat the oil in a deep fryer or Dutch oven over high heat until a deep fry thermometer attached to the side of the pot registers 375°F. Working in batches and being careful not to overcrowd the pot, carefully add the pies to the hot oil and cook them until golden brown, about 5 minutes. Using a slotted spoon, transfer the cooked pies to paper towels to drain.

Read about the Whiffies Fried Pies truck on page 275.

Chipotle Mayonnaise

I ONCE WORKED with a guy we called Mayonnaise. He was white, and he was bland, thus the nickname. (Come to think of it, so was I.) A hit of chipotles could have saved him from his bland self. In this recipe inspired by Whiffies, canned chipotles are used to great effect.

MAKES ABOUT 2 1/4 CUPS

2 cups mayonnaise

1/4 cup sour cream

2 chipotle peppers

1/2 teaspoon paprika

1/2 teaspoon ground cumin

1/2 teaspoon mild chili powder

1 1/2 tablespoons freshly squeezed lemon juice

1 teaspoon salt

1/2 teaspoon granulated sugar

Place the mayonnaise, sour cream, chipotle peppers, paprika, cumin, chili powder, lemon juice, salt, and sugar in a food processor or blender and puree until smooth. The Chipotle Mayonnaise can be refrigerated, covered, for up to 2 weeks.

A CORNUCOPIA OF CRAWFISH.

CRAWFISH PIES

THE INSPIRATION FOR THE SWAMP SHACK'S PIE came from Jazz Fest, the annual two-week spring music and food bacchanal known formally as the New Orleans Jazz & Heritage Festival. At Jazz Fest, crawfish pies and oyster patties and *cochon de lait* po' boys are big draws, on a par with the music itself. I've eaten my share of crawfish at Jazz Fest but I'll go out on a limb here and say Trey Corkern's recipe makes pies that trump the ones I've had back in Louisiana.

A swivel seat on the porch is the ideal perch.

MAKES 10 TO 12 PIES

FOR THE FILLING

1 pound peeled crawfish tails (steer clear of the stuff from China)

1 medium-size yellow onion, chopped

1 red bell pepper, stemmed, seeded, and chopped

1 green bell pepper, stemmed, seeded, and chopped

2 ribs celery, chopped

2 tablespoons chopped garlic

1 tablespoon freshly squeezed lemon juice

4 tablespoons (^{1}/2 stick) salted butter

^{1}/4 cup all-purpose flour

1^1/2 teaspoons Creole seasoning

1^1/2 teaspoons salt

^{1}/2 teaspoon freshly ground black pepper

^{1}/4 teaspoon white pepper

^{1}/4 teaspoon dried thyme

^{1}/4 cup crawfish stock or other seafood or chicken stock

^{1}/2 cup heavy (whipping) cream

^{3}/4 cup cooked white rice

^{1}/2 cup chopped scallions

^{1}/4 cup Creole Cream Cheese (recipe follows)

^{1}/4 cup grated white cheddar cheese

FOR THE CRUST

1 cup all-purpose flour, plus more for rolling out the dough

^{1}/4 cup cake flour

^{1}/2 teaspoon salt

8 tablespoons (1 stick) salted butter

About ^{1}/2 cup ice water

2 quarts peanut oil, for frying the pies

1 egg, beaten with 1 tablespoon water

1 Make the filling: Drain the crawfish tails in a colander over a bowl, setting aside the liquid.

2 Place the onion, red and green bell peppers, celery, garlic, and lemon juice in a food processor and puree them. Set the pureed vegetables aside.

3 Melt the 4 tablespoons of butter in a large skillet over high heat. Let it brown a little, then add the 1/4 cup of all-purpose flour and whisk constantly until the flour is lightly browned, 2 to 3 minutes. Add the pureed vegetables to the skillet, stir to mix, and cook until heated through, about 5 minutes. Add the Creole seasoning, salt, black and white peppers, thyme, and the reserved crawfish

Trey Corkern does it all himself.

the 8 tablespoons of butter into pats and pinch them into the flour mixture. Make a well in the flour mixture and add ¼ cup of the ice water. Continue to pinch the dough, adding more ice water just until the dough holds together. Once you have a good firm dough, knead it by hand on a lightly floured surface for about 15 minutes. If you did it right, your forearms should hurt. Form the dough into a ball, and allow it (and yourself) to rest for at least 10 minutes.

7 Cut the ball of dough in half, wrap in plastic, and place that half in the refrigerator. Using a rolling pin, roll out the second half of dough without adding any flour. Then sprinkle the dough lightly with flour, flip it over, and roll it again until it is about ⅛ inch thick. When you think you're done, roll it out and flip it again, dusting it with more flour. Using a cereal bowl about 4 inches in diameter, with a defined rim, trace circles on the dough with a knife and cut them out. Repeat with the second ball of dough.

8 Heat the peanut oil in a deep fryer or Dutch oven over medium-high heat until a deep fry thermometer attached to the side of the pot registers 360°F.

9 Spoon 2 tablespoons of the filling in the center of one half of a circle of dough. Using a pastry brush, paint the edge of the dough with the egg mixture. Fold the other half of

liquid and cook, whisking, for 1 minute. Add the crawfish stock and let boil for 2 minutes.

4 Add the cream and let the mixture return to a boil while whisking it for 2 minutes, then remove it from the heat, add the rice, scallions, Creole Cream Cheese, and cheddar cheese and stir to combine.

5 Transfer the filling mixture to a large bowl and let cool to room temperature, then refrigerate it until cold, about 1 hour. Once the filling is cold, gently stir in the crawfish tails.

6 Meanwhile, make the crust: Mix both flours and the salt on a large, clean work surface. Cut

the dough over the filling to make a half-moon shape. Crimp the edge of the dough with a fork to seal it. Repeat with the remaining dough and filling. Working in batches and being careful not to overcrowd the pot, carefully add the pies to the hot oil and cook them until puffed and golden brown, about 5 minutes. Using a slotted spoon, transfer the cooked pies to paper towels to drain.

Creole Cream Cheese

THIS MAY BE the most fetishized ingredient in present-day Louisiana. The good folks of Slow Food have included it in their Ark of Taste, a compendium of endangered foods, wherein Creole cream cheese is described as "similar to Neufchâtel and other fresh farmhouse-style cheeses with a taste somewhere between ricotta and crème fraîche, and with an underlying hint of buttermilk." Enjoy the cheese on toast or crackers and with fresh and dried fruit.

MAKES ABOUT 4 CUPS

I gallon skim milk

1/2 cup buttermilk

8 drops of liquid rennet (see Note)

YOU'LL ALSO NEED

I piece of butter muslin or cheesecloth

1 Combine the skim milk, buttermilk, and liquid rennet in a large pot and heat over medium heat to a temperature of 110°F, about 10 minutes. Remove the milk mixture from the heat, cover the pot with a towel, and let stand at room temperature for 24 hours. Do not stir.

2 After 24 hours, place a large colander lined with butter muslin or cheesecloth in the sink and pour the milk mixture into the colander. Let the cheese drain for 10 minutes, then refrigerate it overnight after pulling the edges of the cloth over the top of the cheese and setting the colander in a bowl to catch drips. Once it has drained, you will have Creole cream cheese. Remove the cloth and store the cheese in the refrigerator, covered, for up to 2 weeks.

N O T E : Liquid rennet is available in the refrigerated section of natural food stores.

LAST SEEN: SW 5th Avenue and Stark Street, Portland, Oregon

THE SWAMP SHACK

TREY CORKERN knows how to broadcast Louisiana credibility. When I visited his Spanish moss–draped trailer, he displayed, alongside the register, a calendar from the Saturn Bar, the avant-funk New Orleans dive. (If you know New Orleans, you know that the Saturn, decorated with those rocket-booster neon light fixtures, may be that city's most beloved dive bar.)

But some facets of The Swamp Shack only come into focus when you sit on one of the swivel stools at the counter running the length of his trailer. That's where you'll learn that Trey was born in Franklinton, Louisiana, that he's a photographer by education, and that, for a while at least, he worked the line at Galatoire's, the fabled New Orleans Creole restaurant.

A hot iron is always key.

Adding that halo of powdered sugar.

La Dominique Crêperie—crepes as artwork.

Parker House
Peach Waffle with
almond-pecan
streusel.

WAFFLES
& their
KIN

CHAPTER 2

Waffles are the ideal street food.

That's what the guy working the window at the FlavourSpot trailer in Portland, Oregon, told me. I countered that most Americans think of waffles as knife-and-fork breakfast food, drizzled with syrup, maybe sprinkled with powdered sugar, sometimes flanked by sausage links. The man scoffed. He said that, at the FlavourSpot, they actually call their waffles "Dutch tacos." The implication was that such a coinage might help clear up misconceptions. It does not.

In Portland, it seems, waffles are mutable. And waffles are omnipresent. They're walking-around food. Dig a little and you realize that's the case in much of the waffle-eating world. I'm thinking of Belgium, where the good people of Wafels & Dinges in New York City got their inspiration. Closer to home, I'm thinking of the Dipper Dan I patronized as a boy, slurping waffle cones stacked with double scoops of butter pecan ice cream.

There's something outsize, however, about the Portland waffle aesthetic. In Portland they not only use waffles as conveyances for bacon and sausage, they lard their batters with breakfast sausage. They not only serve waffles with chicken, they serve waffles with chicken gravy.

STARTER WAFFLES

WAFFLES ARE QUICK BREADS, pliable, accommodating, easy to tuck and roll. This basic recipe, inspired by Parkers Waffles & Coffee, will get you started. With these words as your guide, you'll make waffles with texture, waffles with integrity. Not too puffy, not too dense. Just right.

A finishing touch—Scott Trimble gilds his lilies.

Set and ready for the morning rush.

MAKES 4 WAFFLES

2 cups all-purpose flour

3 tablespoons granulated sugar

I teaspoon baking powder

$^{1}/_{2}$ teaspoon baking soda

I teaspoon salt

3 large eggs, lightly beaten

4 tablespoons ($^{1}/_{2}$ stick) butter, melted and cooled slightly

2 cups buttermilk

Vegetable oil spray (optional)

Parkers' Maple Butter (optional, recipe follows), for serving

1 Combine the flour, sugar, baking powder, baking soda, and salt in a large mixing bowl and whisk to mix thoroughly.

2 Place the eggs and butter in another mixing bowl and whisk to combine. Whisk in the buttermilk. Pour the buttermilk and egg mixture into the bowl with the dry ingredients and stir gently until combined. Let the batter rest for a few minutes.

3 Heat a waffle iron following the manufacturer's instructions and, if necessary, lightly coat the surface with vegetable oil spray to prevent the waffles from sticking. Pour one

Waffle as ham and egg envelope, encased in foil to catch any yolky drips.

quarter of the waffle batter into the waffle iron, close it, and cook the waffle until both sides are golden brown, about 5 minutes. Repeat with the remaining batter. Keep the waffles in a warm oven until ready to serve with the Maple Butter, if desired.

Parkers' Maple Butter

IF YOU'RE PLANNING to walk with waffle in hand, smear one side with the maple butter, fold the waffle in half, and tuck the resulting crescent in a pouch made from, say, waxed paper. Walk, but watch for leaks.

MAKES ABOUT I CUP

8 tablespoons (I stick) salted butter

1/2 cup pure maple syrup, preferably Grade B
   (see Note)

Place the butter and maple syrup in a small saucepan over low heat and stir constantly until the butter melts. Pour the Maple Butter into a small bowl and let cool at room temperature to a spreadable consistency. Smear the butter on waffles or pancakes. The butter can be refrigerated, covered, for 1 week or frozen for up to 2 months.

N O T E : Grade B maple syrup is the darkest of the commercial grades of maple syrup and has an intense maple flavor.

LAST SEEN: SW 4th Avenue and College Street, Portland, Oregon

PARKERS WAFFLES & COFFEE

SCOTT AND ABBIE TRIMBLE bought their trailer on Craigslist in the summer of 2009. It had previously been a pizza trailer. In July they parked it in the Portland State University pod of food carts.

Waffles with maple butter came first for the husband and wife team. Then waffles and gravy. Then waffles and chili. By the time they hit waffle-wrapped Reubens, their experimentation had reached its ridiculously sublime conclusion. With that concoction on the top of my mind, waffles and gravy seemed, well, normal.

SAUSAGE GRAVY AND WAFFLES

THIS RECIPE, INSPIRED by Parkers Waffles & Coffee, is theoretically portable. Fold your waffle just so and you have a cone that might hold that sausage gravy for thirty seconds or so before it leaks through. Better, if you're at Parkers, eat this one on the trunk of a car. Of course, at home, the kitchen counter works.

A shoebox of big flavors.

MAKES ENOUGH SAUSAGE GRAVY FOR 2 WAFFLES

1/2 pound pork sausage meat

2 tablespoons all-purpose flour

2 cups milk, or more as needed

Freshly ground black pepper

2 warm waffles (from Starter Waffles, page 43)

Chopped fresh parsley (optional), for garnish

1 Place the sausage in a skillet over medium-high heat and cook until browned and cooked through, 4 to 5 minutes, stirring the sausage to break it into bite-size pieces. Using a slotted spoon or spatula, transfer the sausage to paper towels to drain. Leave all of the sausage fat in the skillet.

2 Whisk the flour into the fat and let it cook for about 1 minute. Slowly add the milk and let the mixture come to a boil, whisking constantly. Reduce the heat and let the gravy simmer until thickened, about 2 minutes. If the gravy is too thick, add more milk while continuing to stir. Season the gravy with pepper to taste.

3 Return the cooked sausage to the skillet and stir until heated through. Pour the sausage and gravy over the warm waffles. Garnish the waffles with the parsley, if desired.

Sausage gravy blankets a hot waffle, making for a hearty start to the day and a sobering end to the night.

BACON OR SAUSAGE WAFFLES

THE LITTLE BLUE WAFFLE WAGON ladies roll their waffles in a manner reminiscent of burritos. The waffles emerge from the order window dusted with powdered sugar and sheathed in blue-and-white checkered tissue. I'm keen on this meaty recipe, inspired by Andrea and Emmy, but the waffle ladies also take plain waffles and smear them with lemon curd, vanilla ginger pear compote, or whipped and sugared cream cheese, too.

Trustworthy—a menu that's short and to the point.

A blue tarp for a blue wagon.

MAKES 4 WAFFLES

2 cups all-purpose flour

3 tablespoons granulated sugar

1 teaspoon baking powder

1/2 teaspoon baking soda

1 teaspoon salt

3 large eggs, lightly beaten

4 tablespoons (1/2 stick) butter, melted and cooled slightly

2 cups buttermilk

Vegetable oil spray (optional)

1/2 pound bacon or sausage, cooked and crumbled

1 Combine the flour, sugar, baking powder, baking soda, and salt in a large mixing bowl and whisk to mix thoroughly.

2 Place the eggs and butter in another mixing bowl and whisk to combine. Whisk in the buttermilk. Pour the buttermilk and egg mixture into the bowl with the dry ingredients and stir gently until combined. Let the batter rest for a few minutes.

3 Heat a waffle iron following the manufacturer's instructions and, if necessary, lightly coat the surface with vegetable oil spray to prevent the waffles from sticking. Stir the crumbled bacon or sausage into the waffle batter (you could add both). Pour one quarter of the waffle batter into the waffle iron, close it, and cook the waffle until both sides are golden brown, about 5 minutes. Repeat with the remaining batter. (Apologies for insulting your intelligence; recipe conventions dictate that I tell you that.) Keep the waffles in a warm oven until ready to serve.

As good tasting as it is good-looking.

LAST SEEN: Hawthorne Boulevard and SE 33rd Avenue, Portland, Oregon

LITTLE BLUE WAFFLE WAGON

ANDREA HAWK AND EMMY ERVIN are lapsed waitresses who decided, after slinging hash and eggs for years, that they would make a living by cooking as well as slinging. In July of 2008 they bought a Shasta, one of those teardrop-shaped campers that you pull behind a pickup. And they parked it in a gravel lot between a lighting store and a psychologist's office.

In the grand Portland tradition, they staked their business on waffles—and on coffee from the local Stumptown Coffee Roasters. Working three irons, set on what was once the camper's bunk bed platform, they dish waffles through a small window to regulars who gather in the gravel lot to eat on 1950s–era TV trays.

A HOLE HERE AND THERE IS PART OF A WAFFLE'S CHARM.

WAFFLE BREAKFAST TACOS

THE BREAKFAST TACO is the signature food of Austin. Made with flour tortillas, traditionally stuffed with chorizo and eggs or bacon and eggs, breakfast tacos have given rise to a wide range of riffs, from the breakfast "panaani" at the Whip In convenience store to the waffle recipe here from Jason Umlas at Lucky J's.

Go light on the ladle. The batter bubbles up as soon as it hits the hot waffle iron.

Note the extra propane tanks—portable fuel to fire the irons.

SERVES 4

FOR THE BREAKFAST POTATOES

1 tablespoon chili powder

1 tablespoon store-bought seasoned salt

1 tablespoon paprika

1 cup canola oil, for frying the potatoes

1 cup diced (3/4-inch) red potatoes

1 cup diced (3/4-inch) red onions

FOR THE WAFFLE TACOS

1 tablespoon canola oil

4 large eggs, beaten

4 slices of bacon, cooked and crumbled

3/4 cup (about 3 ounces) shredded cheddar cheese

4 Lucky J's Waffles (recipe follows)

1 Make the breakfast potatoes: Place the chili powder, seasoned salt, and paprika in a small bowl and stir to mix. Set the chili powder mixture aside.

2 Heat the 1 cup of oil in a large skillet over high heat. Add the potatoes and onions and cook until the potatoes are crisp and the onions are browned, 10 to 12 minutes. Drain the potatoes and onions and toss them with the chili powder mixture. Keep the breakfast potatoes warm while making the waffle tacos.

3 Make the waffle tacos: Place the 1 tablespoon of oil in a large skillet over medium heat. Add the eggs and cook, stirring often.

LUCKY J'S

JASON UMLAS focused on East Asian studies at Brown University. Inspired, he lived in Tokyo for six months. Then he moved to Los Angeles, where he cooked at various restaurants including, God help us all, The Cheesecake Factory. While in LA he also fell, more felicitously, under the spell of Roscoe's House of Chicken 'n Waffles, the iconic Hollywood restaurant.

When I met Jason he had settled in Austin, where he was frying birds in the tiny red Lucky J's trailer on Burnet Road. Behind the trailer, flanking a hardware store, Jason had installed picnic tables. On a Sunday afternoon I watched customers perched at those picnic tables pull brown-bagged vodka bottles from their backpacks and pour Bloody Marys while Jason bopped back and forth from the waffle irons in the trailer to a turntable and speakers set up in the parking lot, where he was spinning Sergio Mendes and Brasil '66, the O'Jays, and Jimi Hendrix.

When the eggs are about halfway done, add the bacon, cheese, and breakfast potatoes (see Note) and cook, stirring, until the eggs are set to taste.

4 Place a waffle in another skillet and heat it over medium-high heat for about 1 minute. Turn the waffle over and spoon the egg mixture on top. Fold the waffle in half. Keep the waffle taco warm while you make the remaining ones.

NOTE: If you'd prefer to serve the breakfast potatoes alongside the tacos instead of in the mix, that's cool.

Lucky J's Waffles

THE WAFFLES HERE ARE LIKE WHITE BREAD, meant to bolster breakfast tacos, not to get in the way. This recipe, unapologetically plain and inspired by Lucky J's, gets the job done, and then gets out of the way, letting all the good stuff you pile on top come to the fore.

MAKES 4 WAFFLES

Heavy-duty cast-iron waffle irons generate a lot of steam.

2 cups all-purpose flour

I teaspoon salt

I tablespoon baking powder

3 large eggs

1/4 cup vegetable oil

Vegetable oil spray (optional)

1 Combine the flour, salt, and baking powder in a mixing bowl and whisk to mix thoroughly.

2 Place the eggs, oil, and 1 cup of water in a large mixing bowl and whisk to combine. Whisk in the dry ingredients, slowly adding up to 1/2 cup more water until the batter has a loose consistency. Let the batter rest for 15 to 20 minutes.

3 Heat a waffle iron following the manufacturer's instructions and, if necessary, lightly coat the surface with vegetable oil spray to prevent the waffles from sticking. Pour about 1/2 cup of the waffle batter into the waffle iron, close it, and cook the waffle until both sides are golden brown but not crisp, about 5 minutes. Repeat with the remaining batter. Keep the waffles in a warm oven until ready to serve.

Don't skimp—homemade waffles deserve pure maple syrup.

CROQUE MONSIEUR "TACOS"

JASON UMLAS HAS A THING for hot sauces. Last time I looked, he was stocking more than twenty varieties, including a brand called Texas Soda Pop, which played very well off the confectioners' sugar garnish on a waffle taco take on the croque monsieur made with chicken, Swiss cheese, and ham.

Crispy chicken, skillet-grilled ham, and melted cheese encased in a fresh waffle—it's kind of French.

Wishbones denote good luck—and good chicken.

SERVES 4

FOR THE CHICKEN

2 cups all-purpose flour

I tablespoon salt

I tablespoon freshly ground black pepper

I tablespoon chili powder

I tablespoon store-bought seasoned salt

I tablespoon paprika

2 cups buttermilk

2 cups canola oil, for frying the chicken

4 chicken tenders (about I pound total)

FOR THE CROQUE MONSIEUR "TACOS"

4 slices ham (see Note)

4 Lucky J's Waffles (page 50)

8 slices Swiss cheese

I teaspoon confectioners' sugar

Hot sauce (optional)

1 Prepare the chicken: Mix 1 cup of the flour with the salt and pepper in a small shallow bowl and set it aside. In a separate shallow bowl, mix the remaining 1 cup of flour with the chili powder, seasoned salt, and paprika and

set it aside. Pour the buttermilk into another small bowl.

2 Pour oil to a depth of 1 inch into a cast-iron skillet and heat over medium-high heat until the oil registers 340°F on a deep fry thermometer.

A Croque Monsieur "Taco" from Lucky J himself. You might need a few napkins to wipe the sugar off your beard.

3 Dredge the chicken tenders first in the flour, salt, and pepper mixture, shaking off the excess flour. Then dip the chicken tenders in the buttermilk until thoroughly coated. Dredge the buttermilk-coated tenders in the flour and seasoning mixture and shake off the excess flour.

4 Cook the chicken tenders in the hot oil until golden brown and cooked through, about 5 minutes. Using a slotted spoon, transfer the chicken tenders to paper towels to drain.

5 Make the Croque Monsieur "Tacos": Warm the slices of ham in a skillet over medium-high heat for about 1 minute. Set the ham aside.

6 Place a waffle in the skillet and heat it for about 1 minute. Turn the waffle over and place 2 slices of Swiss cheese on top. Place a slice of warmed ham on top of the cheese. Place a chicken tender on one side of the waffle and fold the waffle in half. Repeat with the remaining waffles, cheese, ham, and chicken. Sprinkle the waffles with the confectioners' sugar and hot sauce, if desired, before serving.

NOTE: You can substitute 8 slices of cooked bacon for the ham.

AUSTIN:
THE AIRSTREAM AESTHETIC

San Antonio has long been known as the premier street food city in Texas. That reputation was built on the work of the Chili Queens, Mexican women who, in the late 1800s and early 1900s, sold chili con carne from jerry-rigged stands on Military Plaza and then on Market Square.

sold by men and boys who pushed charcoal-burning carts through the streets. In the early 1920s Delphino Martinez worked just such a cart on Congress Avenue. And Matt, his elementary school–aged son, worked alongside, stoking the coals. (Out of that grew Matt's El Rancho, the fifty-plus-year-old Austin Tex-Mex institution.)

Matt was not the only seat-of-his-pants entrepreneur to build an Austin business on street food. In the late 1970s, Maria Corbalan, a native of Argentina, invested her tax return in a taco trailer, which she painted to resemble an adobe bungalow. Over time that trailer begat an outsize restaurant, Maria's Taco Xpress, that has come to codify the hippified Tex-Mex genre.

And still the Austin street food scene booms. Drive down Cesar Chavez Street and a trailer pops into view every few blocks. They're selling pork *al pastor,* sliced from a spinning cone of pineapple-topped meat and tucked into a corn tortilla, or scrambled eggs and chorizo, sluiced with

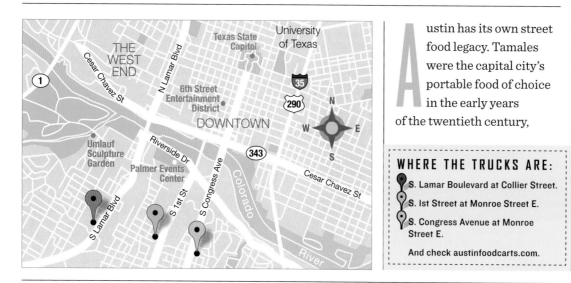

A ustin has its own street food legacy. Tamales were the capital city's portable food of choice in the early years of the twentieth century,

WHERE THE TRUCKS ARE:

- S. Lamar Boulevard at Collier Street.
- S. Ist Street at Monroe Street E.
- S. Congress Avenue at Monroe Street E.

And check austinfoodcarts.com.

chile de árbol salsa and folded into a steaming white wheat tortilla.

In the fall of 2009, more than one thousand licensed mobile food vendors worked Austin's streets. (Just five years prior, the number hovered around five hundred.) Some of those recent additions are workaday trucks, peddling an odd and unrooted mix of burgers and burritos to day laborers. But a goodly number of the new carts are comparable to Man Bites Dog, parked since November of 2009 in the South Austin Trailer Park & Eatery, alongside Torchy's Tacos and Holy Cacao.

Man Bites Dog claims a rectangular concession trailer. Jeremiah Allen, the proprietor, is a onetime bartender who until recently worked for a start-up company making a device that measures alcohol levels in breast milk. Nowadays he serves chicken sausage dogs with sweet corn relish and Frito pies topped with chopped wienies.

Gourdough's Big Fat Donuts opened in October of 2009. Perched alongside a drive-thru espresso stand on South Lamar Boulevard, it is of a similar ilk. College students play Hacky Sack in the pebble parking lot. Speakers blast the latest band that claims to be the rightful heir to the Grateful Dead legacy. This is not breakfast food for morning commuters. Gourdough's opens at eleven and closes as late as three in the morning. And the menu includes a yeast doughnut gorged with hot pepper jelly and slicked with cream cheese icing.

Gourdough's does business in a retrofitted Airstream trailer. Those silver trailers are a defining element of the Austin retail culture. On South Lamar alone, a realtor, a pet groomer, and DeFresh Mode, a raw foods trailer serving "meatless goodness," all do business in Airstreams.

A more recent entry in the unconventional structure category is the shipping container restaurant, pioneered by La Boîte, a pastry and coffee café perched on a South Lamar hill between a yoga studio and The Texas Cuban trailer. Peeled back like a stylish sardine can, outfitted with blond veneer walls, fronted by oversize folding windows that open onto a patio, La Boîte may not foretell the future of portable restaurants. But it turns heads. (And its sausage brioche, made with maple sausage, is stellar.)

Change in the Austin scene is sure to come. Rapid expansion will likely compel new regulations from the city government and new solutions from business owners. The most plausible next step for street food in Austin may be adoption of the Portland pod model.

Among the players hoping to serve that need will be the Whip In, a reinvented convenience store off I-35 that flies under the banner "South Asian food, South Austin mood." They're planning the Whip In Spot, a "six-pack of trailers," featuring food carts parked in a beer garden.

- - - - - - - - - - - - - - - - - -

Top: **France meets Austin.**

Middle: **Corral of Austin eats.**

Bottom: **Cuban with a smile.**

LIEGE WAFFLES

LIEGE IS A UNIVERSITY CITY on Belgium's eastern fringe. Most of the inhabitants speak French. And most of the inhabitants eat waffles as a street food. Liège-style waffles come with a hoary story of origin that involves the prince-bishop of Liège, his chef, his sweet tooth, a brioche recipe, some sugar, and a cast-iron waffle maker. These waffles, inspired by Wafels & Dinges, are not hoary. Instead, they're slightly puffy, made from a yeast dough, not a batter, are a little sour, and wholly addictive.

The Belgian flag flies high at Wafels & Dinges.

MAKES 6 TO 8 WAFFLES

1 envelope (¹/4 ounce) active dry yeast

4¹/2 teaspoons granulated sugar

¹/8 teaspoon salt

¹/3 cup warm water

2 cups all-purpose flour

3 large eggs

1 cup (2 sticks) butter, melted and cooled slightly

1 cup pearl sugar (see Note)

Vegetable oil spray (optional)

Spekuloos Spread (optional, recipe follows), for serving

1 Place the yeast, granulated sugar, and salt in a mixing bowl. Add the warm water and stir until the sugar and salt dissolve. Let the yeast mixture sit in a warm place until it starts to bubble, about 15 minutes.

2 Place the flour in a large mixing bowl and make a well in the center. Pour the yeast mixture into the well, add the eggs and butter, and knead gently with your hands until a dough forms. Cover the bowl tightly with plastic wrap and let the dough sit at room temperature until it rises and doubles in volume, 30 to 45 minutes.

Liege waffles are made from a yeast dough, not a batter. Here dough on the rise awaits its final calling.

3 Gently mix the pearl sugar into the dough and let it rest for 15 minutes more.

4 Heat a waffle iron to its highest temperature, following the manufacturer's instructions, and, if necessary, lightly coat the surface with vegetable oil spray to prevent the waffles from sticking. Place a Ping-Pong to tennis ball-size portion of dough in the waffle iron, close it, and cook the waffle until both sides are golden brown, 3 to 5 minutes. Repeat with the remaining batter. Each waffle will emerge a different size and shape. They will have what you call "character." Serve the waffles with the Spekuloos Spread, if desired.

N O T E : Pearl sugar is a large-crystal sugar. It's available at specialty food stores.

Spekuloos Spread

THIS CARAMEL GOO has the consistency of thin peanut butter and the richness of Nutella. Biscoff is the brand of spread that Thomas DeGeest uses for his waffles, but you can take the following recipe in hand and, inspired by Wafels & Dinges, make your own cookie condiment.

MAKES ABOUT 3/4 CUP

5 ounces Biscoff cookies (about 20 cookies; see Note)

1/2 cup confectioners' sugar

8 tablespoons (1 stick) butter, at room temperature

1 teaspoon pumpkin pie spice

1/2 teaspoon ground cinnamon

1/2 teaspoon salt

Place the cookies in a food processor and process them to a fine powder. Add the confectioners' sugar, butter, pumpkin pie spice, cinnamon, and salt and blend until smooth. Refrigerate, tightly covered, when not in use.

N O T E : Biscoff cookies are available in most grocery stores, or you could save up the snack-size packets from Delta flights.

LAST SEEN: 14th Street between Third and Fourth Avenues, New York, New York

WAFELS & DINGES

THOMAS DeGEEST, the former IBM management consultant who owns Wafels & Dinges, likes to wear a T-shirt that reads "Belgian Ministry of Cultural Affairs, Special Envoy for Waffles." His truck, painted school bus yellow, is a diesel Grumman with a wide bay of windows that affords eaters a glimpse of the waffle men at work, flipping their waffles on rectangular, gas-fired irons with the sort of frenetic energy usually employed by cocaine-snorting DJs.

In the world of Wafels & Dinges, a waffle is a foil for toppings (that's what *dinges* are—toppings, like bananas, walnuts, and Nutella). As for the waffles themselves, DeGeest makes Brussels waffles, which are rectangular, light, and crisp. And he makes Liège waffles, which are irregularly shaped, slightly sour, and pleasantly chewy.

DeGeest and company broadcast tweets that instruct regulars who want free *dinges* to "Tell us what superpower you would like to have." Or, "Make your best Jack Nicholson face."

PEANUT RICE PANCAKES

IN SOUTH KOREA they are known as *hotteok,* Ki Nam, the man who squats behind the cart and smokes cigarettes, told me. Since I first tasted his rice cakes, I've noticed a couple of variations including a dough that's a shade of green, owing to the addition of green tea powder. This recipe, inspired by Koo's Grill, produces a cake that, when bitten, reveals a scalding hot core of molten sugar that will scorch the roof of your mouth. So go slow.

A short stack of pancakes filled with a sweetened peanut surprise.

On chilly days, peanut rice pancakes warm body and soul.

MAKES 8 SMALL PANCAKES

I teaspoon active dry yeast (from I envelope)

2 tablespoons granulated sugar

$^1/_4$ cup warm water

I cup all-purpose flour

$^3/_4$ cup rice flour

$^1/_2$ teaspoon salt

$^1/_2$ cup milk

$^1/_4$ cup roasted peanuts, chopped

$^1/_4$ cup packed brown sugar

2 tablespoons honey

$^1/_2$ teaspoon ground cinnamon

About $^1/_2$ cup vegetable or peanut oil, plus oil for forming the cakes

1 Place the yeast and granulated sugar in a small bowl or measuring cup. Add the warm water and stir until the sugar dissolves. Let the yeast mixture sit in a warm place until it starts to bubble, about 15 minutes.

2 Sift the all-purpose and rice flours and salt into a large mixing bowl. Pour the yeast mixture and the milk into the flour mixture and, using your hands, form the dough into a sticky ball. Cover the bowl tightly with plastic wrap and let the dough sit in a warm spot until it doubles in size, about 2 hours.

3 Place the peanuts, brown sugar, honey, and cinnamon in a bowl and stir to mix. Set the peanut mixture aside.

4 Punch down the dough and divide it into 8 equal pieces. Rub your hands with oil and form

a disk that is about 2½ inches in diameter and ¼ inch thick from one of the pieces. Place 1 tablespoon of the peanut mixture in the center and spread it out evenly. Fold the dough over the filling, pressing the edges to seal it inside and flattening the dough into a free-form disk. Repeat with the remaining dough and filling.

5 Pour enough oil into a large skillet to just cover the bottom and heat it over medium-high heat. When the oil is hot, add the disks of dough, 1 or 2 at a time, and using an offset spatula that has been rubbed with oil, press down as they cook until they are about ¼ inch thick. Cook the pancakes until golden brown, 3 to 4 minutes on each side, continuing to press on them with the spatula. Transfer the pancakes to paper towels or a wire rack to drain. Repeat with the remaining dough, adding more oil as necessary. Serve the pancakes warm.

At Koo's Grill, paddles flatten the pancakes as they cook.

LAST SEEN: 450 South Western Avenue, Los Angeles, California

KOO'S GRILL

THE QUILTED metal cart, set alongside the entrance to the California Market in Koreatown, is flanked by a giant vending machine claw game and a drink machine that vends chai lattes.

Rice cakes, those chewy Korean standards, cooked by a crew of Mexican women, are a buck a pop. Think of a round take on Pop-Tarts, filled with a mix of honey, cinnamon, brown sugar, and chopped peanuts. They're cooked on a griddle, smashed flat by a metal device that resembles an air hockey paddle, and tucked in a folded disposable plate that acts as an insulating jacket. These rice cakes may be the best street food deal in America.

MOROCCAN CHICKEN CREPES

IN MOROCCO, CREPELIKE *BEGHRIR* BREADS are popular. Smooth on one side and pocked with tiny air bubbles on the other, they are typically eaten with honey and butter. In the recipe here, inspired by Fliphappy Crêpes, the crepes do heavy lifting with a Moroccan-inspired chicken filling.

- -

Fliphappy provides crepes and a place to enjoy them.

MAKES 8 CREPES

¹/4 cup olive oil

I red bell pepper, stemmed, seeded, and cut into strips

2 carrots, diced

3 cloves garlic, chopped

Salt and freshly ground black pepper

2 tablespoons (¹/4 stick) butter

2 large onions, cut into thin slices

I teaspoon granulated sugar

8 crepes (from Fliphappy Crepe Batter, recipe follows)

4 cups smoked or roasted chicken chunks

I cup Buttermilk-Feta Dressing (page 63)

¹/4 cup Fliphappy Harissa (page 63)

1 Preheat the oven to 375°F.

2 Lightly coat a rimmed baking sheet with 1 tablespoon of olive oil. Combine the bell pepper, carrots, and garlic on the baking sheet, drizzle 2 more tablespoons of olive oil over the vegetables, and toss to coat. Season the vegetables with salt and black pepper to taste. Bake the vegetables until roasted, 20 to 30 minutes, stirring occasionally.

3 Meanwhile, melt the butter in the remaining 1 tablespoon olive oil in a large skillet over medium-high heat. Add the onions and stir to coat. Cook the onions until softened, about 5 minutes, then reduce the heat to medium. Stir in the sugar and continue to cook the onions, stirring occasionally, until caramelized, about 20 minutes longer. Set the onions aside.

4 To assemble the crepes, spoon some of the roasted vegetables in the center of each crepe. Top the vegetables with 1/2 cup of chicken and some of the caramelized onions. Spoon 1 to 2 tablespoons of the Buttermilk-Feta Dressing on each crepe and drizzle some *harissa* on top. Wrap up the crepes, folding over one end to enclose the filling.

Fliphappy Crepe Batter

CREPES ARE UNDERSTOOD to be delicate. Vulnerable, even. But this recipe, from the Fliphappy Crêpes ladies, makes relatively durable crepes. In addition to the

Moroccan-style chicken filling, Andrea and Nessa wrap their crepes around everything from pulled pork to the ingredients traditionally stuffed inside a Cuban sandwich.

MAKES ABOUT 8 CREPES

3 large eggs, beaten

1 1/2 cups milk

About 2 cups all-purpose flour

About 8 tablespoons (1 stick) butter, melted

1 Whisk the eggs, milk, and 1/2 cup of water together in a large mixing bowl. Gradually add the flour, mixing in only enough to combine all of the ingredients. Stir 7 tablespoons of the butter into the crepe batter.

2 Heat a crepe pan or heavy-bottomed non-stick 10-inch skillet over medium-high heat.

Ring for harissa on this well-used bell, like so many before you.

Coat the bottom of the pan with about 1/4 teaspoon of the remaining butter. Pour about 1/2 cup of crepe batter in the middle of the pan and, using a crepe paddle or an offset spatula, spread the batter evenly, working in a circular motion from the center of the pan to the outside edge. Be careful to cover the bottom of the pan completely with as thin a layer of batter as possible. Let the crepe cook until it starts to brown slightly, about 2 minutes, then gently flip it, and cook for 30 seconds more. Remove the crepe from the pan, being very careful not to tear it. This takes practice. Don't get frustrated if your countertop becomes littered with crepe debris. Transfer the crepe to a piece

LAST SEEN: 400 Josephine Street, Austin, Texas

FLIPHAPPY CREPES

PECAN TREES provide the canopy. Interconnected tarps give further shade. For a patio, there's a pebbled yard, scattered with picnic tables and spray-painted TV trays. Speakers play lusty Donna Summer one minute, reedy Edith Piaf the next. Neighbors include the International Union of Elevator Constructors, Local 133. At the core of this scene is a silver 1966 Avion trailer with a kitchen stuffed inside.

Andrea Day-Boykin and Nessa Higgins were early leaders of the local avant-garde street food scene. Inspired by a trip to Portland, they opened Fliphappy Crêpes in the spring of 2006. "I fell in love with the trailer," Nessa told me. "Andrea was the food person." By adopting the Airstream-style trailer, they set a precedent many followed. And by curating an inviting public space where customers could gather, they dictated that aesthetics mattered, especially on the street.

of parchment paper and cover it with another piece of parchment paper. Repeat with the remaining crepe batter, adding more butter to the pan as necessary and stacking the crepes between pieces of parchment paper to keep them separate.

Buttermilk-Feta Dressing

THINK OF BUTTERMILK RANCH DRESSING. But think of a really good rendition of the stuff. That's the cool, calm, collected taste in this recipe, inspired by the work of Nessa and Andrea at Fliphappy Crêpes.

MAKES ABOUT I CUP

I cup (about 4 ounces) crumbled feta

1/4 cup buttermilk

1/4 cup sour cream

1/4 cup mayonnaise

I clove garlic, peeled and crushed

I tablespoon white wine vinegar

1/2 teaspoon salt

1/4 teaspoon freshly ground black pepper

Using your hands or a fork, break the feta into small crumbles. Place the buttermilk, sour cream, mayonnaise, garlic, wine vinegar, salt, and pepper in a food processor or blender and puree until smooth. Pour into a container and fold in the feta. The dressing can be refrigerated, covered, for up to 1 week.

Fliphappy Harissa

THROUGHOUT MUCH OF NORTHERN AFRICA, *harissa* is a table sauce applied liberally to everything from flatbread to scrambled eggs. In its use of chile flakes, this *harissa* recipe, inspired by Fliphappy Crêpes, compares favorably to a wide range of hot sauces, including the chile oils of China and Korea.

MAKES ABOUT 1/2 CUP

3 tablespoons crushed red pepper flakes

I clove garlic, peeled and crushed

1/2 teaspoon smoked paprika

I tablespoon red wine vinegar

3/4 teaspoon salt

1/4 teaspoon granulated sugar

1/4 teaspoon freshly ground black pepper

1/2 cup olive oil

1 Bring 2 cups of water to a boil in a small saucepan over high heat. Add the red pepper flakes and turn off the heat. Let the pepper flakes soak for 30 minutes, then drain them, discarding the liquid.

2 Place the soaked pepper flakes, garlic, paprika, wine vinegar, salt, sugar, and black pepper in a blender and puree. With the motor running, add the olive oil in a steady stream. This fireball of a sauce can be refrigerated, covered, for up to 1 week.

LEMON CREPES

ZBIGNIEW CHOJNACKI parks his red Jeep Cherokee behind the cart and uses it for storage. That's where he keeps the plastic goods for La Dominique Crêperie. And the crates of lemons. He takes pride in sourcing the best ingredients. He hand cuts all of his fruits and vegetables. His meats are organic and his eggs are free range. He refuses to accept that street food is lowest common denominator food. To watch him craft a lemon crepe is to watch a man who cares deeply about the simple details that, in aggregate, make for great eats. This recipe was inspired by his work.

MAKES 4 CREPES

4 lemons

4 crepes (from Zbigniew Chojnacki's Crepe Batter, page 67)

$1/4$ cup granulated sugar

$1/4$ cup confectioners' sugar

1 Rinse the lemons and pat them dry with paper towels; then zest them. Squeeze the juice of the lemons through a fine sieve, discarding the seeds.

2 Place a crepe in a hot skillet to reheat it slightly. Sprinkle 1 tablespoon of granulated sugar on top of the crepe, followed by a quarter of the lemon zest. Drizzle some lemon juice all over the crepe and then, using a spatula, fold the crepe in half and in half again to create a cone shape.

3 Transfer the crepe to a plate and sprinkle more lemon juice over it, followed by a dusting of 1 tablespoon of confectioners' sugar. Repeat with the remaining crepes.

LAST SEEN: Market at 33rd Street, Philadelphia, Pennsylvania

LA DOMINIQUE CREPERIE

ZBIGNIEW CHOJNACKI is a sculptor of Polish birth who fled his homeland in 1984. He found great success in America. Out of his Philadelphia studio emerged intricately patterned jewelry and raku-textured female busts and torsos. But when art commissions slowed in 2007 he took a different tack. As a boy in Poland Zbigniew had made crepes with his mother. In 2007 the Philadelphia street scene lacked great crepes. So Zbigniew bought a one-man trailer, outfitted it with two crepe irons, and began again.

La Dominique Crêperie's menu is limited. Zbigniew's style is unhurried. His manner is idiosyncratic. A lanky man with an easy cartside manner, Zbigniew does not like to make breakfast crepes. They're unwieldy beasts, he says, overstuffed with sausage and such to suit his customers. Better to seek Zbigniew out in the afternoon when the crowds have died down and he can take his time, zesting lemons to order for a perfectly simple sugared lemon crepe.

Curls of lemon zest fresh from the fruit highlight this crepe. If you don't own a zester, go buy one.

COCONUT VEGGIE CHICKEN CREPES

THE COMBINATION OF COCONUT, vegetables, and chicken is not—as far as I can tell—Polish. Nor is it French. French Caribbean, maybe. But for Zbigniew Chojnacki it's a big seller at La Dominique Crêperie, a favorite of college students who rationalize that, owing to the veggies tucked inside, these crepes constitute a balanced meal.

MAKES 4 CREPES

3 tablespoons vegetable oil

I teaspoon minced garlic

I cup unsweetened coconut milk

1/4 cup chicken broth

2 teaspoons soy sauce

1/2 cup heavy (whipping) cream

4 cups cubed skinless, boneless chicken breasts

I cup shredded carrots

1/2 cup thinly sliced onion

2 cups broccoli florets, blanched (see Note)

Salt and freshly ground black pepper

4 hot crepes (from Zbigniew Chojnacki's Crepe Batter, recipe follows)

Read about the La Dominique Crêperie truck on page 64.

1 Heat 1 tablespoon of oil in a small saucepan over medium heat. Add the garlic and cook until fragrant, about 3 minutes. Add the coconut milk, chicken broth, and soy sauce and bring to a boil. Reduce the heat and let simmer until slightly thickened, about 10 minutes. Remove the coconut sauce from the heat, stir in the cream, and set aside.

2 Heat the remaining 2 tablespoons of oil in a large skillet over medium-high heat. Add the chicken and brown, stirring occasionally. Add the carrots and onion, reduce the heat to medium, and cook until the chicken is cooked through, 5 to 6 minutes more. Stir in just enough of the coconut sauce to coat the chicken and vegetables. Add the broccoli

Zbigniew takes pride in using the best ingredients possible.

and cook until heated through, 1 to 2 minutes. Season the chicken and broccoli mixture with salt and pepper to taste.

3 To assemble the crepes, spoon some of the chicken and broccoli mixture in the center of each crepe, dividing it evenly among them. Wrap up the crepes, folding over one end to enclose the filling.

NOTE: To blanch the broccoli, bring 8 cups water to a boil. Add the broccoli and cook it for 2 minutes. Immediately drain and plunge the broccoli in ice water to stop the cooking, then drain it again. Pat the broccoli dry with paper towels.

Zbigniew Chojnacki's Crepe Batter

ZBIGNIEW MAKES HIS BATTER the night before he intends to use it. Flour, melted butter, milk, and water are the ingredients, he tells me. "Simple, yes?" he asks, smiling, knowing that, while the ingredients are indeed simple, the techniques of crepe making are perfected over a lifetime. Having

A pinch of this, a dab of that add up to scratch cooking from a metal box.

the right equipment helps. Zbigniew works two Krampouz brand industrial-grade crepe irons. The recipe here was inspired by his crepes.

MAKES ABOUT 15 CREPES

2 large eggs

3/4 cup whole milk

1 cup all-purpose flour

About 4 tablespoons (1/2 stick) butter, melted

1 Whisk the eggs, milk, and 1/2 cup water together in a large mixing bowl. Gradually mix in the flour, followed by 3 tablespoons of the melted butter.

2 Heat a crepe pan or heavy-bottomed nonstick 10-inch skillet over high heat. Coat the bottom of the pan with about 1/4 teaspoon of the remaining butter. Pour about 1/4 cup of the crepe batter in the middle of the pan and, using a crepe paddle or an offset spatula, spread the batter evenly, working in a circular motion from the center of the pan to the outside edge and keeping the crepe batter at the edge as thin as possible. Cook the crepe until the batter sets up, 1 to 2 minutes. Carefully flip the crepe over and cook it until very slight golden patches begin to appear on the bottom, 1 to 2 minutes.

3 Transfer the crepe to a piece of parchment paper and cover it with another piece of parchment paper. Repeat with the remaining crepe batter, adding more butter to the pan as necessary and stacking the crepes between pieces of parchment paper to keep them separate. Any leftover crepes can be refrigerated, wrapped in plastic then in aluminum foil, for up to 3 days. Reheat in a low oven for 10 minutes.

TRENDING:
Soft Openings and New Vocabularies

IN 2009 street food carts and trucks took on the tropes of restaurants. In media-driven markets like New York and Los Angeles, truck owners invited the press to cocktail parties where they might get a chance to meet the chef. I still remember walking by a Portland cart with a notice announcing a "soft opening" posted in the sole window that fronted the five-foot wide shack on wheels.

Along the way to prominence, street food spawned its own vocabulary. Take a word like *nonstaurant*, which refers to a nontraditional restaurant in a nontraditional setting. When a cook subleases a dinner space from a restaurant that's only open for breakfast and lunch, he's operating a nonstaurant. When a chef opens a doughnut shop in her parent's garage, she's opening a nonstaurant. Ditto pop-up restaurants, conceived as marketing efforts for savvy corporations. And, yes, so-called nouveau street food.

On the other end of the spectrum is the coinage "B & M restaurant." As in, "That place is so lame; it's nothing but a B & M." In this case, the *b* stands for bricks and the *m* stands for mortar. In the world of street food, bricks-and-mortar businesses are passé.

Also current is *vend-rification.* The term, which has snide connotations, references both the gentrification of traditional catering and taco trucks and the consumer's ongoing fascination with the ways of trucks and carts.

Making a play for ascendancy is the British term *mobiler.* While Americans usually define their street food by conveyance—truck food, trailer food, cart food—the British coinage is expansive, taking into account the working definition of street food that I applied in this book: food sold by vendors who possess the possibility of mobility.

FRIED FRENCH TOAST

DEEP OIL IMMERSION IS IMPORTANT HERE. At Chef Shack, Carrie Summer and Lisa Carlson employ the same deep fryer for French toast that they use for their doughnuts spiced with cardamom (you'll find the recipe on page 265). What emerges from the oil are toasts that do justice to the concept of toast. Too often French toast is anemic stuff, a limp cousin to milk toast. Not here. Pile on any kind of seasonal fruit. Some sausage or bacon wouldn't hurt. And neither would a crowning sprinkle of confectioners' sugar.

Bread bobs in bubbling oil. The result? Spectacular French toast.

Look for the big red dot.

Read about the Chef Shack truck on page 141.

SERVES 4

8 large eggs, beaten

1 cup whole milk

2 tablespoons turbinado sugar, such as Sugar in the Raw

1/4 teaspoon salt

1/4 teaspoon ground cinnamon

Vegetable oil, for frying

8 slices day-old whole wheat bread

Pure maple syrup or honey, for serving

1 Place the eggs, milk, sugar, salt, and cinnamon in a mixing bowl and whisk to combine.

2 Pour oil to a depth of 2 inches into a heavy-bottomed skillet and heat it over high heat.

3 Soak the bread in batches in the egg mixture then immediately transfer it to the skillet and cook, turning once, until golden brown, 2 to 3 minutes total. Drain on paper towels. Repeat with the remaining bread.

4 To serve, drizzle maple syrup or honey over the French toast.

TAQUERIA
EL ULTIMO TACO

TACO
TORTA
GORDITA
QUESADI
BURRIT
TOSTA
FLAU

MELIN
LIMON
PIÑA
SANDIA

AGUAS FRESCAS
E FRUTAS NATURALES

The place for creamy eggs served hot on an open-faced tortilla.

WELCOME
OPEN

(206) 722 9977

TACOS

Taco buses, not trucks, are primary conveyances in some cities.

A curried omelet served with an artfully carved hot dog, Ton-Ton, Philadelphia.

A beckoning smile and the promise of home-cooked Japanese food.

Damian Mosley tried six different recipes

before he settled on the one he would serve at Blacksauce Curbside Kitchen, his traveling biscuit café, which does business in Baltimore. In the end, when kneading, cutting, and baking biscuits, he decided to follow his mother's lead. Smart man.

As interpreted by Damian, a onetime doctoral candidate, his mother's biscuits are bruisers. Squarish and pleasantly dense, some are flavored and colored with sweet potato. Some, on the other hand, are chalk white. All are good foils for a roster of fillings that includes roasted pork with apricot jelly. And, my favorite, jerk crab, made with a hash of sweet white meat spiked with allspice and cayenne.

Brunch from Blacksauce, eaten as you peruse the goods at the farmers' market operating catercorner from the truck, reinforces the notion that, although most of us think of biscuits as grandmotherly food, they adapt to being stuffed with most anything and eaten on the run. You could say the same thing about all of the dishes that follow. Sure, they're grouped under the lose rubric of brunch food, but they're better understood as good eats that you just might enjoy at the beginning of your day.

GRAPEFRUIT FIZZ

THIS IS AN IDEAL SUMMER TONIC, Nancye Benson told me as I drank her Grapefruit Fizz from a Mason jar. Three pulls in, I couldn't help but think that—as is the case with fresh-squeezed orange juice—her tonic would stand up well to a slug of vodka.

Stools and other sorts of seating are street food luxuries.

Beneath these architectural embellishments, a trailer lurks.

SERVES 2

1 grapefruit

3 basil leaves

2 teaspoons agave nectar (see Note)

Ice

2 pints soda water

Juice the grapefruit and add the basil. Pour the mixture into a blender and whir until the basil is pulverized. While the blender is running, add the agave nectar. Place ice in 2 pint glasses. Pour the grapefruit juice mixture over the ice, dividing it evenly between the 2 glasses. Top each serving with soda water, setting the remaining soda water aside for another use. Quaff.

NOTE: Agave nectar, a Mexican sweetener made from the agave plant, is available in grocery stores alongside the sugar or honey.

Read about the Moxie Rx truck on page 75.

EGGS AND GREENS

THIS DISH OF EGGS, MUSHROOMS, smoked salmon, and salad greens is atypical cart food. But then again Moxie Rx, from which this recipe came, is an atypical cart. When I met its proprietor, Nancye Benson, she was waxing poetic about the promise of food carts and wondering aloud whether, as the interest in this way of doing business booms, the sorts of cooks who catalyzed the movement would be displaced by sharp-elbowed folk.

While some street food vendors keep you moving, Moxie Rx encourages idling.

A sign of good eats on North Mississippi Avenue.

SERVES 6

1 large leek

6 tablespoons olive oil

Kosher salt

Freshly ground black pepper

1/4 cup freshly squeezed lemon juice

2 cloves garlic, minced

1 teaspoon chopped fresh thyme or
   lemon thyme leaves

1/2 pound cremini mushrooms, thinly sliced

3 ounces thinly sliced smoked salmon, torn into
   small pieces

6 large eggs

6 ounces salad mix

1/3 cup pine nuts, toasted (see Note)

1 Preheat the oven to 350°F.

2 Cut the leek in half lengthwise and rinse it well under cold running water. Cut the white and light green parts of the leek lengthwise into thin slivers, discarding the dark green parts. Toss the leek with 2 tablespoons of the olive oil and salt and pepper to taste. Spread the leek out on a rimmed baking sheet. Bake the leek until golden and crisp, 7 to 10 minutes, tossing it with a fork as it bakes so it doesn't burn at the edges of the pan. Remove the pan from the oven and set the leek aside.

3 Combine 3 tablespoons of the olive oil and the lemon juice, garlic, thyme, 1/2 teaspoon of salt, and 1/4 teaspoon of pepper in a large mixing bowl. Add the mushrooms and salmon and mix gently to coat.

4 Heat the remaining 1 tablespoon of olive oil in a very large nonstick skillet over medium heat. Crack the eggs into the pan, spacing them evenly. When the whites are set, 2 to 3 minutes, carefully turn the eggs over and cook until set to taste.

5 Add the salad mix to the bowl with the mushrooms and salmon and toss to coat. Divide the salad mixture among 6 plates. Top each with a fried egg, some pine nuts, and some leek slivers. Season the salads with more salt and pepper to taste.

N O T E : To toast the pine nuts, set a dry skillet over medium heat (do not use a nonstick skillet for this). Add the pine nuts and heat them until lightly toasted and aromatic, 3 to 5 minutes. Keep an eye on the pine nuts; you don't want them to burn. Transfer the toasted pine nuts to a heatproof bowl to cool.

The menus at Moxie.

LAST SEEN: North Mississippi Avenue at North Shaver Street, Portland, Oregon

MOXIE RX

AT THE CORE of this prop–styled hippy encampment is a sea foam–green trailer that could, with great effort, be moved. At the prow of the trailer, which serves as the kitchen, Nancye Benson, the proprietor, has installed a few bar stools. Alongside the Moxie Rx trailer, Nancye and her partner have constructed a wood-timbered dining room that looks from one angle like a hobo hut, from another like a showcase for an encampment of postmodern architects. Mounted on the walls are muffin tins, fish molds, and Bundt cake pans. Inside the trailer stand cake pedestals heaped with peach muffins and fig and anise sandwiches. On the stereo lilting singer-songwriters sing earnest songs.

CURRY RICE OMELET

THINK OF SPANISH TORTILLAS, those firm potato and egg cakes. Think of any number of croquettes. This recipe, inspired by the Philadelphia truck Ton-Ton, results in something similar: A substantial omelet, girded with starch and, as Keiko Naka prepares it, spiked with curry.

At the Ton-Ton window, awaiting an omelet.

MAKES 4 OMELETS

Vegetable oil

1/2 onion, chopped

4 white mushrooms, sliced

I teaspoon Madras-style curry powder

4 cups cooked rice

Salt and freshly ground black pepper

8 eggs, beaten

Hot sauce, for serving

1 Heat 2 tablespoons of vegetable oil in a heavy skillet over medium-high heat. Add the onion and mushrooms and cook until softened, about 5 minutes. Add the curry and stir to mix. Add the rice, season it with salt and pepper to taste, and stir to mix. Set the seasoned rice aside, but keep it warm.

2 Heat 1 tablespoon of oil in a nonstick skillet over medium heat. Add one quarter of the eggs, quickly spreading them to make a round omelet. Place one quarter of the seasoned rice in the center of the omelet and fold the top and bottom sides of the omelet over the rice. Cover the skillet with a plate. Flip the omelet over and onto the plate. Repeat with the remaining eggs and rice mixture to make a total of 4 rice omelets, adding more oil as necessary.

3 Serve the omelets with hot sauce, sharing them with people who've been nice to you.

Read about the Ton-Ton truck on page II5.

Chopsticks suit street food like this omelet filled with curried rice.

HUEVOS CON CHORIZO

BREAKFAST BURRITOS

WALK INTO A LATIN GROCERY and you might see three or four different types of chorizo. The Spanish-style stuff is usually cured and has a firm texture, while the Mexican version is usually fresh, with the consistency of ground pork. I've also seen Portuguese and Philippine versions and, in Louisiana, a kissing cousin known as *chaurice.* The Mexican version of chorizo served by Seattle's El Camión is heavy on paprika. It inspired the breakfast burritos here.

The menu is varied at El Camión, and like many new wave vendors, they take credit cards.

Sleek and black, the El Camión trailer is a modern marvel.

Read about the El Camión truck on page 231.

MAKES 4 BURRITOS

4 small (6 inches each) flour tortillas

I can (15 ounces) black beans

6 ounces good-quality Mexican chorizo

8 large eggs, beaten

Salt and freshly ground black pepper

I cup shredded Jack cheese

1/2 cup Calexico Pico de Gallo (page 222)

1 Heat a skillet over medium heat and warm the tortillas one at a time in the skillet until pliable, about 30 seconds on each side. As you work, wrap the tortillas in a clean kitchen towel to keep them warm.

2 Put the black beans in a saucepan and warm them over low heat, stirring occasionally.

3 Heat a large skillet over medium-high heat. Remove and discard the casings from the chorizo, crumble the chorizo into the skillet, and cook it until browned, 4 to 5 minutes.

4 Reduce the heat to medium, add the eggs to the skillet, and cook, stirring, until the egg and chorizo mixture is set to taste. Add salt and pepper to taste, then divide the scrambled eggs and chorizo and the black beans equally among the 4 tortillas. Top each with 1/4 cup of the Jack cheese and a spoonful of *pico de gallo,* then fold up the tortillas.

SEATTLE:
REALIZING ITS STREET POTENTIAL

When the Skillet truck rolled onto the streets of Seattle in the summer of 2007 its shtick was novel.

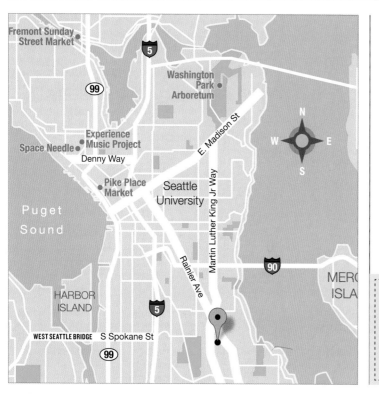

J osh Henderson and Danny Sizemore were white-tablecloth restaurant refugees slinging a better brand of hash from a better brand of trailer. That was news. That was hip.

Their menu was simple: Kobe burgers topped with blue cheese, house-made bacon jam, and arugula. Hazelnut-crusted chicken sandwiches.

WHERE THE TRUCKS ARE:
Be sure to visit the taco buses that line Rainier Avenue S, near where it crosses Martin Luther King Jr., Highway. And check roaminghunger.com.

Poutine swamped with brown gravy, pocked with cheese curds. Peach cobbler baked in cast-iron skillets. In those days the Skillet boys posted the GPS location of their shiny 1962 vintage Airstream on a blog. Such a method seems quaint now. Back then it was cutting-edge. Those were the days when the media was reporting that Seattle was at the center of the street food revolution. There was little evidence for such an assertion.

Yes, there was a furtive taco truck that played hide-and-seek with the authorities before parking, once and for all, in the drive-thru of what looked to be a shuttered Hardee's near the bars of Capitol Hill. (Last time I checked, that lime green taco truck was still parked, abandoned, in the drive-thru. And Rio Bravo, the restaurant alongside, was still selling mole chicken tacos and grapefruit *jarritos* to the students who continued to flock from a nearby community college.)

And, yes, there were a few enterprising vendors selling cream cheese-slathered hot dogs to drinkers frequenting the bars of Ballard and Belltown. (That unlikely combination dates back to at least the 1970s, when Hadley Long began selling hot dogs with cream cheese on bagel-like bread in Pioneer Square.)

But by and large the street food scene in Seattle was in gestation. And that's still where it is. Seattle is not a democratic street food scene like Portland. It's not a fulcrum of the boutique truck food movement like Los Angeles. Seattle is more like the rest of the larger cities in this country. It's a city stumbling toward the realization that street food vendors are catalysts of community, that street food consumers buy goods based on high quality as well as low price.

Helping Seattle realize that potential are people like Kamala Saxton, one of the principals in Marination Mobile, the current cause célèbre of the Seattle street food world. Marination has won a national reputation for Spam *musubi* and *kalua* pork slider riffs on Hawaiian curb food. Now Kamala, who has a master's degree in sports marketing, is looking for ways to give back. Among the ideas she's pondering is a not-for-profit business incubator that is focused on new immigrant entrepreneurs. If efforts like that gain momentum, Seattle might emerge as a leader of the street food movement after all.

In the meantime, the Skillet boys have been learning a few lessons in how to survive cold and rainy Seattle winters (they are now selling jars of their bacon jam by mail order). That taco truck, abandoned in the drive-thru, has been joined by a fleet of taco buses. And a decidedly mobile pig-shaped truck, selling pork sandwiches and slaw, now pulls to the curb at Second Avenue and Pike Street during fair-weather weekdays (read more about the MAXimus/miniMUS truck on page 161).

read more about the MAXimus/miniMUS truck on page 161).

- - - - - - - - - - - - - - - - - - -

Left to Right:

Top Row: On line at Marination Mobile. Inside the carton.

Middle Row: Mulita goodness from El Camión. MAXimus/miniMUS pig at rest.

Bottom Row: Taco buses rule Seattle. Dante works the dog griddle.

IF YOU'RE VERY LUCKY, THIS IS WHAT YOUR BRUNCH WILL LOOK LIKE.

CHORIZO TACOS
WITH EGGS

SERVED IN CARDBOARD BOATS imprinted with a red-and-white plaid, these tacos, jumbled with paprika-spiked chorizo, trail a ruddy and flavorful skein of grease. In this recipe, inspired by the work of the Montanos at El Ultimo Taco, the eggs are *plancha*-fried, their yolks and whites barely combined. This is taco truck fare at its simple best.

Taco trucks in Houston are rolling art galleries of hand-painted signage.

MAKES 4 SMALL TACOS

I small onion, chopped

1/4 cup chopped fresh cilantro

4 small (6 inches each) flour tortillas

6 ounces good-quality fresh Mexican chorizo

8 large eggs, lightly beaten

1 Combine the onion and cilantro and set aside.

2 Heat a skillet over medium heat and warm the tortillas one at a time in the skillet until pliable, about 30 seconds on each side. As you work, wrap the tortillas in a clean kitchen towel to keep them warm.

3 Heat a large skillet over medium-high heat. Remove and discard the casings from the chorizo, crumble the chorizo into the skillet, and cook it until browned, 4 to 5 minutes.

4 Reduce the heat to medium, add the eggs to the skillet, and cook, stirring, until the egg and chorizo mixture is set to taste. Divide the scrambled eggs and chorizo equally among the 4 tacos. Garnish each with some of the onion and cilantro mixture, then fold up the tortillas, if desired.

LAST SEEN: 7403 Long Point Road, Houston, Texas

EL ULTIMO TACO

THE STUCCO WALLS of an adjacent car stereo dealership throb with what sounds like a south of the border riff on rap. Spray from a car wash, set perpendicular to the stereo dealer, settles over the shiny white taco truck owned by Frederico and Vera Montano.

The menu, painted on the side of El Ultimo Taco's truck, advertises an encyclopedia of Mexican eats, from *tortas* to *gorditas,* but the wheelhouse dishes here are breakfast tacos, tucked in flour tortillas, capped with raggedy onions and hashed cilantro. Eat from the fold-down stainless steel shelf that runs the length of the truck, in sight of the trash can that's strapped to the back bumper, and you can hear the low murmur of Spanish in the kitchen and the frequent scrape of the cook's spatula on the flattop grill.

NOPALITOS AND EGGS TACOS

NOPALITOS, MADE FROM the pads of prickly pears, are tucked into a flour tortilla and topped with cilantro. They taste vegetal—the perfect foil for rich scrambled eggs. Serve these eggs, inspired by El Ultimo Taco, with *salsa verde* and an *agua fresca.*

Don't you expect that a line of Hot Wheels taco trucks will soon hit the market?

Read about El Ultimo Taco on page 81.

MAKES 4 SMALL TACOS

4 small (6 inches each) flour tortillas

2 tablespoons (1/4 stick) butter

1/4 cup diced onion

1/4 cup jarred nopalitos, rinsed and cut into strips

8 large eggs, beaten

Salt and freshly ground black pepper

2 tablespoons chopped fresh cilantro, for garnish

1 Heat a skillet over medium heat and warm the tortillas one at a time until pliable, about 30 seconds on each side. As you work, wrap the tortillas in a clean kitchen towel to keep them warm.

2 Melt the butter in a skillet over medium heat. Add the onion and cook until soft, 3 to 5 minutes. Add the nopalitos and cook until heated through, about 3 minutes.

3 Add the eggs to the skillet and cook, stirring, until the egg mixture is set to taste. Season the egg mixture with salt and pepper to taste. Divide the mixture equally among the 4 tacos, and garnish each with some of the cilantro, then fold up the tortillas, if desired.

Melon Agua Fresca

STEP UP TO THE WINDOW of a taco truck and you might spy small plastic barrels of *agua limón* (lemon) or *agua piña* (pineapple) on a shelf by the register. The translation of *agua fresca* is fresh water or cold water and these are, in essence, light, thirst-quenching blends of water and fruit. Served at El Ultimo Taco in stubby white foam cups, these drinks pack a morning punch and inspired this recipe.

SERVES 6

6 cups cubed, peeled, and seeded watermelon or cantaloupe

6 cups cold water

3 tablespoons freshly squeezed lime juice

6 tablespoons granulated sugar

Ice, for serving

Place the watermelon, water, lime juice, and sugar in a blender and puree until very smooth. Pour the *agua fresca* through a strainer into a pitcher and chill it before serving it poured over ice.

STUFF TO GO ON TOP

BREAKFAST AND BRUNCH are meals in need of accessories. Hash browns require ketchup and Tabasco sauce, at the least. Biscuits beg for jelly. And eggs tucked in tacos require salsas, both red and green. I'm keen on the green stuff, brightened with tomatillos, cooled by avocados.

A generous supply of salsas served from *molcajetes*.

Read about the El Camión truck on page 231.

Salsa de Chipotle

CANNED CHIPOTLE PEPPERS in *adobo* sauce should always be in your kitchen cabinet. They pack a smoky punch and they keep forever. You'll find canned chipotles in the Mexican section of the supermarket.

MAKES ABOUT 2 1/2 CUPS

2 tablespoons olive oil

1/2 cup diced onion

2 cloves garlic, minced

2 cups seeded and chopped tomatoes

3 canned chipotle peppers in adobo sauce, drained

1 teaspoon dried oregano

1 teaspoon salt

Pinch of sugar

Heat the olive oil in a skillet over medium-high heat. Add the onion and garlic and cook until just starting to soften, about 1 minute.

Add the tomatoes, chipotle peppers, oregano, salt, and sugar and cook over low heat until the flavors blend, about 10 minutes. Remove the salsa from the heat, let it cool, then puree it in a blender until smooth.

Guacamole Salsa Verde

I LIKE THE CHUNKY CONSISTENCY of the salsas that El Camión displays on the ledge of its truck. There's a generosity to the roster, which spans a range of tolerance for heat, from this one—inspired by the work of El Camión's proprietor, Scott McGinniss—which is fairly mild, to the habañero, an orange-hued smoker.

MAKES ABOUT 2 CUPS

1/2 pound tomatillos, husked and quartered

1/2 cup chopped white onion

3 fresh jalapeño peppers, stemmed, seeded, and minced

2 cloves garlic, chopped

2 tablespoons fresh lime juice

1 1/2 teaspoons salt

1 ripe avocado, pitted, peeled, and cut into small chunks

1/4 cup chopped fresh cilantro

Place the tomatillos, onion, jalapeños, garlic, lime juice, and salt in a food processor and pulse until a chunky puree forms. Transfer the tomatillo mixture to a bowl and gently fold in the avocado and cilantro.

MIGAS TACOS

A TEX-MEX STANDARD, *migas* are built on a base of stale corn tortillas that have been crisped, sauced, and scrambled with eggs. Traditionally served as a breakfast plate, *migas* are now popular in Austin as taco fillings. In this recipe, adapted from Torchy's Tacos, the texture and lime-kissed taste of the corn tortillas play well off the flour tortilla wraps. By the way, if you're curious about the word *migas,* the Spanish translation is "crumbs."

Migas are all about texture. These await a heavy hit of Roasted Red Salsa.

MAKES 4 SMALL TACOS

FOR THE MIGAS

2 cups vegetable oil, for frying

4 corn tortillas (6 inches each), cut into 1/4-inch strips

FOR THE TACOS

4 small (6 inches each) flour tortillas

1 tablespoon butter

1 tablespoon milk

4 large eggs, beaten

2 tablespoons chopped roasted Hatch-style green or Anaheim chiles

2 tablespoons Calexico Pico de Gallo (page 222)

1/2 cup shredded cheddar or Jack cheese

1 avocado, peeled, pitted, and sliced

Roasted Red Salsa (recipe follows), for serving

You can't miss Torchy's oversize logo in Austin.

Read about the Torchy's Tacos truck on page 234.

1 Make the *migas:* Heat the oil in a deep fryer or Dutch oven over high heat until a deep fry thermometer attached to the side of the pot registers 350°F. Carefully add the corn tortilla strips to the hot oil and cook until crisp, about 2 minutes. Using a slotted spoon, transfer the tortilla strips to paper towels to drain, then set them aside.

2 Make the tacos: Heat a skillet over medium heat and warm the flour tortillas one at a time until pliable, about 30 seconds on each side. As

you work, wrap the tortillas in a clean kitchen towel to keep them warm.

3 Melt the butter in the milk in a skillet over medium-high heat. Add the eggs, and once the eggs start to form a skin on the bottom, add the green chiles and the fried tortilla strips. Cook, stirring, until the egg mixture is set to taste, about 2 minutes.

4 Divide the egg mixture equally among the 4 flour tortillas. Top each with some of the *pico de gallo,* shredded cheese, and sliced avocado, then fold up the tortillas, if desired. Serve the tacos with the Roasted Red Salsa.

Roasted Red Salsa

THIS RED TABLE SAUCE from Torchy's Tacos gets its bass note from roasted tomatoes and its treble note from chopped cilantro. In addition to complementing the Migas Tacos, it's the perfect analogue for ketchup when you're hungry for hash browns.

MAKES ABOUT 2 CUPS

16 ripe plum tomatoes, cut in half lengthwise

2 tablespoons (1/4 stick) butter

I cup chopped white onion

6 cloves garlic, minced

4 serrano peppers, stemmed, seeded, and minced

1/2 cup diced green chiles or Anaheim chiles

I bunch cilantro

I tablespoon store-bought vegetable demi-glace (see Note)

I tablespoon key lime juice

I tablespoon kosher salt

I teaspoon freshly ground black pepper

1 Preheat the broiler.

2 Line a rimmed baking sheet with aluminum foil. Arrange the tomato halves on top, skin side up, and broil them until the skins begin to char, 4 to 5 minutes. Watch the tomatoes carefully. Set the broiled tomatoes aside to cool.

3 Melt the butter in a skillet over medium heat. Add the onion, garlic, and serrano peppers and cook until slightly caramelized, 6 to 8 minutes. Let the onion mixture cool.

4 When the onion mixture is cool enough to handle, place it and the tomatoes in a blender. Add the green chiles, cilantro, vegetable demi-glace, key lime juice, salt, and black pepper and puree until smooth. The salsa can be refrigerated, covered, for up to 1 week.

N O T E : You'll find vegetable demi-glace, a base for making sauces, in supermarkets next to the bouillon.

EJOTES AND EGG TACOS

AT TAQUERIA LAS PALMITAS green beans—runner beans, more than likely—are blanched, salted, and fried on a flattop grill and mixed with loosely scrambled eggs. Tucked into a puffy corn tortilla, they taste righteous. Almost healthy. Especially when compared to the more common taco truck egg lineup of *salchicha* (sausage) and *jamón* (ham).

Maria Molina has the touch. Her tortillas are feathery light each and every time.

A humble cart that dishes world-beater tacos.

MAKES 4 SMALL TACOS

1/2 cup fresh green beans, cut into 1-inch pieces

Ice water

4 small (4 inches each) Las Palmitas Corn Tortillas (recipe follows)

2 tablespoons (1/4 stick) butter

8 large eggs, beaten

Salt and freshly ground black pepper

1 Bring a pot of water to a boil. Add the green beans and cook them for about 1 minute. Immediately drain the beans and submerge them in ice water to stop the cooking. Drain again and dry the beans on paper towels.

2 Heat a skillet over medium heat and warm the tortillas one at a time, about 30 seconds on each side. As you work, wrap the tortillas in a clean kitchen towel to keep them warm.

3 Melt the butter in a skillet over medium heat. Add the eggs and cook, stirring frequently. Just before the eggs are set to taste, stir in the blanched green beans and cook the eggs for about 1 minute longer. Season with salt and pepper to taste. Divide the egg

LAST SEEN: 7106 Bellaire Boulevard, Houston, Texas

TAQUERIA LAS PALMITAS

TORTILLAS HECHO A MANO— that's what the sign says, taped to the order window of a diminutive white trailer sharing a parking lot berth with a dry cleaner and a botanica specializing in herbs and tinctures.

While many Houston proprietors decorate their trailers with a restraint characteristic of circus sideshow banners, Taqueria Las Palmitas broadcasts a conservative aesthetic. The glossy white truck is free of markings, save blue lettering at top left, spelling out the business name.

As promised, the tortillas are made by hand, on a press worked by Maria Molina, a native of Michoacán. On the day I visited, Indira Molina, her high school–age daughter, worked the window, translating orders for her mother and parceling out the electric green *salsa verde* that enlivens their breakfast tacos.

mixture equally among the 4 tacos, then fold up the tortillas, if desired.

Las Palmitas Corn Tortillas

GREAT BREAD IS SIMPLE STUFF: grain and water. Serve it fresh, serve it hot, and people fall at your feet. On the Las Palmitas truck, Maria Molina and her daughter Indira work a cast-iron press mounted on the front ledge. Chances are your efforts won't yield tortillas that are as feathery as theirs, but you should try this recipe, inspired by them, anyway.

Morning ammunition, stacked and ready to be cracked.

THE HOSTAGE SITUATION:
A Visit to the South West Comisaria

THE CITY OF HOUSTON licenses mobile food commissaries. Mobile food vendors are required to report to one of those privately owned commissaries each day. That's where taco trucks get cleaned and sanitized. That's where they dump waste water. And load up on clamshell boxes, Mexican Coca-Colas, and bags of masa. That's where operators get propane tank refills. At some commissaries, they can get a brake job, too.

On a suggestion from my friend Robb Walsh, the dean of taco truck scribes, Angie Mosier—who took the photographs for this book—and I stopped by the South West Comisaria on Beechnut Street, tucked behind Doña Tere Tamales. The main building is a drive-through warehouse. Out back is a series of interconnected sheds, beneath which drivers were using pressure hoses to wash down their trucks.

As Angie snapped pictures, I made an inventory of the commissary's goods. And I tried to get a handle on how the place works. All for you, dear reader. That's where the trouble began.

A man approached. He asked me what I was doing. I tried to explain about our book project. I offered my card. He took it. On the back, he scribbled down the license plate number of my rental car. I made a snide remark. I made a mental note to learn Spanish, once and for all. He called the cops.

When I told him that I would just leave, he summoned three mechanics from the shop next door. None were carrying wrenches, but they blocked our way. One man smiled, as if to say, "Yes, this seems crazy, but . . ." All three suggested that Angie and I wait until the policeman came.

Almost an hour passed before the squad car arrived. During that time, I learned that the man who called the cops was named Ned. His brother, who owns the commissary, was away. Ned was in charge. He feared that Angie and I were there to case the joint. He talked about thieves cutting holes in the roof and rappelling into the building.

When the cop came, he counseled me to ask for permission before poking around a place of business. And he told Ned that while he can make someone leave his place of business, he cannot prevent someone from leaving. The policeman did not use the word hostage. And neither did I. But that's what it felt like.

As the cop drove away, Ned and I shook hands. I slapped him on the back. He slapped me on the back. We both smiled. We almost hugged. And Angie and I wheeled out of the lot, in search of a *torta* trailer we'd heard about.

2 cups masa harina

1¹/3 cups water

1 Place the masa harina in a large mixing bowl, then add the water and stir until a dough begins to form. Knead the dough on a work surface until the masa and water are completely blended, about 5 minutes. Divide the dough into 12 equal-size balls.

2 Place each ball of dough between 2 pieces of plastic wrap and press it into a 4-inch disk. Peel off the plastic just before cooking.

3 Heat an ungreased cast-iron skillet or *comal* over high heat. Cook the tortillas until a bread-like skin forms on the outside, 30 seconds per side. As you work, wrap the tortillas in clean kitchen towels to keep them warm.

SCRAPPLE, EGG, AND PROVOLONE HOAGIES

NICK HASLIDIS CRACKS EGGS to order. He whips them with a fork, the way you do at home. What you probably don't do at home is pour those eggs onto a griddle so that they spread into a thin and vaguely rectangular-shaped omelet and then gather and fold that thin omelet over a plank of griddled scrapple (see Note) and a couple of slices of provolone, tucking in the corners of the omelet in the manner of a burrito. Since most of us lack a three-foot griddle, here's a cheat, inspired by Nick's work.

- -

LAST SEEN: 33rd Street and Spruce Street, Philadelphia, Pennsylvania

JOHN'S LUNCH TRUCK

NICK HASLIDIS didn't plan to work a lunch cart. That's an old man's game. Then his father, John Haslidis, fell sick and Nick stepped up. When I met Nick the thirty-something had been working a flattop grill in a four-by-six cart for fourteen years. At one point Nick converted a U-Haul truck into a crepe truck and went into business with a friend. But that friendship fell apart and so did that business. And his father needed him.

As Nick and I talked, helicopters fwopped above and ambulances screeched alongside. They were bound for the University of Pennsylvania hospital, just across the street. So were the white-jacketed doctors, who bypassed an adjacent cart selling freshly cut fruit to take their turn in front of Nick's window and scarf up a breakfast of scrapple and eggs on a hoagie roll.

MAKES 4 SANDWICHES

2 tablespoons vegetable oil

8 slices scrapple ($1/4$ inch thick)

About 5 tablespoons butter, at room temperature

8 large eggs, beaten

Salt and freshly ground black pepper

4 Italian sandwich rolls

8 slices provolone cheese

1 Heat the oil in a large skillet over high heat. Add the scrapple and cook until well browned and heated through, about 5 minutes per side. Set the cooked scrapple aside.

2 If the skillet looks dry, add up to 1 tablespoon of butter. Reduce the heat to medium, add the eggs, and cook, stirring often, until set to taste. Season the eggs with salt and pepper to taste. Remove from heat.

3 Using a knife, split the rolls lengthwise, stopping just short of cutting all the way through. Spread about 1 tablespoon butter inside each roll. Place 2 slices scrapple in each roll and top them with the scrambled eggs, dividing the eggs evenly among the 4 rolls. Top the eggs in each roll with 2 slices provolone. Scarf a hoagie while walking somewhere.

CHES MADE ON SARCONE BREAD

EGGS, CHEESE, AND BROCCOLI RABE—NOW THAT'S BREAKFAST!

BREAKFAST SANDWICHES
WITH BROCCOLI RABE AND PROVOLONE

FOR BREAKFAST MIKE DATT of MikeyD's Grill toasts slices of pound cake on a flattop grill. But sandwiches are his forte, including a morning torpedo of broccoli rabe and eggs, cooked hash house omelet-style, draped with sharp provolone and laced with red pepper flakes and garlic. Herewith, a recipe inspired by Mike's griddle work (add the pepper flakes and garlic if your morning stomach can handle them).

A proud Mike with another specialty—Philly cheesesteak done right (see page 155).

MikeyD's Grill—minimalist space, maximalist taste.

Read about MikeyD's Grill truck on page 156.

MAKES 4 SANDWICHES

2 tablespoons ($1/4$ stick) butter

8 eggs, lightly beaten

2 cups broccoli rabe pieces (1 inch), blanched (see Note)

Salt and freshly ground black pepper

4 Italian sandwich rolls

8 slices provolone cheese

1 Melt the butter in a large skillet over medium-high heat. Add the eggs and cook, stirring often. Just before the eggs are set to taste, stir in the broccoli rabe and cook the eggs for 1 minute longer. Season the egg and broccoli rabe mixture with salt and pepper to taste.

2 Using a knife, split the rolls lengthwise, stopping just short of cutting all the way through. Place 2 slices provolone inside each roll, then divide the egg mixture evenly among the 4 rolls.

NOTE: To blanch the broccoli rabe, bring 8 cups of water to a boil. Add the broccoli rabe and cook it for about 2 minutes. Immediately drain and plunge the broccoli rabe in ice water to stop the cooking, then drain it again. Pat the broccoli rabe dry with paper towels.

FALAFEL AND EGG HOAGIES

FIRST, MONA HAGALI lays down a base of provolone atop a splayed loaf of bread. (Provolone may be the signature ingredient of Philly street food.) Then come disks of falafel and the omelet. Instead of ketchup, she reaches for the Sriracha bottle and decorates the whole with a zigzag of garlicky and salty heat. This recipe is an homage to Mona's work at A&M.

Not all trucks are tricked out.

The bare-bones A&M truck.

MAKES 4 SANDWICHES

2 tablespoons vegetable oil, or more as needed

2 cups thinly sliced onions

I red bell pepper, stemmed, seeded, and cut into strips

8 large eggs, beaten

Salt and freshly ground black pepper

4 Italian sandwich rolls

4 tablespoons (1/2 stick) butter, at room temperature

8 slices provolone cheese

8 Falafel (recipe follows, or use a box mix)

Sriracha, for serving

1 Heat the oil in a large skillet over medium-high heat. Add the onions and bell pepper strips and cook until lightly browned, about 7 minutes. Using a slotted spoon, transfer the onions and bell pepper to a bowl and cover them to keep warm.

2 If the skillet looks dry add some more oil. Reduce the heat to medium, add the eggs, and cook, stirring often, until set to taste. Season the eggs with salt and black pepper to taste.

3 Using a knife, split the rolls lengthwise, stopping just short of cutting all the way through. Spread about 1 tablespoon of butter inside each roll. Place 2 slices of provolone in each roll and top them 2 falafel in each sandwich. Add the scrambled eggs and onion and bell pepper mixture, dividing the eggs and vegetable mixture evenly among the 4 rolls. Top with a spritz of Sriracha.

Falafel

YOU COULD GO with a boxed falafel mix, but why be lazy when you have this easy recipe, inspired by Mona's work at A&M? Leftover falafel balls can be wrapped in aluminum foil and refrigerated for up to two days. They reheat easily.

MAKES 18 TO 20 FALAFEL

2 cups dried chickpeas (garbanzo beans)

I teaspoon baking powder

$^1/_2$ cup chopped onion

I large egg, beaten

4 cloves garlic, crushed

I teaspoon ground cumin

I teaspoon ground coriander

$^1/_4$ teaspoon crushed red pepper flakes

$^1/_2$ cup chopped fresh parsley

$^1/_4$ cup chopped fresh cilantro

I teaspoon salt

I teaspoon freshly ground black pepper

2 quarts vegetable oil, for frying

Falafel and eggs with a squirt of Sriracha.

1 Put the chickpeas in a large bowl and add water to cover by 2 inches. Soak the chickpeas overnight.

2 Rinse and drain the chickpeas, then place them in a food processor and pulse to break into flakes the size of small oats. Add the baking powder, onion, egg, garlic, cumin, coriander, red pepper flakes, parsley, cilantro, salt, and black pepper and puree until the mixture is smooth but still grainy. Refrigerate the falafel mixture for about 15 minutes.

3 Heat the oil in a deep fryer or Dutch oven over medium-high heat until a deep fry thermometer attached to the side of the pot registers 325°F. Roll the falafel mixture into Ping-Pong-size balls. When the oil is hot, carefully add the falafel balls, a few at a time, to the hot oil and cook them until they are dark golden brown, about 5 minutes. Using a slotted spoon, transfer the falafel to paper towels to drain.

LAST SEEN: In the alley behind Drexel University's LeBow Engineering Center, Philadelphia, Pennsylvania

A&M

MONA HAGALI'S halal food truck anchors a United Nations conclave of eight Drexel University vendors, including Pyramid Pizza and Mai's Oriental Food. The exterior of her truck is scarred. The interior is comfortably clean. Mona's menu is diverse—confusing, even. As if she's trying to serve the wants of her Middle Eastern neighbors, a scattering of Africans, and stoned students, too.

That dictate translates as pork roll hoagies, made with a bologna-like meat. And falafel omelets. And okra sandwiches, stuffed with dusky green fritters. And, for the spliffers, her take on the "Big Fat Jimmy," a student truck standard piled with, among other goods, mozzarella sticks, fries, shaved steak, and liquid cheese product.

SRIRACHA:
America's Postmodern Hot Sauce

When you want heat, look for the rooster.

AMONG AMERICA'S STREET FOOD VENDORS Sriracha hot sauce is reaching a level of ubiquitousness that is almost comparable to Tabasco. It's the condiment with which Mona Hagali of A&M in Philadelphia garnishes her falafel omelet-stuffed hoagies. It's the condiment supplied by the Kogi trucks that travel the streets of Los Angeles, vending kimchi-garnished tacos to the young, hip, and hungry.

The orange-red sauce is loaded with garlic and capsaicin. It also comes with a good backstory, as I learned when I stopped off to visit Huy Fong Foods in Rosemead, a city in the San Gabriel Valley outside Los Angeles.

"I made this sauce for the Asian community," David Tran, Huy Fong Foods' founder, told me one afternoon, seated in the conference room at the company headquarters. "I knew that, after the Vietnamese resettled here, they would want their hot sauce for their *pho*," a beef broth and noodle soup that is a de facto national dish of Vietnam.

"But I wanted something that I could sell to more than just the Vietnamese," said David, a man of Chinese heritage, born in Vietnam. What David eventually developed in Los Angeles, in the early 1980s, was his own take on a traditional Asian chile sauce. In Sriracha, a seaside town in the Chonburi province of Thailand, where chunky chile pastes are favored, natives may not recognize his puree.

Some consumers believe Sriracha to be a Thai sauce. Others link it to Vietnam. However, in the United States, Sriracha as manufactured by Huy Fong Foods has become an American sauce, a polyglot puree with roots in different places and peoples. The ingredient list on the bottle is written in Vietnamese, Cantonese, English, French, and Spanish. And the serving suggestions, printed alongside, include pizzas, hot dogs, hamburgers, and, for French speakers, pâtés.

Like many immigrants of his generation, David Tran's journey from Vietnam to America was epic. Unlike many of his contemporaries, Mr. Tran's travels, and the travels of his family members, were fueled by chile sauces. From 1975 onward David made sauces from peppers grown by his older brother on a farm just beyond Long Binh, a village north of the city then known as Saigon. Though he never devised a formal name for his products, David decorated each cap with a rooster, his astrological sign.

Production was family focused. David ground the peppers. His father-in-law washed the sauce containers, repurposing Gerber baby food jars obtained from U.S. servicemen. His brother-in-law filled the jars with sauce. Itinerant jobbers bought the sauces from Mr. Tran and sold them to *pho* shops and other informal restaurants.

By 1979, many of the Tran family's friends were leaving Vietnam. "We never were threatened," David recalled. "But we knew it was time to go. And I had enough money saved to buy our way out." And so his family left.

Sriracha was the fourth sauce David Tran produced and bottled in the United States. He did not anticipate the popularity his sauce would develop. He believed the sauce to be good. He liked to tell people that all he did was grind peppers, add garlic, and leave it alone.

Over the past decade a number of imitators have entered the Sriracha category. Each includes an image of its namesake animal on the center of the bottle, where Huy Fong has long placed its rooster. Some copied Huy Fong's signature script. Others employed similar green caps on the bottles. The competition has proved no great hindrance to Huy Fong sales. In 1996 Huy Fong Foods expanded, increasing both its processing and storage capacity to meet the spiking demand.

More than ten million bottles of Sriracha now roll off the Rosemead line each year. With the purchase of a nearby warehouse, the company has begun storing its peppers where Wham-O once manufactured those icons of the 1950s and 60s pop culture, the Hula Hoop and the Frisbee.

Plump dumplings via NYC Cravings.

Flea market tacos in Austin.

A hash of lettuce and cilantro graces most Korean tacos.

Roots Jambalaya from The Swamp Shack, Portland.

UNEXPECTED pleasures

CHAPTER 4

Some foods are made for walking about.

Easy to pick up. Easy to take with. Drumsticks come with natural handles. Hot dogs come with buns. Other foods are less well-endowed. This chapter includes some unconventional treats that are not easily or quickly conveyed from cooktop to mouth.

Also here are the just plain hard-to-categorize. I'm thinking of egg foo yong, served from a battered truck parked at the edge of the University of Pennsylvania campus. And mutton stew, slurped from a Styrofoam bowl while shopping for bootleg DVDs at an Austin flea market.

Wandering the U.S. in search of great eats, I ate a coconut milk-perfumed stew, cooked by a recent Malaysian immigrant to San Francisco. She talked of how the dish could be frozen and served as savory popsicles. On that same trip, I took my place in line at 51st State, a swank truck focused on celebrating the regional foodways of America. The truck serves, on occasion, cornmeal-fried quail drizzled with maple syrup and paired with jalapeño cheese grits. That quail isn't typical street food. It's more like restaurant food that went out for a smoke and stayed to hang out on the curb. And so it is with the recipes that follow. They are truck food dishes because they're cooked in trucks. And sometimes that's enough.

KOREAN SHORT RIBS
WITH KALBI MARINADE

I'M NOT SURE WHAT THE SPRITE in the *kalbi* marinade does to the short ribs other than establish that the recipe is a thumb of the nose to traditionalists. That said, recipes for barbecued chickens marinated in Dr Pepper are fairly common. And I'm keen on redeye gravy made with Coke instead of coffee.

Street Food 101: Keep the menu simple.

Kogi-ready to roll from the compound.

Read about the Kogi truck on page 212.

SERVES 4

FOR THE MARINADE

2 cups soy sauce

2 cups maple syrup

1¼ cups granulated sugar

1 yellow onion, peeled and quartered

4 scallions, white and light green parts coarsely chopped

¹/3 cup cloves garlic, peeled

1 small kiwi fruit, peeled and cut into large chunks

¹/2 Asian pear, peeled, cored, and cut into large chunks

³/4 cup (half of a 12-ounce can) Sprite or 7UP

¹/2 cup freshly squeezed orange juice

¹/3 cup Asian (dark) sesame oil

4 tablespoons sesame seeds, toasted (see Notes)

¹/3 cup mirin (sweet rice wine)

1¹/2 teaspoons freshly ground black pepper

2¹/2 pounds boneless beef short ribs (see Notes), thinly sliced and lightly trimmed

1 Make the *kalbi* marinade: Place the soy sauce, maple syrup, sugar, onion, scallions, garlic, kiwi, Asian pear, Sprite, orange juice, sesame oil, sesame seeds, mirin, and pepper in a blender and puree until smooth. You'll have about 6 cups of marinade. It can be refrigerated, covered, for up to 1 week.

2 Place the short ribs in a large resealable plastic bag, add the marinade, and massage it into the meat. Let the short ribs marinate in the refrigerator for at least 2 hours.

SHORT RIBS IN ALL OF THEIR SPLENDOR—SERVED AS A TACO WITH PLENTY OF GREEN GOODNESS.

3 Set up a grill for indirect grilling. If you are using a gas grill, light only half of the burners. If you are using a charcoal grill, mound the coals on one side of the grate. Preheat the grill to medium.

4 Drain the ribs, discarding the marinade. Place the ribs on the grate away from the heat, cover the grill, and cook the ribs until the meat is very tender and has shrunk back from the ends of the bones, 1½ to 2 hours. If you are using a charcoal grill, you'll need to add more coals after 1 hour.

NOTES: To toast the sesame seeds, set a dry skillet over medium heat (do not use a non-stick skillet for this). Add the sesame seeds and heat them, tossing occasionally, until lightly toasted and aromatic, 3 to 5 minutes. Keep an eye on the sesame seeds; you don't want them to burn. Transfer the toasted sesame seeds to a heatproof bowl to cool.

You can make Korean cut short ribs by butterflying the meat, leaving slices of the rib bone intact or, as suggested here, you can use boneless short ribs. Ask a butcher to wrangle the boneless ones, cutting the meat into slices as thin as ¼ inch.

BARBECUE:
Roadside Apparitions and Realities

DRIVING OUT OF AUSTIN through the Hill Country, I broke for a barbecue stand. It was a crossroads lean-to, cobbled from timbers and roofing tin. Around back was one of those black barrel smokers, made from industrial piping. Cloaked in swirling smoke, fronted by a sign that reads something like Skeeter's Place, the whole setup looked like an apparition, like the barbecue stand of my dreams. Turns out that it was a dream of sorts. When I got out of my car, I saw that the stand was a mere facade and the smoke was coming from a machine. It was a set for the filming of a commercial.

Roadside barbecue is a fixture in the American South, my native region. Talk with Old Guard barbecue men and you learn that some of the region's beloved restaurants began when an enterprising cook dug an earthen pit by the highway near a busy intersection, laid in wood, refashioned a metal bedspring as a grill, and capped the pit with a sheet of roofing tin. There are fewer roadside stands these days. But some honest road food proprietors remain on the job. (By my definition, road food is the rural analog to urban street food.)

I've yet to find the Hill Country barbecue stand of my dreams. But I'm keen on a place in a gas station parking lot on the outskirts of Jackson, a Tennessee town between Memphis and Nashville. Shane Dempsey, the owner, sells smoked chicken quarters from a decommissioned U-Haul truck with a window cut in the side. "I can drive fifty-five miles an hour in this thing," he told me, "and it'll still be smoking."

SPAM MUSUBI

TRAVEL IN HAWAII and you'll notice these tiles of rice and Spam, bound in wraps of nori, displayed in hot boxes on the counters at neighborhood convenience stores. Spam is a vestige of World War II, when canned meat rations fed soldiers stationed on the islands. In this *musubi* recipe, inspired by the Marination Mobile, those pink slabs of pork get a quick fry in a pan and a douse of soy.

From this window Hawaiian-inspired beauty emerges.

Streetside accessorization is part of the ploy.

MAKES 8 MUSUBI

I can (12 ounces) Spam

1/4 cup soy sauce

3 tablespoons mirin (sweet rice wine)

3 tablespoons granulated sugar

4 sheets of nori, cut in 2-inch wide strips (see Notes)

4 cups cooked sushi rice

Furikake (see Notes)

1 Remove the Spam from the can and set the can aside. Cut the Spam horizontally into 8 equal slices. Cook the slices in batches in a skillet over medium-high heat until a crisp crust forms on both sides, about 2 minutes per side. Transfer the cooked Spam to paper towels to drain.

2 Combine the soy sauce, mirin, and sugar in a small saucepan over medium-high heat and let come to a boil. Reduce the heat so that the soy sauce mixture simmers, then add the drained Spam slices, turning them to coat completely. When the soy sauce mixture has thickened, use a slotted spoon to remove the Spam from the pan. Discard the soy sauce mixture.

3 Remove both the top and bottom from the can of Spam. Place a piece of nori on a work surface. Position the Spam can upright on one

end of the nori. Using the can as a mold, fill it with some of the rice, pressing down on the rice with your fingers until it is about 1/2 inch thick (it helps to moisten your fingers with water when doing this). Sprinkle *furikake* (see Notes) over the rice, seasoning it to taste, and top the rice with a slice of Spam followed by another layer of rice. Press hard on the rice to compress it. Carefully remove the can. Wrap the nori around the rice and Spam, moistening the ends with a bit of water to help seal the nori. Repeat with the remaining nori, rice, and Spam, then revel in the porky goodness that is Spam.

NOTES: The Sushi Chef brand of nori is widely available; it comes in .45-ounce packages.

Furikake is a Japanese condiment made from a combination of flavorings including ground dried fish, sesame seeds, and seaweed. It can be found at Asian groceries or ordered online.

A hit of heat benefits sliders and tacos alike.

LAST SEEN: 2500 First Avenue, Seattle, Washington

MARINATION MOBILE

KAMALA SAXTON, a principal in Marination Mobile, loves the intimacy of street food. "If I'm in a restaurant, I don't always get to talk to the owner or meet the chef," she told me. "On a truck like mine, you have no choice. There's no divide. We're the people taking your order and cooking your food."

Slate blue and slick, the Marination Mobile looks hip. But beneath that cool exterior is the chassis of an old linen services truck. And beneath the high concept food lurks a simple idea. "What we did was pay tribute to the lunch trucks of Hawaii," said Kamala, who claims both Hawaiian and Korean lineage

and who argues, convincingly, that those Hawaiian lunch trucks vend our nation's foremost fusion on wheels.

On the Marination Mobile menu you'll find kimchi quesadillas, *kalbi* (short rib) tacos with slaw, and *kalua* pork sliders. Kamala calls the chile-kicked sauce for the sliders "nunya sauce." As in, if you ask for a recipe, you get the reply, "That's nunya business."

BARBACOA DE BORREGO

"FUZZY GOAT," that's what I understood Cruz Suarez to be saying. "You're eating fuzzy goat." I learned later that the fuzzy goat was actually old lamb or, as you may know it, mutton. This recipe, inspired by Santa Rosa Tacos de Barbacoa, results in smoke-tinged barbecue, which is, of course, the English translation of *barbacoa*. The tender meat makes the perfect filling for tacos.

A jumble of chopped lamb, onions, and cilantro.

SERVES 10 TO 12

2 teaspoons salt

2 teaspoons freshly ground black pepper

2 teaspoons chili powder

7 to 8 pounds mutton shoulder with bones, or
   3 to 5 pounds boneless mutton shoulder

1 Set up a charcoal grill for indirect grilling by mounding the coals on one side of the grate. Preheat the grill to medium-high.

2 Mix the salt, pepper, and chili powder in a small bowl to make a rub. Massage the spices into the mutton shoulder.

3 Place the mutton shoulder in the center of the grill rack. Cover the grill and cook the meat until it begins to fall apart, 2½ to 3 hours. Use an instant-read meat thermometer to test for doneness, inserting it into the thickest part of the meat without touching a bone, if any. The mutton is done when the internal temperature reaches 170°F. You will need to add fresh coals to the grill after each hour of cooking.

4 Transfer the mutton shoulder to a cutting board and let it rest for 20 to 30 minutes. Pull the meat apart or chop it into bite-size pieces to use in tacos.

Read about the Santa Rosa Tacos de Barbacoa truck on page 106.

HIGH-SPEED CLEAVER WORK IS KEY AT SANTA ROSA.

CONSOME DE BORREGO
(MUTTON SOUP)

I WANT TO LIKE *MENUDO.* But I just can't get past the tripe. I tell you this to establish that I'm not always a bravado eater. That's important to know when I tell you that I love this mutton *consomé,* inspired by Santa Rosa Tacos de Barbacoa. It's a rich soup, almost elegant.

SERVES 6 TO 8

2 tablespoons olive oil

2 medium-size carrots, diced

2 celery ribs, diced

I large onion, thinly sliced

I cup cooked chickpeas (garbanzo beans)

2 cloves garlic, coarsely chopped

I teaspoon salt

I teaspoon freshly ground black pepper

7 to 8 pounds mutton shoulder with bones, or 3 to 5 pounds boneless mutton shoulder, seasoned for Barbacoa de Borrego (page 104)

I small white onion, chopped, for garnish

1/2 cup chopped fresh cilantro, for garnish

Jalapeño peppers, sliced, for garnish

Lime wedges, for serving

Soup so rich you'll need to rethink your definition of consommé.

LAST SEEN: At La Pulga market, South Pleasant Valley Road at Elmont Drive, Austin, Texas

SANTA ROSA TACOS DE BARBACOA

WHAT DOES A FLEA MARKET taste like in Austin? *Elotes* (corn), peddled from a custom-fabricated roasting trailer, swabbed with mayonnaise, sprinkled with cheese and chile powder. *Pupusas* (masa cakes), stringed with cheese and served on a paper plate, piled with shreds of pickled cabbage and carrots.

Walking the dirt aisles of La Pulga outdoor market, as generators clack and rattle, you can buy jeans appliquéd with marijuana leaves. And hand-tooled belts. And ten-packs of tube socks. Beneath a corner tent you can get your car rewired. Alongside, another vendor sells stereo decks and molar-rattling speakers that he'll install while you wait.

But the real reason to visit this weekends-only market is the food. After a morning of wandering, I zeroed in on the *barbacoa* stand of Cruz Suarez. His line was longest. And, true to form, his eats proved to be the best.

1 Preheat a charcoal grill to medium-high. Don't put the cooking grate in place yet.

2 Place the olive oil, carrots, celery, sliced onion, chickpeas, garlic, salt, and black pepper in a heavy-duty roasting pan or disposable aluminum pan and stir to mix. Place the pan in the bottom of the grill and surround it with hot coals. Add enough water to cover the vegetables. Place the cooking grate on the grill and let it heat up for a few minutes.

3 Place the mutton shoulder on the grill grate directly over the pan with the vegetables. Cover the grill and cook the meat until it begins to fall apart, 2½ to 3 hours. Use an instant-read meat thermometer to test for doneness, inserting it into the thickest part of the meat without touching a bone, if any. The mutton is done when the internal temperature reaches 170°F. The juices from the meat will drip into the pan with the vegetables. Check the water level in the pan as the meat cooks and add more if necessary to keep the vegetables just covered. This will be the soup broth in the finished dish. You will need to add fresh coals to the grill after each hour of cooking.

4 Transfer the mutton to a cutting board and let it rest for 20 to 30 minutes. Then, carefully remove the pan with the soup from the coals.

A wide choice of condiments complements mutton.

You may need someone to help you. Skim any excess fat from the surface of the soup.

5 Chop the mutton with a cleaver. Put some of the meat in bowls, setting the remaining meat aside for another use, such as taco filling. Ladle the soup over the meat, and top it with the chopped onion, cilantro, and slices of jalapeño. Serve the soup with lime wedges.

THAI CHICKEN KARAAGE

CHICKEN NUGGETS WITH CHARACTER. With crunch and fierce chiles. With oomph. Nuggets that challenge you to rethink nuggets. That's what this recipe from Paul Qui, Moto Utsonomaya, and Ek Timrek gets you. It uses the Japanese cooking technique *karaage,* where poultry or meat is marinated, dusted with a starch, and then fried. The herbs are key here. Don't stint. As for the chile sauce, if you can't find the brand suggested, you can substitute another Thai sauce so long as it's sweetened with palm sugar.

A colorful entrance to the kinetic world of East Side King.

SERVES 4 TO 6

I cup Asian fish sauce

I cup distilled white vinegar

I cup granulated sugar

I head garlic, peeled and minced

4 Thai chiles, coarsely chopped

I cup chile sauce, preferably Mae Ploy brand

6 skinless boneless chicken thighs (about I pound total), cut into chunks

1/2 cup cornstarch

Vegetable oil, for frying the chicken

1/4 medium-size onion, thinly sliced

2 jalapeño peppers, thinly sliced

Salt

Cilantro, mint, and basil sprigs, for garnish

Lime slices, for garnish

1 Place the fish sauce, vinegar, sugar, garlic, Thai chiles, and 1 cup of water in a large mixing bowl and stir to mix. Place 1/2 cup of the fish sauce mixture in a small mixing bowl. Add the chile sauce, stir to mix well, cover the

To cut through the heat, that cooling thatch of greens is key.

EAST SIDE KING

EVERY MUSICIAN NEEDS a diverting side project, a band that allows him to put aside his oboist day job and, say, rip through the Hoodoo Gurus catalog. That same logic applies to a cadre of chefs from Uchi, the hip and genre-defining Austin sushi restaurant. Late in 2009 three of those chefs opened a punk rock concession stand behind the Liberty bar in east Austin. The team consists of Paul Qui, a chef de cuisine at Uchi, along with sushi chefs Moto Utsonomaya and Ek Timrek. Their fare is crisp sweetbreads with kimchi. And a salad of deep-fried brussels sprouts (see page 126). And cucumber kimchi-garnished pork buns, inspired by Paul's stint at Momofuku in New York.

This is late-night grub, cooked after the boys close down Uchi. They work in a trailer with two flat tires that looks like it's been tagged by an early career Basquiat. Appropriate to the carnival-of-drunks vibe that defines the back patio at the Liberty, all food, prepared by an interchangeable crew of the three sushi vets, hits the bar-top tables served in tinfoil-wrapped cardboard boats of county fair corn dog provenance.

Behind this bar lurk great street eats.

bowl, and place it in the refrigerator. You'll use this as sauce for the cooked chicken. Let the sauce return to room temperature before using.

2 Add the chunks of chicken to the large mixing bowl and stir to coat them well with the fish sauce mixture. Cover the bowl and let the chicken marinate in the refrigerator for 24 hours.

3 Place the cornstarch in a shallow bowl. Remove the chicken from the marinade, shake off the excess liquid, and discard the marinade. Dredge the chicken in the cornstarch.

4 Pour oil to a depth of 2 inches into a cast-iron skillet and heat over high heat until it registers 350°F on a deep fry thermometer. Working in batches and being careful not to overcrowd the skillet, carefully add the chicken to the hot oil and cook, turning once, until golden brown, 5 to 7 minutes. Using a slotted spoon, transfer the chicken to paper towels to drain.

5 Place the onion, jalapeños, and drained chicken in a mixing bowl and stir to mix. Add the reserved sauce and generously toss the chicken mixture with it and season with salt to taste. Garnish the chicken with the cilantro, mint, basil sprigs, and the lime slices.

TAMARIND-GLAZED FRIED CHICKEN DRUMMETTES

FRIED CHICKEN TAKES WELL TO SWEETNESS, especially to syrup and honey. Think of the modern chicken and waffles phenomenon, with its taproot at Roscoe's House of Chicken 'n Waffles in Hollywood. And think of the honey-dripped fried chicken popular in Virginia. The brown sugar in this recipe, inspired by the Asian Soul Kitchen, gets you to the same place. The sweet-sourness of the tamarind tamps things down before they get out of control.

SERVES 4

1/2 cup cider vinegar

1/2 cup firmly packed brown sugar

1 package (14 ounces) tamarind pulp (see Notes)

1 teaspoon minced peeled fresh ginger

3 whole cloves

1 tablespoon grated orange zest

2 teaspoons salt

1 cup all-purpose flour

2 tablespoons cornstarch

1 teaspoon freshly ground black pepper

16 chicken wing drummettes (the meaty portion of the chicken wing)

Peanut oil, for frying the chicken

1/2 cup sesame seeds, toasted (see Notes)

LAST SEEN: South Grand Avenue between West Third and Fourth Streets, Los Angeles, California

ASIAN SOUL KITCHEN

THIS PROJECT IS THE WORK of the husband and wife team of Akiko Konami and Richard Wright (no, not that Richard Wright). The vibe is multiculti. They keep Mexican Cokes iced in the cooler, along with Mitsuya brand cider. In addition to fried chicken and collard greens, Akiko and Richard serve *panko*-battered salmon croquettes that owe a debt of inspiration to Baltimore crab cakes.

If Asian-inflected soul food sounds like a conceit to you, they back up their cooking with a sound rationale. "You go to any inner-city neighborhood in America," lead cook Ralph "Snook" Barnes told me,

A sunshine yellow truck serving deep-fried soul food.

"and you'll find Asian people frying chicken for black customers."

1 Combine the cider vinegar and brown sugar in a small saucepan over medium heat and cook, stirring, until the brown sugar dissolves, about 5 minutes. Whisk in the tamarind pulp, ginger, and cloves, stirring to break up the tamarind pulp, and cook until the mixture becomes a thick glaze that coats the back of a spoon, about 15 minutes. Stir in the orange zest and 1 teaspoon of the salt. Remove the tamarind glaze from the heat and keep it warm.

2 Place the flour, cornstarch, pepper, and the remaining 1 teaspoon of salt in a shallow bowl and stir to mix. Dredge the chicken drummettes in the flour mixture.

BOX OF ASIAN SOUL KITCHEN'S FRIED GOODNESS AND GREENS.

3 Pour oil to a depth of 2 inches into a cast-iron skillet and heat over high heat until it registers 350°F on a deep fry thermometer. Working in batches and being careful not to overcrowd the skillet, carefully add the drummettes to the hot oil and cook until golden brown, 5 to 7 minutes. Using a slotted spoon, transfer the cooked chicken drummettes to paper towels to drain.

4 Toss the drained chicken drummettes in the tamarind glaze and sprinkle them with the toasted sesame seeds before serving.

N O T E S : Tamarind pulp is sold in Indian and Mexican grocery stores and some supermarkets. Look for a brand such as Goya, which already has its seeds and strings removed.

To toast the sesame seeds, set a dry skillet over medium heat (do not use a nonstick skillet for this). Add the sesame seeds and heat them, tossing occasionally, until lightly toasted and aromatic, 3 to 5 minutes. Keep an eye on the sesame seeds; you don't want them to burn. Transfer the toasted sesame seeds to a heatproof bowl to cool.

CIVIC IDEALISM:
How to Curate a Cart Scene

CITY GOVERNMENTS TEND TO VIEW street food in one of two ways. Some see carts as nuisances, as threats to so-called legitimate brick-and-mortar businesses. Those cities do their best to outlaw street food, basing their decision on health and sanitation arguments or decades-old laws that give back-door exclusivity to loose collections of hot dog vendors and pretzel mongers.

The other sort of city government regards street food carts and trucks as small businesses in the making. Mayors and council people in these enlightened cities think street food vendors help foster small business. They believe that street food brings more people into the streets, which is a key component in making a city safe and pleasantly livable.

The curation of street food—like the curation of street life—is not effortless. The mayor of Cleveland, Ohio, knows this. In June of 2009 he announced his intention to create a food cart program that would, in the words of the local newspaper, "turn Cleveland's sidewalks into an urban buffet."

Mayor Frank Jackson's vision of the plan was a nonprofit organization that would manage the program, selecting and overseeing the carts. The city's economic development office would lend the program money for the purchase of new carts. Once up and running, the cart operators would pay a monthly usage fee, which would in time pay down the $400,000 debt incurred for the new carts. Civic idealism, it seems, comes with a price tag.

GREENS
WITH TURKEY NECKS

FOR THE LONGEST TIME preserved pork was the preferred flavoring for greens in the American South. More recently, however, health concerns have compelled cooks and eaters—especially Southerners—to look to other proteins for flavor. This recipe, inspired by the Asian Soul Kitchen, uses smoked turkey necks to their fullest potential.

The logo suits the truck, showcasing cultures in complement.

Read about the Asian Soul Kitchen truck on page 110.

SERVES 4 TO 6

1/4 cup vegetable or olive oil

I medium-size onion, diced

2 cloves garlic, minced

I pound smoked turkey necks

I teaspoon salt

I teaspoon crushed red pepper flakes

3 large bunches collard, turnip, or mustard greens

I tablespoon granulated sugar

Pepper vinegar, or a favorite hot sauce

1 Heat the oil in a large stockpot over medium-high heat. Add the onion and cook until translucent, about 2 minutes. Add the garlic and cook, stirring with a wooden spoon, until softened, about 2 minutes. Be careful not to let the garlic brown. Add 8 cups of water and let come to a boil. Add the smoked turkey necks, salt, and red pepper flakes. Reduce the heat to medium-low and cook until the flavor develops, 30 to 45 minutes.

2 Meanwhile, rinse the greens well. Remove and discard the thick center veins of the greens and coarsely chop the leaves. After the turkey necks have cooked for 30 to 45 minutes, add the greens to the pot and stir. At first the greens will take up lots of room, but as you stir them they will wilt.

3 Sprinkle the sugar over the greens, stir to mix, and cover the pot. Reduce the heat to low and let the greens simmer until they are dark green and very soft, 45 minutes to 1 hour.

4 To serve the greens, remove the turkey necks from the pot and pull the meat from the bones. Return the meat to the pot and stir to mix. Season the greens with pepper vinegar to taste.

CHICKEN MUGS

CORNSTARCH IS THE KEY in this recipe, inspired by Keiko Naka at Ton-Ton Japanese Food Cart. Frying in a cornstarch batter yields a fine-grained crust that is shatteringly crisp and, compared to some thick-skinned Southern-style chicken, fairly innocuous. The ginger supplies a subtle heat. If you want more fire, reach for a Korean-style chile paste.

Grab a mug of bird and go.

From the menu to the cart itself, Ton-Ton is stylish as can be.

SERVES 4

2 cloves garlic, minced

2 teaspoons grated peeled fresh ginger

2 tablespoons soy sauce

I teaspoon granulated sugar

16 chicken wing drummettes (the meaty portion of the chicken wing)

I cup cornstarch

Peanut oil, for frying the chicken

YOU'LL ALSO NEED

Four 8-ounce paper coffee cups, for mugs

1 Combine the garlic, ginger, soy sauce, and sugar in a large mixing bowl. Add the chicken drummettes, stir to coat well, and let marinate in the refrigerator, covered, for at least 1 hour.

2 Place the cornstarch in a shallow bowl and dredge the chicken drummettes in it.

3 Pour oil to a depth of 2 inches into a cast-iron skillet and heat over high heat until it registers 350°F on a deep fry thermometer. Working in batches and being careful not to overcrowd the skillet, carefully add the drummettes to the hot oil and cook until golden

brown, 5 to 7 minutes. Using a slotted spoon, transfer the cooked chicken drummettes to paper towels to drain.

4 Place 4 drained chicken drummettes in each of 4 paper coffee cups so that you can ambulate and eat. For drivers, they fit in cup holders, too.

LAST SEEN: Market Street at 33rd Street, Philadelphia, Pennsylvania

TON-TON JAPANESE FOOD CART

KEIKO NAKA, the pigtailed proprietor of Ton-Ton Japanese Food Cart, was born in Tokyo. When I met her, she was wearing a white shirt and a blue apron and wielding a pink-handled knife. Her cart looked Hello Kitty cute. Her sign, rendered in a flourish of black, calls to mind both restrained calligraphy and exuberant graffiti.

For grab-and-go, Keiko sells *onigiri*—cellophane-wrapped triangles of seaweed stuffed with hashed tuna, mayo, and salted rice (you'll find the recipe on page 124). I ordered a curried rice omelet (page 76) and a fried chicken "mug."

Standing in line with a paper cup full of marinated fried chicken elegantly hacked into serving pieces, I learned that *ton-ton* is Keiko's take on the sound a cleaver makes when hitting a cutting board.

Daily specials on display, all priced at a pittance.

CHICKEN PEANUT STEW

THE PRESENCE OF PEANUTS in a stew or soup is usually a mark of African influence. Never mind that the peanut is a New World plant. Never mind, too, that the peanut is not a true nut at all. It's a legume—a pea. In this recipe, inspired by Buraka, peanuts provide both texture and flavor.

Buraka, the cart, a compact and colorful beacon of goodness.

SERVES 6

I tablespoon olive oil

2 pounds boneless, skinless chicken breasts and thighs, cut into bite-size pieces

4 medium-size red potatoes, diced

I onion, chopped

2 cloves garlic, peeled and crushed

I teaspoon ground cumin

I teaspoon ground coriander

I teaspoon freshly ground black pepper

I teaspoon crushed red pepper flakes

I teaspoon salt

3/4 cup chunky natural peanut butter

I can (15 ounces) chickpeas (garbanzo beans), rinsed and drained

1 Heat the olive oil in a large skillet with a tight-fitting lid over medium-high heat. Add the chicken and cook until browned, 3 to 5 minutes. Remove the chicken from the skillet and set it aside.

2 Reduce the heat to medium-low, add the potatoes, onion, and garlic to the skillet and cook, stirring, until the vegetables soften, 2 to 3

Scratch cooking in huge pots and tight confines.

minutes. Sprinkle the cumin, coriander, black pepper, red pepper flakes, and salt over the vegetables and stir to mix well. Add 1 cup of water and the browned chicken and stir to mix. Increase the heat to medium-high and let the water come to a boil. Immediately reduce the heat, cover the skillet, and let the chicken and vegetables simmer for about 15 minutes, stirring occasionally.

3 Add the peanut butter, stirring to blend well. Add the chickpeas, cover the pan again, and let simmer until the chicken is cooked through and the potatoes are fork tender, about 10 minutes longer.

A styrofoam coffin of spicy stew, water on the side.

LAST SEEN: Library Mall, 700 block of State Street, Madison, Wisconsin

BURAKA

When Markos Regassa left Ethiopia to study business at the University of Wisconsin, his aim was to apply his education and open an import-export company. Instead, in 1992 he opened a bright yellow cart on the Library Mall and started serving the foods of Africa. One year later, he opened a small restaurant, too.

His food is not strictly Ethiopian. Regassa's coconut curry chicken, chock-full of yellow-fleshed yams, was inspired by a Kenyan dish. But all dishes, no matter their origin, come with *injera*, the spongy Ethiopian flatbread made with a blend of teff and other grains.

NEW YORK CITY:
FROM STREET MEAT TO SCHNITZLED COD

To understand New York City street food you must understand street meat. That's what my friend Zach Brooks calls flattop-cooked chicken or lamb served over rice and doused with white sauce and hot sauce. He's the mind behind Midtown Lunch, the Web-based catalog of good eats squirreled away in the skyscraper gulch.

I n Midtown Manhattan street meat is often known as halal food, a reference to food prepared in a manner that respects Islamic law. (Think of a Muslim take on Jewish kashruth and you're close.) Some carts have no real signage save a placard that reads simply HALAL. No matter what the placard reads, chances are that the umbrella positioned above it will advertise the Broadway production of *The Lion King*.

At the Biryani Cart, a Southeast Asian relative of the halal cart, the repertoire goes beyond meat and rice. A Vendy Award favorite (see page 264 for more about the Vendys), the Biryani Cart has diversified, adding Indian-inspired burritos wrapped in *paratha* (Indian flatbread) as well as seafood over rice.

For the longest time, street meat—along with dirty-water hot dogs—defined the pavement dining options in Midtown Manhattan. (That's a gross but reasonably accurate generalization, one that holds fairly well in Manhattan but lacks traction in Brooklyn, where Red Hook soccer fields vendors have been selling *pupusas*—masa cakes—since the 1970s.)

WHERE THE TRUCKS ARE:

⚲ 6th Avenue at 46th Street.

⚲ 3rd Avenue at 46th Street.

⚲ Broadway at Broome Street.

And check newyorkstreetfood.com.

And then a change came. New York City shed its white tablecloth restaurant insecurities. An appetite for great food—served without pretense—spiked.

A new breed of street food vendors, most working trucks, not carts, began hopscotching the city, stopping in the 40s for lunch and at Union Square for dinner. They sold their goods based on taste and provenance, not low price. They devised marketing strategies. They built websites and pipelined their lives into blogs.

Early adopters included Jerome Chang. A onetime Le Cirque pastry chef, he rolled onto the streets in 2007. The Dessert Truck, doing business in a converted postal vehicle, earned cred selling chocolate mousse with a peanut butter core, goat cheese cheesecake with rosemary caramel, and meringues with berry "gelée" and whipped crème fraîche.

And still the trucks rolled. Hamburgers, sourced from grass-fed cattle, advertised by way of flat-screen TVs mounted on truck broadsides, showing said cattle grazing in bucolic pastures. Dumplings, stuffed with organic edamame or Thai basil and chicken, sold by way of haiku tweets, like this one: "summer storm bodes gray / the dumpling truck perseveres / spreading dumpling love."

As the decade reached its close, while most New Yorkers were still eating street meat and hot dogs, the buzz hounds were all focused on the New Guard, like the Schnitzel & Things truck, owned by Oleg Voss and Jared Greenhouse.

Oleg learned to love the de facto national dish of Austria while working at an investment bank in Vienna. Jared likes the sound that battered cod, chicken, or pork make when they hit hot oil. Judging by the crowds, New Yorkers like that sound, too.

- - - - - - - - - - - - - - - - - - -

Left to Right:
Top Row: Calexico in SoHo. Biryani's Kati roll in Midtown.

Middle Row: Meru Sikder of the Biryani Cart. Wafels & Dinges.

Bottom Row: Schnitzel window. Doug Quint waits to take a Big Gay Ice Cream order

A LUSCIOUS BED OF PORK SAUCE LURKS UNDERNEATH THE BIRD.

TAIWANESE FRIED CHICKEN

THE KOREAN-STYLE FRIED CHICKEN served in the second-story restaurants and karaoke taverns that line 32nd Street, the Main Street of New York City's Koreatown, has won attention of late. The chicken is usually fried twice, in the manner of Belgian frites. And the resulting crust is papyrus thin. But Korea is not the sole Asian country with a knack for fried bird. Witness this Taiwanese riff, inspired by the good folks at the NYC Cravings truck.

The line at NYC Cravings.

SERVES 4

1 cup soy sauce

1/4 cup mirin (sweet rice wine)

3 tablespoons granulated sugar

2 tablespoons minced garlic

2 tablespoons Chinese five-spice powder

2 teaspoons freshly ground black pepper

1 whole chicken (about 3 pounds), quartered

2 egg yolks

1/2 cup cornstarch

2 cups sweet potato starch (see Note)

2 tablespoons garlic powder

Peanut oil, for frying the chicken

Cooked rice, for serving

Taiwanese Pork Sauce (optional, recipe follows), for serving

1 Combine the soy sauce, mirin, sugar, garlic, 1 tablespoon of the five-spice powder, and the pepper in a large bowl. Add the chicken to the soy sauce mixture, turning it to coat all sides. Let the chicken marinate, covered, in the refrigerator overnight.

2 Beat the egg yolks with the cornstarch in another bowl. Add the yolk mixture to the bowl with the chicken and stir to mix well.

3 Place the sweet potato starch, garlic powder, and the remaining 1 tablespoon of five-spice powder in a large shallow bowl and stir to mix. Working with one chicken quarter at a time, dredge the chicken in the sweet potato starch mixture and let sit for a few minutes.

4 Pour oil to a depth of 2 inches into a cast-iron skillet and heat over high heat until it registers 350°F on a deep fry thermometer. Working in batches and being careful not to overcrowd the skillet, carefully add the chicken quarters to the hot oil and cook, turning once, until golden brown and cooked throughout, about 12 minutes. Using tongs, transfer the cooked chicken to paper towels to drain. Serve the chicken over the rice with the pork sauce, if desired.

Low-cost branding.

NOTE: You can find sweet potato starch at Asian markets.

Taiwanese Pork Sauce

CALL THIS GRAVY IF YOU LIKE. That's what it is: Pork gravy with soy sauce, inspired by the NYC Cravings folk. In my native American South, this is the kind of stuff we mop up with biscuits, the stuff we plop on mashed potatoes, the gilding with which we anoint a fried chicken thigh. Serve it over rice or fried bird. Your call.

MAKES ABOUT 4 CUPS

Peanut oil

10 shallots, thinly sliced

1 pound ground pork

2 tablespoons soy sauce

1 teaspoon salt

1 teaspoon freshly ground black pepper

1 teaspoon granulated sugar

1 Pour oil to a depth of about 1 inch into a heavy, medium-size saucepan and heat over medium heat for 1 to 2 minutes. Add the shallots and cook until brown and crisp, 2 to 3 minutes. Using a slotted spoon, transfer the shallots to paper towels to drain. Do not wipe out the pan.

2 Add the ground pork to the pan and cook over medium-high heat, breaking the meat up with a spoon, until browned, about 5 minutes. Add the soy sauce, salt, pepper, sugar, and enough water to cover the meat. Return the browned shallots to the pan, reduce the heat, and let the sauce simmer until the water has cooked off, about 45 minutes.

LAST SEEN: 24th Street between Park Avenue and Madison Avenue, New York, New York

NYC CRAVINGS

IN THE SUMMER OF 2009, twenty-somethings Thomas Yang, his sister Diana Yang, and their friend Eric Yu retrofitted an Italian bread truck, painted it cream with a bamboo green trim, and rolled it out under the banner NYC Cravings. Their trope was Taiwanese food. Their specialty was Taiwanese fried chicken.

As interpreted by NYC Cravings, fried chicken is a dark-meat quarter bird, marinated in five-spice powder and soy sauce, cooked in deep, roiling oil, served over rice, and swamped with a "secret pork sauce." Nestled on the side in that same foam clamshell is a hash of soured cabbage, which ameliorates what little grease lingers on the bird.

They offer dumplings too, but these are no match for the gut punch of that Taiwanese fried chicken. More recently, NYC Cravings has added *zongzi*, a bamboo leaf–stuffed tetrahedron of glutinous rice pocked with, among other items, peanuts, sweet Chinese sausage, and dried shrimp.

EGG FOO YONG

AT YUE KEE, in the shadow of the Kappa Alpha house at Penn, an order for egg foo yong gets you two chicken and onion omelets swamped in brown gravy over a mound of white rice.

SERVES 4 TO 6

1 cup chicken broth

2 tablespoons soy sauce

1 tablespoon mirin (sweet rice wine)

1 1/4 teaspoons freshly ground black pepper

1 tablespoon cornstarch, dissolved in 3 tablespoons water

1 teaspoon Asian (dark) sesame oil

3/4 cup shredded cooked chicken

1/2 cup finely grated onion

1/2 cup bean sprouts

1/2 cup grated celery

5 extra-large eggs, well beaten

1 teaspoon kosher salt

Vegetable oil, for cooking

Cooked rice, for serving

1 Combine the chicken broth, soy sauce, mirin, and 1 teaspoon of the pepper in a small saucepan over medium-high heat. Bring to a boil then reduce the heat to low. Stir in the cornstarch mixture and cook, stirring constantly, until the sauce thickens, about 5 minutes. Add the sesame oil and stir to mix. Remove the brown sauce from the heat and keep it warm.

2 Combine the chicken, onion, bean sprouts, celery, eggs, salt, and remaining 1/4 teaspoon of pepper in a bowl.

3 Add enough oil to a cast-iron skillet to cover the bottom and heat over medium-high heat. Ladle in about 1/4 cup of the chicken and egg mixture for each omelet, being careful not to crowd the skillet, and cook, turning once, until golden brown and crunchy on both sides, about 1 1/2 minutes per side. Remove the omelets from the skillet and keep them warm in a low oven until all of the egg mixture has been cooked, adding more oil to the skillet as necessary. Serve the omelets 2 to a person over rice topped with the brown sauce.

LAST SEEN: 38th Street near Walnut Street, Philadelphia, Pennsylvania

YUE KEE

IN THE MANNER OF a derelict diner, Yue Kee, which has been doing business since 1983 across from the Wharton business school, is surly and efficient. On the day I visited, Bi Pang, the proprietor, along with her husband, Tsz Pong, jockeyed from the wok to the order window, as college kids pretending to study quantum physics stood in line.

Craig LaBan, restaurant critic for the *Philadelphia Inquirer*, once gave this beat-to-hell, zinc-colored truck two bells, the local equivalent of two stars. Among other eats, he cited the sparerib tips with black bean sauce and the pork belly with medicinal herbs and bok choy.

He liked the egg foo yong, too, a Chinese-American dish often dismissed as retrograde, but that, prepared well—as it is here—reminds me that an omelet has universal appeal.

TUNA ONIGIRI

WHEN I ASKED KEIKO NAKA, the proprietor of Ton-Ton Japanese Food Cart, the origins of this dish, she shrugged and smiled and told me, "This is what we would take to a picnic." In Tokyo, where these triangles of rice are street food staples, *onigiri* are sold in a wide variety of flavors, from preserved plum to salmon. A typical convenience store might stock twenty or more flavors. Keiko stocks nine. Tuna is her most popular.

A handful of nori, rice, and tuna.

Everything is handmade, even the menu board.

Read about the Ton-Ton truck on page 115.

MAKES 8 ONIGIRI

1 can (5 ounces) solid white tuna, drained and flaked with a fork

2 tablespoons mayonnaise

1 teaspoon soy sauce

1/2 teaspoon chili powder

4 cups warm cooked sushi rice

8 sheets of nori, cut in 2-inch wide strips (see Note)

1 Place the tuna, mayonnaise, soy sauce, and chili powder in a small bowl and stir to mix. Set the mixture aside.

2 Moisten your hands with cold water. Take 1/2 cup of the rice and place it in one hand.

Make an indention in the middle of the rice with your thumb. Put about 1 tablespoon of the tuna mixture in the indention. Encase the tuna filling in the rice, first forming it into a ball, then working it into a triangular shape. Repeat with the remaining rice and tuna filling.

3 Wrap each triangle of rice in 1 or 2 strips of nori. Moisten with water to seal. Serve the *onigiri* immediately or wrap them tightly in plastic wrap and refrigerate.

NEW ORLEANS STREET NOODLES: Meet Old Sober

NEW ORLEANS BOASTS a long tradition of street commerce. In *Creole Sketches*, Lafcadio Hearn documented the comings and goings, as well as the appearance and demeanor, of New Orleans food peddlers of the late 1800s. Most were women of African extraction. They sold pralines. They sold fish and vegetables. And, most famously, they sold calas, fried rice fritters.

"The Cala woman was a daily figure on the streets till within the last two or three years," wrote the editors of the 1901 edition of *The Picayune Creole Cook Book.* "She went her rounds in bandana tignon, guinea blue dress, and white apron, and carried on her head a covered bowl in which were the dainty and hot Calas. Her cry, *'Belle Cala! Tout Chaud!'* would penetrate the morning air, and the olden Creole cooks would rush to the doors to get the first fresh, hot Calas."

Today New Orleans street food is still a driver of the culinary economy. A few mobile enterprises, like the Lucky Dogs carts and the Roman Candy Man wagon, remain in place as tradition bearers. Freelance praline sellers still walk the French Quarter, while unlicensed catering trucks do drive-bys of local colleges and high schools, selling crab patties and shrimp pies.

Taco trucks arrived in the wake of the levee failures that followed Hurricane Katrina. In the post-Katrina economy, those taco trucks did most of their business in sight of construction sites. More recently they've moved to the margins of the city or, in some cases, begat brick-and-mortar taquerias. Many of the traditional vendors, on the other hand, have begun focusing more intently on carnivals and festivals. The second line parades associated with Mardi Gras Indian celebrations are especially important.

Working from a cherry-red concession trailer, Danielle Brown sells Sno-Balls drenched in bubble gum and red velvet cake flavorings. On occasion, she parks near the intersection of Claiborne Avenue and Robertson Street. But she does most of her business at second line parades. "I'll park at one end of the parade," she told me. "And my husband will park at the other. And we'll be steady making Sno-Balls."

Also working the second line circuit is Linda Green. She sells paper cups of frozen Kool-Aid, concoctions she calls hucklebucks, and foam cups of ya-ka-mein, a kind of low-rent riff on *pho* that many drinkers call "old sober." (The reference, Linda says, is to the sobering qualities of hot noodle soup.)

Although Linda likes the second line crowds best, she also works the New Orleans Jazz & Heritage Festival each spring. Eats served at Jazz Fest are not in the strictest definition of the word street food, but they certainly reflect the democratic ideals that inform the best street feeds.

Ya-ka-mein in all its noodley glory.

FRIED BRUSSELS SPROUTS

NOT MUCH STREET FOOD is vegetable based (unless you count tofu dogs, which I don't). Part of the problem is that it's difficult to eat a bowl of greens while walking. The answer is brussels sprouts, which, as showcased in this recipe from the East Side King boys, eat like popcorn shaken from a sack.

Paul Qui will take your order.

A back alley scene in Austin.

Read about the East Side King truck on page 109.

SERVES 4 TO 6

I cup sweet chili sauce, preferably Mae Ploy brand

I cup distilled white vinegar

I clove garlic, minced

4 Thai chiles, minced

2 tablespoons vegetable oil

I pound brussels sprouts, quartered

1/2 cup thinly sliced red cabbage

1/2 cup thinly sliced green cabbage

1/4 cup alfalfa sprouts

1/4 cup thinly sliced onion

I large jalapeño pepper, thinly sliced

Salt

1/8 cup torn fresh mint leaves

1/8 cup torn fresh cilantro leaves

1/8 cup torn fresh basil leaves

1 Place the chili sauce, vinegar, garlic, and Thai chiles in a small mixing bowl. Mix well and set aside.

2 Heat the oil in a large skillet over high heat. Add the brussels sprouts and cook them until the cores of the sprouts are approaching golden brown and the edges are caramelized, about 1½ minutes.

3 Toss the red and green cabbage, alfalfa sprouts, onion, and jalapeño in a large mixing bowl. Add the brussels sprouts and the chili sauce mixture. Season with salt to taste and garnish with the mint, cilantro, and basil.

STILL LIFE WITH BRUSSELS SPROUTS, GREENS, AND FRIED BUN

ELOTES

THE TYPICAL CHEESE used for *elotes* is *cotija añejo,* dry, grainy stuff from Mexico. It's fairly salty. Grated "parmesan," shaken from those green cylindrical cans, is a common substitute. I'm not saying you should follow suit. I'm just saying that's what some people do. Here's the right way, inspired by the *elotes* from Melissa's Roasted Corn. You can grill the corn over charcoal or cook it indoors in a skillet. If you prefer to eat yours *en vaso* (in a cup), see the variation on the facing page.

Elotes equal joy—even for the corn.

Pop art worthy of Lichtenstein.

SERVES 6

6 ears corn, in their husks

1/2 cup mayonnaise

3 cups crumbled Cotija añejo or shredded
    queso fresco

3 tablespoons chili powder

Salt

1 Soak the corn, in the husks, in water to cover for about 30 minutes.

2 If you are grilling the corn, set up a charcoal grill for direct grilling and preheat it to high.

3 Remove the husks and corn silk from the corn and grill the ears on the grill or cook them in a dry cast-iron skillet over high heat until the kernels just begin to turn brown, about 2 minutes per side, 8 minutes in all, turning with tongs.

4 Slather the corn with the mayonnaise, roll it in the crumbled cheese, and sprinkle it with the chili powder and salt to taste. You might want to snag a roll of paper towels.

ELOTES EN VASO

FOR *ELOTES EN VASO*, wait until the grilled or charred corn is cool enough to handle, then cut the kernels off the cobs, using lengthwise strokes of a chef's knife. Place the kernels from each ear of corn in an individual dish, or *vaso*. Top each serving of corn with a dollop of mayonnaise, some of the crumbled cheese and chili powder, and a sprinkling of salt to taste. Garnish the *elotes en vaso* with lime wedges and serve them with plastic spoons.

Don't stint on the chili powder.

LAST SEEN: 9612 Beechnut Street, Houston, Texas

MELISSA'S ROASTED CORN

CORN MAY BE the most elemental Mexican street food: Boiled in the husk. Roasted in the sheath. Unsheathed, grill blackened, and slathered with mayonnaise and cheese. Or shaved into slabs, tumbled into a cup, and layered with *crema* and powdered chiles.

In the Fruitvale neighborhood of Oakland, California, I ate my fill from a vendor who was dealing corn from a beer cooler on wheels. In Austin, Texas, at a Saturday morning flea market, I ate cobs that had been roasted in an orange firebox on wheels. And in Houston, at Melissa's Roasted Corn, I enjoyed *elotes en vaso*—corn in a cup. Too many versions of this dish are built on a base of canned or frozen corn. But Melissa roasts an honest *espiga*, shaving that ear of corn into sheets of kernels and folding these into cool *crema*.

Speaking of corn, one eat I missed on my Houston trips was *pan de elote*, or corn bread, as served by the LALA trailer on Telephone Road near Hobby Airport. According to Houston chowhound Jay Francis, the proprietor, who was born in Monterrey, Mexico, bakes round loaves studded with hypersweet whole-kernel corn. Next time.

ROASTED POBLANOS

STUFFED WITH ARTICHOKE CREAM CHEESE

STUFFED PEPPERS ARE STREET FOOD PARAGONS. In Tucson I fell for güero chile peppers stuffed with cheese, wrapped in bacon, and blistered on a flattop grill (you'll find the recipe on page 134). At a street festival in South Pittsburg, Tennessee, I once ate a banana pepper stuffed with pimento cheese, rolled in corn flour, and deep-fried. This recipe, from the Maximilianos, is part of that continuum, delivered with a vegan's sensibility.

The Dandelion cart—great vegetarian offerings to go.

MAKES 12 TO 18 STUFFED POBLANOS; SERVES 4 TO 6

I pound vegan cream cheese, or I pound regular cream cheese

^{1}/$_2$ cup eggless mayonnaise, preferably Vegenaise brand

^{1}/$_4$ cup nutritional yeast

^{1}/$_4$ cup apple cider vinegar, preferably Bragg brand

^{1}/$_3$ cup freshly squeezed lemon juice

I green bell pepper, stemmed, seeded, and diced

I red bell pepper, stemmed, seeded, and diced

I red onion, diced

2 large carrots, diced

2 ribs celery, diced

2 cups chopped artichoke hearts, well drained (see Notes)

2 teaspoons dried oregano

^{1}/$_2$ teaspoon crushed red pepper flakes

12 to 18 poblano peppers

20 dried corn husks from a package (see Notes), soaked for 10 minutes in cold water to cover and drained

Cumin Rice (recipe follows)

1 Mix the cream cheese, mayonnaise, nutritional yeast, cider vinegar, lemon juice, green and red bell peppers, onion, carrots, celery, artichokes, oregano, and red pepper flakes in a large bowl and stir to mix. The filling mixture should be medium-thick and pleasantly gloppy. Set the poblano filling aside.

2 Roast the poblano peppers by placing them directly over the flame of a gas burner or under the broiler and rotating them occasionally, until they are charred all over, about 5 minutes. Be careful to watch and rotate the poblanos often to ensure that they blacken but do not burn.

3 Place the roasted poblanos in a plastic or paper bag and seal it tightly to let the peppers steam until cool. When cool enough to handle, using gloves, peel or rub off the charred skin and discard it. Cut a slit in the side of each poblano and remove the seeds.

4 Preheat the oven to 350°F.

5 Spoon the filling into the cavities of the poblanos, dividing it equally among them. Wrap the stuffed poblanos in the soaked corn husks. Place them in a baking dish and cover it with aluminum foil. Bake the poblanos until they are very soft, about 1 hour. Serve the poblanos with the Cumin Rice.

NOTES: Use artichokes from a can or jar and drain them well.

Dried corn husks are available in Mexican grocery stores, some supermarkets, and online (Amazon.com, for example).

Cumin Rice

CUMIN POWDER GOES DEAD FAST. Fresh cumin seeds, on the other hand, especially when toasted as in this recipe from The Dandelion cart, bloom with the persistent musky scent that perfumes many Mexican dishes. Like the stuffed poblanos, this is hippy-fied Mexican, filtered through the lens of a natural foods grocery. And it's really good.

SERVES 4 TO 6

1/4 cup vegetable oil

1 cup diced celery

1 cup diced carrots

1 cup diced onion

1/4 cup whole cumin seeds

4 cups uncooked brown basmati rice

1/4 cup vegetable broth powder

1 Heat the oil in a stockpot over medium-high heat. Add the celery, carrots, and onion and cook until the onion softens, about 5 minutes.

2 Add the cumin seeds and continue cooking the vegetables until fragrant or the cumin seeds begin to pop, about 1 minute.

3 Add the rice, stir to coat it with the oil, and cook until slightly browned, 3 to 4 minutes. Add the vegetable broth powder and 12 cups of water and stir to mix. Let come to a boil, then reduce the heat and let the rice simmer, covered, until tender, at least 1 hour, stirring periodically. If the rice looks dry before it is cooked through, add a little more water.

MADISON, WISCONSIN: CURATING THE INFORMAL CULINARY ECONOMY

Most American street food scenes evolved organically as cooks in need of funds worked to serve customers in need of food.

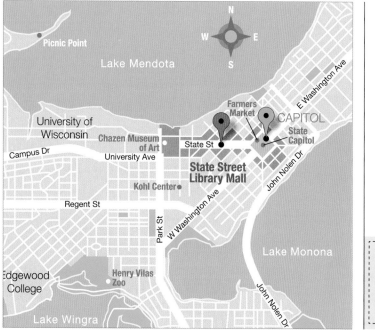

WHERE THE TRUCKS ARE:

📍 Library Mall, State Street.

📍 State capitol apron surround.

The economics were straightforward. Not so, the social dynamics. (My friend Psyche Williams-Forson wrote a book, *Building Houses out of Chicken Legs: Black Women, Food, and Power*, about the entrepreneurial activities of African American women.)

Street food advocates— and, yes, that term defines a category of people, including me—have categorized such traditional relationships, deeming them engines of the "informal economy." That's just a less derisive way to say underground economy, or black market economy.

College towns are hotbeds of informal culinary economics. Doormen at rock-and-roll clubs barter the promise of pizza delivery tomorrow night for free tickets to the show tonight. Graduate students from Thailand, in need of a car for a grocery store run, cook platters of *pad see ew* for their auto-owning dorm mates.

Too few college towns boast eats beyond grill-blackened hot dogs and fryer-scorched chicken drummettes. Madison, Wisconsin, is an exception, offering an alternate multicultural vision, curated by the city for the benefit of its citizens. In Madison, there are two primary groupings of carts: The pedestrian mall that runs alongside the University of Wisconsin library and the apron that surrounds the state capitol grounds. (There are late-night cart clusters on Frances Street and elsewhere, but they serve as mere ballast for drunks.)

I arrived on a September morning, just as a twenty-seven person review panel organized by Warren Hansen, the city's street vending coordinator, was fanning out, clipboards in hand, to evaluate the forty-odd carts that ply the Madison streets. A civil services lifer, Warren took a job as a lifeguard at a City of Madison pool and never looked back. He studied art history while in college here. As boss of the carts in Madison, Warren has applied the curatorial processes of the art world to the cart scene.

The testers are a group of volunteers recruited by Warren. Some are Madison city employees. Others are frequent cart customers,

people Warren interacts with on his daily rounds, eaters he deems discerning. All of the clipboard wielders take their assignments seriously. They look officious, at times absurdly so, kicking cart tires, appraising artwork, scribbling scores. But their work pays dividends to the University of Wisconsin students who step out of the library for a bite at the Buraka cart of yams and *wat*, an Ethiopian stew sopped up with *injera* flatbread. Also benefiting are the state bureaucrats who, instead of accepting a fast food fate, step up to The Dandelion cart for a roasted poblano pepper stuffed with artichoke cream cheese and served with a side of cumin-spiced rice. Idealism in action—that's Madison.

- - - - - - - - - - - - - - - -

Left to Right:

Top Row: A Taste of Mexico mural. X marks the Jamerica truck.

Middle Row: Lindsay Gehl, LMN O'Pies proprietor. Order up at Jamerica.

Bottom Row: Boxes of campus color.

TORITOS

AT THEIR MOST BASIC, *toritos* are stuffed güero chiles, cooked on a flattop grill until they brown and then blister. Seafood trucks in Tucson stuff blond and stubby güeros with shrimp and serve them as appetizers. The cheese-stuffed güeros peddled by hot dog vendors are more common.

Ruiz Hot-Dogs, set in a mesquite-shaded gravel lot on Sixth Avenue, serves one version. Even better, at Oop's Hot Dogs Martin Lizarraga stuffs his chiles with mozzarella and wraps them in bacon. As the bacon crisps on the flattop, the mozzarella turns to a pleasant goo. The following recipe was inspired by Oop's. Serve it alongside your hot dog.

MAKES 6 STUFFED PEPPERS

6 güero chile peppers (small, hot, yellow peppers), Hungarian wax peppers, or hot banana peppers

6 chunks of mozzarella or other white melting cheese, cut into chubby sticks

6 thin slices of bacon

1 Rinse the peppers under cold running water and pat dry with paper towels. Cut a slit in each pepper but leave the stem and bottom point intact. Scrape the seeds out of the cavities and stuff the mozzarella inside.

2 Wrap a slice of bacon around each pepper. Place the stuffed peppers in a skillet over medium-high heat and cook them, turning as needed, until the bacon is brown and crisp. If you are not serving the *toritos* immediately, keep them in a warm oven.

LAST SEEN: East Ajo Way and South 6th Avenue, Tucson, Arizona

OOP'S HOT DOGS

YOU CAN'T MISS THE BLUE VAN painted with a hip-hop–inspired hot dog cartoon character, wearing oversize sunglasses, giving a thumbs-up to passersby. That logo is the masterwork of Oop's proprietor Martin Lizarraga, who learned to construct Sonoran-style hot dogs in his native Hermosillo.

There, Martin told me, crumbled chorizo is a common topping. Chopped bacon, too. And cucumbers mixed with *crema.* Here, health department regulations cut down on such expressive hot dog riffs. Here, a fellow learns to express himself in other ways, through, say, hip-hop hot dog cartoon characters—and *toritos.*

ETHIOPIAN LENTILS
WITH YAMS

THE INTERPLAY OF EARTHY LENTILS and sugar-kissed sweet potatoes defines this Buraka dish. In Africa a call for yams will get you the stringy tubers that are native to that continent. Here, it gets you garnet-hued sweet potatoes.

The city of Madison encourages the decoration of carts.

SERVES 4 TO 6

1 tablespoon olive oil

1 large sweet potato, peeled and cut into 1-inch cubes

1 red bell pepper, stemmed, seeded, and diced

1 onion, diced

3 cloves garlic, minced

1 teaspoon minced peeled fresh ginger

1/2 cup dried split red lentils

1 tablespoon tomato paste

2 teaspoons Berbere Spice Mix
    (recipe follows)

Salt and freshly ground black pepper

1 Heat the olive oil in a heavy skillet over medium heat. Add the sweet potato, bell pepper, onion, garlic, and ginger and cook the vegetables, stirring occasionally until they start to soften, about 8 minutes.

Read about the Buraka truck on page 117.

Buraka proves that vegetable–based meals need not be boring.

2 Add the lentils, tomato paste, spice mix, and 2 cups of water, stir to mix well, and bring to a boil. Reduce the heat and let the lentils simmer until they are soft and all of the water is absorbed, 20 to 30 minutes. Taste for doneness. Season the lentil mixture with salt and black pepper to taste and serve immediately.

Berbere Spice Mix

IN A TYPICAL GROCERY YOU CAN BUY Greek-style seasoning in little yellow canisters, Cajun-style seasoning in fat green canisters, various Mediterranean spice mixes, and on occasion something called Tuscan Sunset spice mix. I've rarely, however, seen a north African *berbere* mix, which is a shame because this stuff tastes great with everything from stews to french fries. This version was inspired by the spices used by the Buraka food cart.

MAKES ABOUT 1/2 CUP

3 tablespoons paprika

5 teaspoons crushed red pepper flakes

2 teaspoons ground cumin

I teaspoon ground cardamom

I teaspoon ground coriander

I teaspoon ground ginger

I teaspoon ground turmeric

I teaspoon salt

I teaspoon freshly ground black pepper

1/2 teaspoon ground allspice

1/2 teaspoon ground cloves

1/2 teaspoon ground cinnamon

Place the paprika, red pepper flakes, cumin, cardamom, coriander, ginger, turmeric, salt, black pepper, allspice, cloves, and cinnamon in a small bowl and whisk to mix well. Store the spice mix in an airtight container.

SING A SONG OF OKRA: Music from the Street

HUNCHED IN A library carrel, with headphones on, I once spent an afternoon listening to street vendor cries. I can still hear the voice of a Gullah vendor from 1950s Charleston, South Carolina, who sang of blackberries in a Little Richard falsetto. I remember listening to Ninevah Whitley, the New York City fishmonger of the 1930s who shouted

Fish man!
Bring down your dish pan!
If you ain't up, get up!
If you ain't down, get down!
Come on down
Get around
Fish ain't but five cent a pound.

At the Library of Congress, I read transcriptions of performances by Si Custis. He was a Mississippi pit master of the 1920s, famous for shouting

Ice cold lemonade!
Made in the shade
Stirred with a spade
Good enough for any old maid!

Those voices are, by and large, gone from the streets of modern day America. One artist working to keep them alive is Olu Dara, a jazz musician born in Natchez, Mississippi, and now living in Brooklyn, New York. In 1998 he cut a solo album, *In the World: From Natchez to New York*. One of the tracks, "Okra," paid homage to the calls of street vendors.

"We called him the Coal Man," Olu told me, speaking of the hawker who, during the 1940s, was a constant on the streets of Natchez. "I don't think I ever knew his real name. He sold coal, but we knew him by his fruits and vegetables. Strawberries, blackberries, dewberries, whatever was growing; that's what he sold. You could smell the freshness before you heard him coming."

Olu's lyrics play like an homage to the men and women who once trundled our avenues and alleyways, selling fruits and vegetables, shrimp and fish, homemade liquor, too. But Olu's music is not bound by the constraints of folklore. With his lyrics, his lilting voice, his bright cornet, his effervescent guitar, Olu has revivified a vocation.

ROOTS JAMBALAYA

THEY WOULDN'T DO IT THIS WAY back in Louisiana. Not with beets. And corn. Assimilation, becoming part of a new place, a new culture, changes a boy. And it influences the way he cooks. That's how this recipe from Trey Corkern at The Swamp Shack came to be. It reflects the dietary inclinations of Portland, as well as inspirations provided by Louisiana.

A handful of roots and rice.

The use of the word "shack" is apt here.

Read about The Swamp Shack truck on page 39.

SERVES 6 TO 8

2 large red beets

3 carrots

3 parsnips

1/2 cup olive oil

1/3 cup minced garlic (8 to 10 cloves)

1/4 cup chopped shallots

1/4 cup Creole seasoning mix

1/4 cup Italian seasoning mix

5 cups vegetable stock

2 cups converted rice

1/2 cup fresh white corn kernels

1/4 cup chopped scallions or fresh cilantro,
    for garnish

1 Rinse and coarsely chop the beets, carrots, and parsnips, leaving the skins on, then set them aside, keeping each separate.

2 Heat the olive oil in a stockpot over medium heat. Increase the heat to medium-high, add the garlic and shallot and cook until fragrant, about 2 minutes, stirring constantly and being careful not to let them burn. Add the Creole and Italian seasoning mixes and stir well.

3 Add the beets to the stockpot and cook, stirring constantly, for 2 minutes. Add the carrots and parsnips and stir well. Add the vegetable stock, stir, cover the pot, and let come to a boil. Add the rice, stir to mix well, and reduce the heat to low. Cover the pot again and let the rice cook until tender, 18 to 20 minutes.

4 Remove the pot from the heat, add the corn kernels, and stir to mix. Cover the pot and let the jambalaya stand for 10 minutes. Stir gently with a fork to fluff the rice and serve topped with the scallions or cilantro.

FRIED GREEN TOMATO SALAD

CHICKPEA-TEMPURA-FRIED: That's the best way to describe the mustard-yellow batter that enrobes these fried green tomatoes. Nestled on a bed of dressed greens, the tomatoes prove that, no matter what Fannie Flagg may have said, Southerners have no lock on the frying of tomatoes—green, yellow, or otherwise. This recipe was inspired by the trailer work of Carrie Summer and Lisa Carlson at Chef Shack.

Crisp on the outside and crisp on the inside—Chef Shack excels at fried green tomatoes.

"Now serving" beckons the crowds.

SERVES 4

FOR THE VINAIGRETTE

1¹/2 tablespoons finely minced shallot

1¹/2 tablespoons red wine vinegar

1¹/2 tablespoons Dijon mustard

¹/4 teaspoon salt

¹/3 cup extra-virgin olive oil

Freshly ground black pepper

FOR THE TOMATOES

2 quarts peanut or canola oil, for frying

¹/2 cup all-purpose flour

¹/2 cup chickpea (garbanzo bean) flour (see Note)

1 teaspoon salt

1¹/2 cups seltzer water

2 large green tomatoes, sliced ¹/4-inch thick

4 large handfuls of mixed salad greens

1 Make the vinaigrette: Combine the shallot, vinegar, mustard, salt, and the olive oil in a small, tightly sealed jar and shake vigorously. Taste for seasoning, adding pepper to taste. Set the vinaigrette aside.

2 Prepare the tomatoes: Heat the oil in a deep fryer or Dutch oven over medium-high heat until a deep fry thermometer attached to the

side of the pot registers 325°F. Combine the all-purpose flour, chickpea flour, salt, and seltzer water in a mixing bowl. Dip the green tomato slices in the batter to coat and carefully place them in the hot oil. Cook the tomatoes, turning them once, until golden brown, 3 to 4 minutes per side. Using a slotted spoon, transfer the tomatoes to paper towels to drain.

3 Toss the mixed salad greens with the vinaigrette and divide the greens evenly among 4 plates. Top each plate of greens with 2 or 3 fried green tomato slices and serve.

NOTE: Chickpea (garbanzo bean) flour is available in health food stores and markets that specialize in Indian and African groceries.

Chef Shack makes the most of the market.

LAST SEEN: Mill City Farmers' Market, 704 2nd Street S., Minneapolis, Minnesota

CHEF SHACK

LISA CARLSON AND CARRIE SUMMER are the chefs behind the polka-dotted Chef Shack. They arrived with keen pedigrees. Lisa had worked the line with, among others, Daniel Humm of Eleven Madison Park in New York City. Carrie's résumé includes a stint as a pastry chef at Morimoto in Philadelphia.

Here, in Minneapolis, the partners work what was once a deep-fried Oreo trailer, cooking a range of foods from Indonesian-spiced beef tongue tacos to chickpea flour–battered fried green tomatoes. Lisa owns the savory end, sourcing grass-fed beef from local favorite Thousand Hills Cattle Company and pork from Tim Fischer. Carrie handles the sweets, including the Chef Shack's signature creation, Indian-spiced mini doughnuts (you'll find a recipe for those on page 265).

Although their business is growing, the Chef Shack women still take a three-month wanderlust vacation each winter. Last time I saw them, Lisa and Carrie were plotting their attack on Singapore and Borneo.

Meru Sikder stands and delivers in NYC.

Falafel and fries from Liba, San Francisco.

Yes—a mac and cheese sandwich!

A Philly Cheesesteak from MikeyD's.

SANDWICH up!

CHAPTER 5

Fried fish sandwiches are ephemeral indulgences. Cooked in 2 or 3 minutes.

Served hot from the grease. Tucked between slices of flimsy white bread. They collapse as they are constructed. And threaten to fall apart as they are consumed.

La Camaronera, a counter-service fish-fry house in Miami's Little Havana neighborhood, has sold fish sandwiches since 1976. Set in a strip mall, alongside a store that sells neutraceuticals and various snake oils including Sexomax and Erectomax, the restaurant is a working man's favorite, operated with joy and ferocity by the Garcia brothers.

Leaning at the bright blue laminated counter, I nibbled an order of *bollitos de carita,* which translates from Spanish as black-eyed pea fritters. Raspy and salty, smelling pleasantly of fresh-dug soil, they called to mind *acarajé,* a food beloved in West Africa. What's more, they served as an ideal preamble to La Camaronera's true specialty, *pan con minuta,* a fried snapper sandwich.

In 2010 Dave Garcia, a linebacker of a man, opened a truck-based variation on the Garcia norm. The Fish Box serves a foreshortened version of the La Camaronera menu. On the day I visited, The Fish Box was parked on the industrial fringe of the city, out near the airport, in a complex of low-slung block buildings occupied by tile importers and installers.

There were no *bollitos de carita* at this location. No oyster cocktails or ketchup-battered spiny lobsters either. But the promise of fresh, local fish cooked in clean, hot oil prevailed. And the *pan con minuta* was prepared with the same care—albeit at a price that's about one third higher. (Call it the truck tax.)

The Fish Box's snapper, filleted into a shingle with the tail still attached, dipped in an egg batter, fried, and served on a poufy Cuban bun, is perfect walking-around food. But, like most good things that emerge from trucks, it's evanescent. Here one moment, it's a pile of crumbs and fin shrapnel the next.

So good, so fresh, so cheap.

FALAFEL BURIED UNDER FETA, TOMATOES, LEMON, AND MORE.

LIBA FALAFEL SANDWICHES

FOR GAIL LILLIAN OF LIBA, the idea of the definitive falafel sandwich recipe is tough to conjure. "The nature of the menu is to mix and match a number of our toppings to complete the sandwich," she told me. "Every sandwich comes in a whole wheat pita from our local Hamati Bakery, and has tahini and *chimichurri* in it. After that, it's up to the customer to finish off the sandwich with any number of our fifteen falafel bar items." The following recipe is a favorite of photographer and recipe developer Angie Mosier.

Liba's extensive condiment bar.

A bright and joyous truck—viva Liba.

MAKES 4 SANDWICHES

4 whole wheat pita pockets

8 Falafel balls (page 93)

1/2 cup tahini

Olive-Orange Relish with Thyme (recipe follows)

Rosemary Peanuts (recipe follows)

Stuff each pita pocket with 2 falafel. Drizzle 1 tablespoon of tahini over each falafel sandwich, then top the sandwiches with a spoonful of olive-orange relish. Sprinkle some Rosemary Peanuts on top and serve.

Olive-Orange Relish
WITH THYME

THE PAIRING OF OLIVES AND ORANGES is characteristic of a Mediterranean palate, which makes sense when you consider that chickpea croquettes are beloved throughout the Mediterranean, whether known as *panisse* in France or *panelle* in Italy.

MAKES ABOUT 2 1/2 CUPS

2 cups fresh orange juice

3 tablespoons minced garlic

2 tablespoons fresh lemon thyme leaves

2 cups pitted kalamata olives

1 Combine the orange juice, garlic, and thyme in a skillet over medium-high heat. Let the mixture simmer until just barely syrupy, 10 to 15 minutes.

2 Place the olives in a food processor and pulse until irregularly chopped.

3 Place the orange juice mixture and the chopped olives in a bowl and stir to mix well. The relish tastes best after chilling for 24 hours. It can be refrigerated, covered, for up to 1 week.

Rosemary Peanuts

GAIL PUTS THESE PEANUTS out on the Liba truck's condiment bar. They're great for snacking and sprinkling on salads, too.

Serve yourself Rosemary Peanuts.

MAKES I POUND

¹/4 cup minced fresh rosemary

¹/8 cup granulated sugar

2 tablespoons kosher salt

¹/2 cup water

I pound raw, unsalted peanuts

1 Combine the rosemary, sugar, salt, and water in a saucepan over medium-high heat and stir until the sugar dissolves. Add the peanuts and stir until coated. Transfer the peanuts to a rimmed baking sheet to cool.

2 Place the cooled peanuts in a food processor and pulse until coarsely chopped. The peanuts can be kept in an airtight container, at room temperature, for up to 1 week.

LAST SEEN: By the loading dock at 155 De Haro Street, San Francisco, California

LIBA

GAIL LILLIAN got her idea for a food truck while traveling in the Netherlands, where Amsterdam falafel cooks mix and match various toppings. "Falafel has been around forever," she told me, as she rang up a credit card sale on her iPhone. "It's the least trendy food there is." But that doesn't mean falafel can't stand a bit of gussying.

Tucked into the well of her truck, where most operators ice down canned soft drinks, Gail displays vases of daisies. On the metal shelf that runs the length of the truck, she stocks jars of rosemary-roasted peanuts, fiery *harissa*, and ginger tomato chutney. From her fryer emerge perfect orbs of chickpea fritters and slender twigs of sweet potato, proving once and for all that those orange tubers can hold up to a bath in roiling oil (you'll find her secret in the recipe on page 13).

As for the truck's name, Liba is Gail's mash-up of the German and Yiddish words for love.

CHICKPEA AND DELICATA SANDWICHES

"IN THE STREETS AND FRY SHOPS of Palermo you will find *panelle,* patties made of chickpea flour and parsley that are deep-fried, salted, and served on a roll, often with a squeeze of lemon." That's Kevin Sandri from the Garden State truck on the origins of his outrageously good sandwich. In his recipe here, he has leveraged that Palermo inspiration to create a vegetarian sandwich.

Don't leave much time between the frying of the patty and the consumption of your sandwich. Like most fried food, it's best when eaten hot.

- -

Garden State's look relies heavily on quilted stainless.

MAKES 6 SANDWICHES

FOR THE CHICKPEA PATTIES

1¹/8 cups chickpea (garbanzo bean) flour (see Note, page 141)

1 teaspoon salt

¹/2 teaspoon freshly ground black pepper

¹/4 teaspoon ground cumin

¹/4 teaspoon cayenne pepper

¹/4 cup chopped fresh flat-leaf parsley

Olive oil, for brushing the baking sheets

FOR THE CARROT-RADISH SLAW

1¹/2 cups grated carrots

3 radishes, trimmed and sliced

1¹/2 teaspoons rice wine vinegar

1¹/2 teaspoons extra-virgin olive oil

Salt and freshly ground black pepper

FOR THE ROASTED DELICATA SQUASH

2 delicata squash (about 1¹/2 pounds total)

2 tablespoons olive oil

1 teaspoon freshly ground black pepper

FOR THE SANDWICHES

6 ciabatta rolls

Olive oil, for brushing the rolls

2 quarts vegetable oil, for frying

Lemon Aioli (recipe follows)

2 cups mixed salad greens

Salt

1 Make the chickpea patty mixture: Place the chickpea flour, salt, black pepper, cumin, and cayenne in a heavy pot over high heat and stir to mix. Gradually add 2 cups of water while stirring with a flat-edged wooden spatula. You want to avoid lots of lumps of flour but a few are okay. Stirring constantly, gradually lower the heat as the chickpea mixture thickens. When most of the water has been absorbed, add the parsley. The chickpea mixture is done once it pulls away from the side and bottom of the pot as you stir it, 10 to 15 minutes.

2 Lightly oil a baking sheet. Transfer the chickpea patty mixture to the pan, spreading it out evenly so that it covers the pan completely. Oil the bottom of a second sheet. Place this pan on top of the chickpea mixture and press on it firmly to create a smooth, even surface. Remove the top pan. Let the chickpea patty mixture cool completely.

3 Make the carrot-radish slaw: Place the carrots, radishes, rice wine vinegar, and olive oil in a bowl and toss to mix. Season the slaw with salt and black pepper to taste. Cover the slaw and set it aside. The slaw should be served at room temperature.

4 Prepare the delicata squash: Preheat the oven to 350°F.

5 Cut each squash in half lengthwise and remove and discard the seeds. If the skins of the squash are tough, peel them (when delicata squash first come into season, you can eat the skin). Cut the squash crosswise into 1/4-inch-thick slices. Place the squash on a rimmed baking sheet and toss with the olive oil and black pepper. Bake the squash until it is easily pierced with a knife, 10 to 15 minutes. Keep the squash warm.

6 Preheat the broiler.

7 To assemble the sandwiches: Using a knife, split the ciabatta rolls lengthwise, stopping just short of cutting all the way through. Lightly brush the insides of the rolls with olive oil and toast them, opened up like a book, under the broiler.

8 Cut the chickpea patty mixture into 12 pieces. Heat the 2 quarts of vegetable oil in a deep fryer or Dutch oven until a deep fry thermometer attached to the side of the pot registers 350°F. Working in batches and being careful not to crowd the pot, carefully

Read about the Garden State truck on page 19.

Open-faced chickpea fritters, crispy, hot, irresistible.

Tables and chairs and umbrellas make a lunch at Garden State downright civilized.

Lemon Aioli

AIOLI HAS BECOME ubiquitous. Over the last couple of years I've eaten truffle aioli. And Tabasco aioli. And ramp aioli. The best versions, however, have been the simplest. As in this lemon aioli. When making aioli, Garden State uses a blend of canola oil and extra-virgin olive oil. I've opted for using only light olive oil here.

MAKES ABOUT I CUP

3 cloves garlic

I teaspoon Dijon mustard

1/8 teaspoon cayenne pepper

Zest and juice of I lemon

2 egg yolks (see Note)

3/4 cup light olive oil

add the chickpea patties to the hot oil and cook them until they are crisp and beginning to brown, about 4 minutes. Using a slotted spoon, transfer the cooked patties to paper towels to drain.

9 Spread some aioli on the inside of each toasted roll, then add some salad greens to each side. Add some of the carrot-radish slaw, then place 3 or 4 slices of squash on top. Lightly salt the chickpea patties. Place 2 patties on top of the squash in each roll and close up the sandwiches.

Place the garlic, mustard, cayenne, lemon zest and juice, and egg yolks in a food processor and puree. With the motor running, slowly drizzle in the olive oil. It should form a thick emulsion, like mayonnaise. Refrigerate the aioli, covered, until ready to use.

N O T E : Because aioli contains raw eggs, prepare it with very fresh eggs that have been kept refrigerated.

BATTERED TRUCKS AND HELLO KITTY CUTE CARTS:
PHILADELPHIA

Los Angeles is the citadel of the modern American street food phenomenon, where every kitchen on wheels gets fifteen minutes of tweeted fame, New York City is where street food folk adopt the PR budgets and branding tropes of their brick-and-mortar cohorts.

Philadelphia is something different, a city of recidivist pleasures, where vendors still work battered trucks and quilted metal carts, dishing the fuel of workaday life to working-class eaters.

Philadelphia trucks, by and large, are rickety. Gun-metal gray and rust-scarred white define their exterior palates. The kitchens are galleys, stuffed to the gills with deep fryer bays and double-wide *planchas,* the sort of equipment usually crammed into diners. Most rely on generators that rattle and hum and drown out all other sounds.

Most of the carts are made of quilted stainless steel, incised with a diamond pattern; many are from Custom Mobile Food Equipment, of Hammonton, New Jersey.

In Philadelphia, groupings of trucks hunker at curbs at various spots, from the Temple University campus, where vendors peddle lo mein this and bagel sandwich that, to the bridge near the old main post office, where a gauntlet of Caribbean-inflected soul food trucks dish ribs and callaloo, goat curry and macaroni and cheese, oxtails and peach cobbler.

Across the Schuylkill River from downtown,

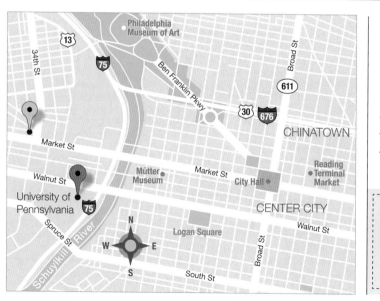

WHERE THE TRUCKS ARE:

- Market Street at 34th Street
- Near the University of Pennsylvania, walk along Spruce Street between 33rd and 38th streets.

Drexel University and the University of Pennsylvania sit cheek by jowl. You can get sophisticated eats here. But even the hippest vendors are focused on food, not folderol.

Walking a street that flanks the Drexel campus I came upon a squad of eight utilitarian trucks. One looked like it was a relic of a Korean War missile strike, retrofitted to dish fried fish. Another was so tagged with graffiti overlays that it resembled an art installation.

Deeper along the corridor that links the two campuses, falafel trucks appeared. Ali Baba, Magic Carpet, Aladdin, Casablanca, each frying chickpeas and stuffing pitas. And Chinese takeaways, too, like Double Dragon, Le Anh, and The Real Le Anh. (The latter sold clamshells of pad thai and bags of pizza rolls.)

I hit my stride when I doubled back toward Drexel. At Walnut Street and 33rd Street stood a trio of carts that confirmed, at least for me, why Philadelphia street food matters. Above the cluster loomed a street sign, stamped with the silhouette of an umbrella-shaded vendor, stipulating when sellers may work the curb and when eaters may follow their trails of steam in search of lunch.

One vendor was a slight Japanese woman, working a pink-handled knife, selling beautifully composed treats of the Hello Kitty school. Another was a Polish man who looked and sounded French and specialized in crepes. The third vendor sold cheesesteaks and hoagies. Just what I expected to find in Philadelphia, until the vendor introduced himself, and I came to understand that Mike Datt, of MikeyD's Grill, was born in northern India, not southern Philadelphia. No matter his place of origin, Mike speaks fluent broccoli rabe and provolone.

- - - - - - - - - - - - - - - - - -

Left to Right:

Top Row: Utz-pure Pennsylvania. Keiko Naka, proprietor of Ton-Ton.

Middle Row: Falafel and egg breakfast hoagie, A&M. The perfect thin crepe.

Bottom Row: A construction worker hits the window for a sandwich. Philly trucks are by and large functional, not fancy.

PHILLY AT ITS CHEESE-BLANKETED BEST.

CHEESESTEAK SANDWICHES

WITH PROVOLONE AND BROCCOLI RABE

AS SERVED IN HOMAGE to Philly by restaurants across this great land, the cheesesteak sandwich may be the most abused regional sandwich. I'm referring to versions made with that insult to protein known as Steak-umm. And I'm talking about versions drenched in the orange liquid goo that industry folks call performance cheese. This recipe, inspired by Mike Datt who once worked at Tony Luke's, corrects some of those wrongs.

The bread is all-important in Philadelphia.

MAKES 4 SANDWICHES

4 tablespoons (1/2 stick) butter

3 cups thinly sliced onions

2 cups I-inch pieces broccoli rabe, blanched (see Note)

1 1/2 pounds roast beef cooked rare, thinly sliced and chopped

Salt and freshly ground black pepper

4 Italian sandwich rolls

8 slices provolone cheese

1 Melt the butter in a large skillet over medium-high heat. Add the onions and cook until lightly browned, about 5 minutes. Add the broccoli rabe and the roast beef and season with salt and pepper to taste. Cook the broccoli rabe and beef mixture until heated through, about 2 minutes.

2 Preheat the broiler.

3 Using a knife, split the rolls lengthwise, stopping just short of cutting all the way

Spatula work on a flattop.

MIKEYD'S GRILL

MIKE DATT was born in New Delhi, India. Prior to opening MikeyD's Grill, his metal hut on wheels, he worked the grill at Tony Luke's, the fabled Philly roast pork stand. During that six-year stint, he learned to rely on sesame-seeded loaves from Sarcone's Bakery, another south Philly institution, in business since 1918.

When I asked Mike about technique and ingredients, he told me that he won't open the cart unless he can get Sarcone's loaves. In years past, Mike said he had to get in line at midnight to get the loaves he needed.

He talked with the same passion about the iron slab on which he cooks. "You know how your mom cooks everything in a frying pan?" he said, in a lilting Indian accent, hardened just a bit by his time in Pennsylvania. "Same with me—I cook everything on the flattop."

through. Open the rolls up like a book and divide the broccoli rabe and beef mixture evenly among them, topping each sandwich with 2 slices of provolone. Place the open sandwiches under the broiler until the cheese melts, about 2 minutes.

NOTE: To blanch the broccoli rabe, bring 8 cups of water to a boil. Add the broccoli rabe and cook for 2 minutes. Immediately drain and plunge the broccoli rabe into ice water to stop the cooking, then drain it again. Pat dry with paper towels.

First a pileup of beef, then the cheese.

CHICKEN CHEESESTEAK SANDWICHES

THIS IS A HERETICAL MOVE—at least for traditionalists. Substituting chicken for beef, like some kind of careless flight attendant, staggering the aisles, handing out cardboard dinners. But as served by MikeyD's Grill, it's a good move.

Regulars know the wait is short—but any wait would be worth it.

MAKES 4 SANDWICHES

About 2 tablespoons vegetable oil

2 whole skinless, boneless chicken breasts (about 1 1/2 pounds), diced

Salt and freshly ground black pepper

3 cups thinly sliced onions

1 green bell pepper, stemmed, seeded, and cut into strips

4 Italian sandwich rolls

4 tablespoons mayonnaise

8 slices provolone cheese

1 Heat 2 tablespoons of oil in a large skillet over medium-high heat. Add the chicken, season it with salt and black pepper to taste, and cook, stirring occasionally, until cooked through, about 8 minutes. Using a slotted spoon, transfer the chicken to a plate.

2 Add a little more oil to the skillet. Add the onions and bell pepper and cook over medium-high heat until slightly browned and soft, about 6 minutes. Return the chicken to the skillet and cook until heated through, 1 to 2 minutes. Taste for seasoning, adding more salt and/or black pepper as necessary.

3 Preheat the broiler.

4 Using a knife, split the rolls lengthwise, stopping just short of cutting all the way through. Open the rolls up like a book and spread 1 tablespoon of mayonnaise inside each. Divide the chicken mixture evenly among the rolls, topping each sandwich with 2 slices of provolone. Place the open sandwiches under the broiler until the cheese melts, about 2 minutes.

Sandwiches nestled within tissue place mats rest on the truck counter.

CUBANO SANDWICHES

A PROPER CUBANO SANDWICH is pressed flat until the weight of the griddle and the goo of the cheese seal shut the envelope into which the pork and ham have been stuffed. While most cubano recipes rely on roast pork shoulder, this sandwich, inspired by Eric Smith and Hector Ward at The Texas Cuban, is built on a base of roast pork tenderloin.

Still life with meat, bread, plantains, and mustard.

An easy fusion of cultures.

MAKES 4 TEXAS-SIZE SANDWICHES

4 Cuban sandwich rolls, or 4 French bread sandwich rolls

4 tablespoons (1/2 stick) butter, at room temperature

Thinly cut dill pickle slices

About I pound sliced roasted pork (see Note)

4 tablespoons store-bought or homemade Mojo Sauce (recipe follows)

I pound sliced ham

8 slices Swiss cheese

Yellow mustard

1 Using a knife, split the sandwich rolls in half and spread butter on the inside and outside of each half. Arrange the pickle slices and the slices of pork on the bottom half of each roll. Sprinkle 1 tablespoon of mojo on top of the pork. Top the mojo with slices of ham, then place 2 slices of Swiss cheese on the ham. Spread yellow mustard on the cut side of the top half of each roll and place these on the sandwiches.

2 Heat a griddle or skillet over high heat. Arrange the sandwiches topside down on the hot griddle or skillet, using the bottom of another skillet to press down hard on the sandwiches as they cook. Cook the sandwiches to toast the roll, 1 minute, then flip the rolls and continue cooking until the cheese melts, about 1 minute more, being careful not

LAST SEEN: South Lamar Boulevard and Collier Street, Austin, Texas

THE TEXAS CUBAN

ERIC SMITH works for a video game designer. He didn't want to commit to a full restaurant for this moonlight entrepreneurial endeavor. "Real restaurants are scary," he told me. "But if I fail here, what am I out? I sell my trailer on eBay and walk away."

Eric is a Texan. His partner, Hector Ward, late of the band Sigmund Fraud, is of Cuban ancestry. Thus the mashup known as The Texas Cuban, set in a rectangular trailer, painted glossy black, parked on a ragged patch of barren land across from a transmission repair shop.

When I asked how the two cultures fused in the trailer, Eric said, "We make our Cuban sandwiches to Hector's Cuban specs. But we make them big—for Texas." While we were talking, and I was thinking about how a Cuban sandwich shop establishes Texas provenance, I noticed that Eric and Hector source that most Texan of soft drinks: Dr Pepper, sweetened with true cane sugar and bottled in Dublin, Texas.

Eric Smith and Hector Ward, proprietors.

to let the rolls burn. Slice the sandwiches in half diagonally before serving.

NOTE: If you decide to roast a pork tenderloin, remember it cooks quickly in a 350°F oven. An average tenderloin weighs a little less than a pound and cooks in about 20 minutes.

Mojo Sauce

GOOD AND GARLICKY—A must for any sandwich that calls itself a cubano.

MAKES ABOUT 1 CUP

1/2 cup olive oil

6 cloves garlic, minced

1/2 cup freshly squeezed lime juice

1/2 teaspoon ground cumin

Salt and freshly ground black pepper

Heat the olive oil in a small, heavy saucepan over medium-high heat. Add the garlic and cook until fragrant, about 1 minute. Add the lime juice and cumin, then season with salt and pepper to taste. Let the mixture come to a boil, then remove it from the heat. The Mojo Sauce can be stored in the refrigerator, covered, for up to 1 week.

SLOPPY JERK PORK SANDWICHES

AT THEIR WORST, sloppy joes taste like ground beef goulash in white bread envelopes. At their best, they taste like these. If you can find a brace of fresh-baked dinner rolls, use them. If you can't, try brown-and-serve rolls from the bread aisle. No matter what you do, don't settle for hamburger buns when making either the jerk pork or jerk chicken sandwiches, inspired by the Jamerica Restaurant cart.

The University Mall resembles a culinary U.N.

Read about the Jamerica truck on page 33.

MAKES 6 SANDWICHES

I habañero pepper, stemmed, seeded, and minced

¹/2 cup chopped scallions

2 tablespoons minced garlic

I teaspoon ground allspice

I teaspoon freshly grated nutmeg

I teaspoon dried thyme

I teaspoon salt

I teaspoon freshly ground black pepper

About 2 tablespoons freshly squeezed lime juice

2 pork tenderloins (about I pound each)

¹/2 cup store-bought Jamaican barbecue sauce

6 fresh-baked dinner rolls

You're in charge of your own Scoville rating.

1 Combine the habañero, scallions, garlic, allspice, nutmeg, thyme, salt, and black pepper in a small mixing bowl with enough lime juice to make about 2 tablespoons of paste. Rub the habañero paste all over the pork tenderloins, then refrigerate the pork, covered, overnight.

2 Preheat a charcoal grill to high.

3 When ready to cook, brush and oil the grill

grate. Place the pork tenderloins on the hot grate and grill until cooked through but slightly pink, about 10 minutes. Use an instant-read meat thermometer to test for doneness; when done the internal temperature of the pork should be 145°F.

4 Transfer the pork tenderloins to a cutting board and let them rest for a few minutes. The final temperature on the instant-read thermometer should be 155°F. Chop the pork into bite-size pieces, toss it in the barbecue sauce, and pile it on the rolls.

VARIATION:

SLOPPY JERK CHICKEN

The heat is ready for the squirting—and don't forget a handful of napkins.

SUBSTITUTE 3 POUNDS of bone-in chicken legs and thighs for the pork tenderloins. They will be cooked through after grilling for about 45 minutes. Or you can bake the chicken in a 375°F oven for about 45 minutes. Let the chicken rest for a few minutes before pulling the meat off the bones and chopping it. Toss the chicken in the barbecue sauce and pile it on the sandwich rolls.

MAXIMUS/MINIMUS: Of Slaw and Soylent Green

Seattle's zinc-toned zoomorphic tribute to the great god pig is a twenty-first-century answer to the twentieth-century Oscar Mayer Wienermobile. A snout, fixed with rivets, protrudes from the hood. Ears flop from the roof. Kurt Beecher Dammeier's metal pig is only incidentally a restaurant that sells sandwiches of pulled pork, with choices of slaws and sauces. Those sauces dovetail with the name of the truck. MAXimus is chili-powder spiked. MiniMUS is comparatively mellow, sweetened with honey mustard. (Both sauces likely get their smoke from lapsang

Here piggy, piggy.

souchong tea infusions.) The pork is pretty good. And the business, which claims a weekday perch at Second Avenue and Pike Street, is successful. But the true source of the commotion is the truck itself. Yes, it's playful. To watch the MAXimus/miniMUS truck turn a corner is to conjure a toy pig in urban slop. But this rendering also projects some sort of postapocalyptic time when porcine paddy wagons might roam the streets, rounding up vegetarians for Soylent Green–inspired feeds.

SAN FRANCISCO: GOBBA GOBBA STREET

"Trucks are a liability," Jonathan Ward of Kung Fu Tacos told me, as I stood alongside his truck, scarfing down a hoisin-slicked duck taco with mango salsa. "If it's raining, you get no business. Get a flat tire, you get no business. It's tough. But it's also a rush, a thrill."

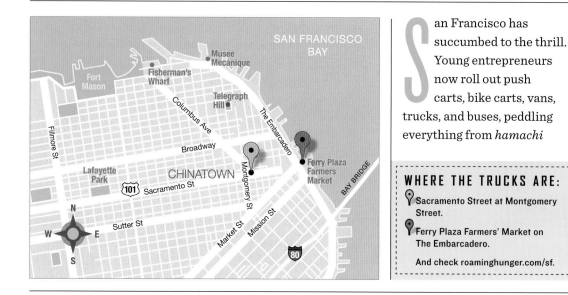

S an Francisco has succumbed to the thrill. Young entrepreneurs now roll out push carts, bike carts, vans, trucks, and buses, peddling everything from *hamachi*

nigiri to curried frog's legs, from nitrate-free hot dogs to vegan tamales. There has, of course, always been a street food scene in the city. On summer afternoons, *paleta* men have long peddled ice cream in the Mission District. You might even make a case that the people who sell their chowder in sourdough bowls on Fisherman's Wharf are street vendors of a sort, or at least inheritors of a long-standing street food tradition.

Meanwhile, in the tourist-free zone, drinkers at the headbanger bar Zeitgeist in the Mission get their nutrition from Virginia Ramos. Known simply as the Tamale Lady, she arrives most evenings wheeling a cart loaded with a cooler weighed down with sweet potato tamales, pork and green chile tamales—all sorts of tamales. She says to the drunks who crowd around, "I don't know you, but I love you."

Patrons of the "salumi-cycle," operated by Boccalone, the pig product

WHERE THE TRUCKS ARE:
Sacramento Street at Montgomery Street.

Ferry Plaza Farmers' Market on The Embarcadero.

And check roaminghunger.com/sf.

specialist and Ferry Building Marketplace tenant, are usually sober. But they're no less fanatical than Tamale Lady patrons. Thirty sandwiches stuffed with cured parts fill the silver Boccalone cooler, which is mounted on the front fork of a cherry-red bike. And when the deliveryman alights, they're gone in a flash of cash and grease.

RoliRoti, on the other hand, works the farmers' market circuit. Thomas Odermatt, the proprietor, is a relatively old hand among the new wave of quality-focused vendors. In business since 2005, he's helped San Francisco understand that truck food can be built on a base of local, organic, and sustainable supplies. (He started with chickens, then moved on to pig knuckles and *porchetta;* you'll find the recipe on page 164.)

Read through this vendor hopscotch and you might think that the street food scene in San Francisco is without a true rudder. And you'd probably be right.

Compared to other cities, San Francisco is without an overarching rubric. There's no defining vendor, like Kogi in Los Angeles. There's no defining tradition, as in the street meat beloved by New Yorkers. There's no defining form, as in the Airstream trailers of Austin. Instead what you have is a sort of free-form expression, loosely defined by a commitment to artisanal eats.

Who's Your Daddy potato chips and Gobba Gobba Hey fall beyond the purview of this book. Both began as guerrilla street food operations, but neither has operated from a truck or cart. And both now sell most of their products through retail outlets. Their stories are, however, instructive and representative of the state of street food in San Francisco.

Bill Horst, the proprietor of Who's Your Daddy, is a salesman by vocation. On the day I met him—in front of Pal's Take Away, the Mission grocery that stocks his stuff— Bill was wearing a dress shirt with cuff links. As we talked,

from the trunk of his Saab he pulled a box of his ruffle-cut chips, jumbled with shards of bacon, sealed in a clear plastic bag. "I just went to Dolores Park with my bags of chips. And that was it," he told me.

Steven Gdula, the man behind the guerrilla food business Gobba Gobba Hey, also frequents Dolores Park. He sells cookie cream sandwiches called gobs. As in black cherry chocolate gobs with lime butter cream frosting. And orange cardamom ginger gobs with saffron icing.

Standing at the counter at Pal's Take Away, in sight of a display of his gobs, Steven and I talked about the state of street food in America. We talked about the boom in guerrilla street food in San Francisco. Trying to put it all in perspective, he said, "It's amazing to me that people are willing to take food from a perfect stranger and put it in their mouth."

Top: **Steven Gdula of Gobba Gobba Hey.**
Middle: **Mobile coffee service.**
Bottom: **RoliRoti porchetta sandwich.**

PORCHETTA

ALTHOUGH THOMAS ODERMATT won his reputation with chicken cookery, he's also a wizard with hunks of pork. Specifically with *porchetta*. That's his recipe below for boned and rolled *porchetta,* which he slices into hunks, spreads with a house-made condiment like onion or fennel jam, and tucks into slices of sturdy bread, mopped with juices from the cutting board.

The RoliRoti crew keeps the line moving.

SERVES 10 TO 12

1 tablespoon finely minced lemon zest

5 tablespoons freshly squeezed lemon juice

1 tablespoon minced garlic

1 tablespoon chopped fresh rosemary

2 tablespoons fennel seeds, toasted and
   lightly crushed (see Note)

4 dried bay leaves, crumbled

1 tablespoon kosher salt

1 tablespoon freshly ground black pepper

1¹/2 teaspoons pinot grigio or similar dry white wine

2 pounds boneless pork loin

1 pork belly (about 5 pounds), with fat and skin on

Onion Marmalade (recipe follows), for serving

YOU'LL ALSO NEED

Butcher's string

1 Place the lemon zest and juice, garlic, rosemary, toasted fennel seeds, bay leaves, salt, pepper, and pinot grigio in a small bowl and mix until a crumbly paste forms.

2 Working with a sharp knife, cut back the fat of the pork loin, making sure not to cut into the loin meat. Rub the pork belly inside and out evenly with herb paste. Put the pork loin inside

Porchettas on the rotisserie.

the pork belly, then tie the roast crosswise at 2-inch intervals with butcher's string. Make sure you use an even tension when tying so that the *porchetta* will cook evenly. Cover the *porchetta* with plastic wrap and refrigerate for 24 hours to let it absorb the flavor of the herb paste.

3 Preheat the oven to 450°F.

4 Place the *porchetta* on a rack in a roasting pan, seam side up. Bake the *porchetta* for 30 minutes, then lower the temperature to 350°F. Continue baking the *porchetta* until an instant-read thermometer inserted into the thickest part of the meat registers almost 140°F, 1 to 1½ hours longer. For the last 5 minutes of cooking place the *porchetta* under the broiler to crisp the skin, rotating the *porchetta* until it is golden brown.

Thomas Odermatt works the board.

5 Remove the *porchetta* from the oven and let rest for 15 minutes before serving. Then, remove and discard the string and carve the *porchetta* into ½-inch slices. Serve the *porchetta* with the Onion Marmalade.

N O T E : To toast fennel seeds, place them in a dry skillet over medium heat (do not use a

⚲ **LAST SEEN**: At the Civic Center farmers' market, Market Street and 7th Street, San Francisco, California

ROLIROTI

SWITZERLAND: THAT'S WHERE Thomas Odermatt learned from his father, a master butcher named Otto Odermatt, to carve pigs and chickens and other beasts. That's where he learned to roast chickens and *porchetta* on rotating spits, twirling in front of a wall of gas-fueled flames.

Thomas mounts his array of spits at the rear of retrofitted trucks that make the rounds, visiting various San Francisco farmers' markets, peddling local, free-range birds that are rubbed with spice mix and then flame-burnished. Beneath those organic birds, on a modified flattop grill, fingerling potatoes sizzle and hiss in a shallow puddle of aromatic chicken juices until the potatoes, like the chicken, are tender and golden.

nonstick skillet for this). Cook, stirring continually, until fragrant and toasted, 2 to 3 minutes. Transfer the toasted fennel seeds to a heatproof bowl to cool.

Onion Marmalade

SWEET ON SWEET WORKS HERE. Pork is a naturally sweet meat, one that takes well to the mellow caramel of onions and the licorice scent of fennel.

MAKES ABOUT 2 CUPS

1 1/2 tablespoons olive oil

7 yellow onions, thinly sliced (use a mandoline, if you have one)

3/4 cup balsamic vinegar

3 tablespoons fennel salt (see Note)

Heat the olive oil in a large skillet over very low heat. Add the onions and cook, stirring occasionally, until they are caramel colored and very soft, about 1 hour. Add the balsamic vinegar and fennel salt and stir to mix. Continue to cook the onions until they taste sweet and the vinegar has reduced to a syrup, about 2 hours longer. The onions can be refrigerated, covered, for up to 2 days.

NOTE: To make fennel salt, place 3 tablespoons of fennel seeds in a dry skillet over medium heat (do not use a nonstick skillet for this). Cook, stirring continually, until fragrant and toasted, 2 to 3 minutes. Add 2 teaspoons of coarse sea salt and stir to blend. Remove the fennel seed mixture from the heat and let cool. Transfer the fennel seed mixture to a spice mill and grind it until the fennel seeds are coarsely crumbled.

LA COCINA:
Helping Street Cooks Go Legit

CALEB ZIGAS calls food vendors who lack permits "informal vendors." At La Cocina, a small business incubator and commissary based in the San Francisco Mission District, his clients are working-class immigrants who make a living by cooking and selling food. Among La Cocina's clients is Veronica Salazar of El Huarache Loco, who specializes in sandal-shaped masa cakes, smeared with *barbacoa,* beans, or cheese, inspired by her hometown of Mexico City.

(She now sells the cakes, called *huaraches,* at local farmers' markets.)

El Huarache Loco is one of La Cocina's success stories. But walking the Mission with Caleb, as he points out hot dog vendors who cook their sausages on cookie sheets positioned over propane burners and furtive *churro* men who sell stick-shaped, cinnamon sugar–dusted doughnuts at the rate of three for a dollar, it's clear that he aspires to catalyzing more sweeping

changes in street vending and street life.

In an effort to bring more vendors under the tent and share best practices, Caleb began staging periodic seminars with titles like "How to Sell From a Mobile Unit (Legally!) in the Bay Area." Also in 2009, La Cocina staged a street food festival; the first proved so popular that it's now an annual August event. Stepping across the aisle, in early 2010 La Cocina received initial approval to curate pushcart food sales in San Francisco parks.

SPICY CHICKEN BURADI ROLL

WRAPPED FOODS ARE UNIVERSAL—as in French crepes, Mexican burritos, and Vietnamese rice paper–wrapped summer rolls. Such foods were engineered for portability, for conveying small bits of this and that from stove to mouth. This recipe, which draws on the broad *roti* tradition of South Asian bread, was inspired by the work of Meru Sikder at the Biryani Cart.

Meru Sikder, king of the *buradi* roll.

MAKES 4 ROLLS

2 tablespoons vegetable oil

2 cups bite-size chunks boneless, skinless chicken (about 1/2 pound)

Freshly ground black pepper

I cucumber, peeled and sliced in half-moon shapes

I white onion, sliced into thin, half-moon slices

2 cups shredded iceberg lettuce

I cup Habañero Mint Sauce (recipe follows)

Salt

4 Chappatis (page 168)

2 tablespoons Sriracha chile sauce

1 Heat the vegetable oil in a large skillet over medium-high heat. Season the chicken with black pepper to taste. Cook the chicken until seared on the outside and cooked through, 5 to 7 minutes. Set the chicken aside to cool.

2 Combine the cucumber, onion, and lettuce in a large mixing bowl. Add the chicken to the bowl along with the Habañero Mint Sauce and gently toss to coat. Season the chicken and vegetable mixture with salt and pepper to taste.

3 Divide the chicken and vegetable mixture equally among the *chappatis,* drizzle Sriracha on top to taste, then roll the *chappatis* up and eat.

A *buradi* roll fresh from the order window.

Habañero Mint Sauce

THE YOGURT TAMPS DOWN THE HEAT of the habañero, but just barely. Inspired by the sauce served by the Biryani Cart, this recipe yields a concoction that goes well with lamb, too, in the manner of, say, a hot mint jelly.

MAKES ABOUT I CUP

I cup plain whole-milk yogurt

I tablespoon finely chopped fresh mint

1/4 teaspoon green habañero sauce, preferably Melinda's, or more to taste

Mix the yogurt, mint, and habañero sauce together until thoroughly incorporated. Taste for seasoning, adding more habañero sauce as necessary. The sauce can be refrigerated, covered, for up to 1 week.

Chappatis

THIS IS A FLATBREAD, lovely and simple, comparable to the pitas of the Middle East and tortillas of Mexico. Traditionally, in South Asia eaters tear off segments of *chappati* and use those shreds to grab bites of food. *Chappatis* can also be formed into cones to hold loose jumbles of food. That's how they're used at the Biryani Cart.

MAKES 6 BREADS

2 cups wheat flour, plus flour for rolling out the chappatis

I teaspoon ghee or clarified butter

I teaspoon salt

1/4 cup water (used to help knead the dough)

1 Mix the wheat flour, ghee, and salt with 2 tablespoons water and knead until a smooth dough forms. Add up to 2 more tablespoons of water if necessary. Let sit for 30 minutes.

2 Separate the dough into 6 equal–size balls and dust the balls with just a bit of flour. Roll out the balls of dough into thin disks.

3 Heat a griddle or cast-iron skillet over high heat. Place a disk of dough on the hot surface and cook until it is light brown with a tortilla-like texture, 2 to 3 minutes. Flip it and cook for 2 to 3 minutes more. Repeat with remaining dough. As you work, keep the *chappatis* warm until ready to serve.

LAST SEEN: Sixth Avenue and 46th Street, New York, New York

BIRYANI CART

A SORT OF PRIMAL PILAF, *biryani* is a composed rice dish popular in, among other South Asian countries, India, Pakistan, and the People's Republic of Bangladesh. Appropriately, Meru Sikder, a onetime banquet chef at a New Jersey hotel, who now lives in Queens, is a Bangladeshi by birth.

Meru opened the Biryani Cart in 2004, selling dark meat chicken *biryani*, studded with wedges of boiled egg and sprinkled with chili powder. His vegetable *biryani*, loaded with chickpeas, carrots, cabbage, peas, and incendiary peppers, compromises neither flavor nor calories.

Instead of the white sauce common at halal carts, Meru supplies yogurt-strafed *raita*. For his *buradi* rolls filled with glazed chicken, he supplies a scorching, and visually arresting, habañero mint sauce.

CREAMED (and Cheesed) TOMATO SOUP

THE PAIRING OF A GRILLED CHEESE sandwich and a bowl of tomato soup is classic. The acid in the tomatoes plays well off the richness of the cheese. But the combo doesn't translate well on the street, where bowls and cutlery are cumbersome. This recipe, inspired by The Grilled Cheese Truck, is about packaging and portion control. Think of the soup as a mere chaser for the grilled cheese. On the truck, they serve it in plastic bullets. At home, you might want to break out proper shot glasses.

Specialization suits the truck food ethic.

MAKES 4 SERVINGS, ABOUT 10 SHOTS

3/4 cup olive oil

1 can (14 ounces) diced tomatoes

3 cloves garlic, minced

1 teaspoon salt

1 teaspoon freshly ground black pepper

1 medium-size onion, diced

1 carrot, diced

1 rib celery, diced

2 tablespoons (1/4 stick) butter

1/4 cup grated Parmesan cheese

1/2 cup heavy (whipping) cream

1 Preheat the oven to 375°F.

2 Pour 1/4 cup of the olive oil onto a rimmed baking sheet. Drain the tomatoes, setting aside the juices. Spoon the drained tomatoes onto the baking sheet and top them with the garlic, salt, and pepper. Drizzle another 1/4 cup of olive oil over the tomatoes and stir to mix well. Bake the tomato mixture until the tomatoes are very soft and beginning to caramelize, 15 to 20 minutes, stirring to ensure even cooking.

3 Heat the remaining 1/4 cup of olive oil in a stockpot over medium-high heat. Add the onion, carrot, and celery and cook the vegetables, stirring often, until softened, about 8 minutes. Add the tomato mixture to the stockpot along with the reserved tomato juices and 1 cup of water. Let the soup come to a simmer, then cook until the vegetables have cooked down and the flavors are well blended, about 20 minutes.

4 Add the butter, Parmesan, and cream to the pot and combine them using an immersion blender. Or transfer the soup to a blender. If you use a blender, be careful; fill it only halfway, making sure there is space at the top for steam to escape or you'll get coated in the tomato soup equivalent of napalm. Serve the soup in shot glasses.

GRILLED CHEESE MAC AND CHEESE SANDWICHES

THESE SANDWICHES ARE ABOUT TEXTURE. About the slight chew of the macaroni noodles that lurk beneath shatteringly crisp slices of toast. These sandwiches, inspired by The Grilled Cheese Truck, are about goofball creativity, too—about adding cheese to cheese in an act of righteous excess. Optional additional fillings served at The Grilled Cheese Truck include caramelized onions and pulled pork.

LAST SEEN: Outside The Brig, 1515 Abbot Kinney Boulevard, Venice, California

THE GRILLED CHEESE TRUCK

"WE'RE MELTING AT THE BRIG." That's a typical tweet blasted into the ether by Michele Grant. Along with Dave Danhi, a chef, she owns The Grilled Cheese Truck. The Brig is a bar in Venice with an accommodating parking lot and, inside, a Jägermeister fountain. Circa 2010 The Brig is the toast of the late night demimonde.

When Michele isn't cooking grilled cheese sandwiches—and serving shot glasses of tomato soup—she advises clients on how to eat healthy diets. (Yes, she's aware of the irony.) When she lets her guard down Michele refers to her sandwiches as glue, the reference being, I assume, to the glue with which night drinkers hold themselves together.

MAKES 2 SANDWICHES

1 tablespoon vegetable oil

4 slices white bread or Texas toast (see Note), toasted

4 slices sharp cheddar cheese

1 cup macaroni and cheese (use your favorite recipe or, God help you, crack open a box)

1 Heat the oil on a griddle or in a large skillet set over medium-high heat.

2 Top all the slices of Texas toast with a slice of cheese. Spoon 1/2 cup macaroni and cheese onto 2 of the slices of bread and top each with one of the remaining 2 slices, cheese side down. Place the sandwiches on the griddle and let cook until the bread is nicely toasted, 2 minutes. Carefully flip the sandwiches and cook on the second side until the macaroni and cheese is warmed through and the Texas toast is golden, 2 minutes more. Reduce the heat if the toast is browning too quickly. To serve, cut the sandwiches in half on the diagonal.

NOTE: Texas toast is just white bread cut in double-thick slices. It's great for toasting.

TEXTURAL COMPLEXITY BY WAY OF NOODLES AND A LITTLE PULLED PORK.

CHEESEASAURUS

YES, THIS IS BASICALLY a grilled cheese sandwich made with Texas toast and cut into dinosaur shapes after cooking. Which is to say, this is more about the idea than the recipe. That said, the results are pretty cool, in a *T. rex* sort of way.

Eons ago, sandwiches like these roamed the earth.

The little box that could.

MAKES 1 SANDWICH

1 tablespoon canola oil

2 slices Texas toast (see Note)

2 slices American cheese, at room temperature

YOU'LL ALSO NEED

A dinosaur-shaped sandwich cutter
    (the DynoBytes brand is a favorite)

Heat the oil on a griddle or in a skillet over medium-high heat. Arrange the slices of Texas toast on the hot surface and top each with a slice of cheese. When the bottom of the bread is browned and the cheese has melted, about 3 minutes, place 1 slice of Texas toast, cheese side down, on top of the other and transfer it to a cutting board. Let the sandwich cool slightly, then position the sandwich cutter on top and press down. Presto.

N O T E : Texas toast is white bread cut in slices that are double the thickness of regular bread slices. The "toast" part happens when the bread is toasted or griddled.

Read about the Brunch Box truck on page 198.

SWEET POTATO WRAP

SWEET POTATOES GIVE THIS WRAP HEFT. That's heft in both the weight and nutritional sense. The sweet potatoes play the part of meat. The poblanos, on the other hand, add an edge of heat and acidity in this recipe, inspired by the Maximilianos of The Dandelion truck.

The crowd awaits vegetarian goodness.

Read about The Dandelion truck on page 131.

SERVES 4

2 poblano peppers

1/2 cup chopped fresh cilantro

I tablespoon garlic, minced

4 tablespoons olive oil

I red bell pepper, stemmed, seeded, and cut into strips

I cup sliced onion

2 large sweet potatoes, baked

4 large (8 to 10 inches each) flour tortillas, warmed

I cup shredded Gouda cheese

1 Roast the poblano peppers by placing them directly over the flame of a gas burner or under the broiler, rotating them occasionally, until they are charred all over, about 5 minutes. Rotate the poblanos often to ensure that they blacken but do not burn.

2 Place the roasted poblanos in a plastic or paper bag and seal it tightly to let them steam until cool. When cool enough to handle, using gloves, peel or rub off the charred skin and discard it. Stem and seed the poblanos, then coarsely chop them. Set the chopped peppers aside.

3 Combine the cilantro, garlic, and 2 tablespoons of the olive oil in a blender and blend well to create a cilantro pesto. Set aside.

4 Heat the remaining 2 tablespoons of olive oil in a skillet over medium-high heat. Add the red bell pepper and onion and cook until soft, about 5 minutes.

5 Scoop the flesh from the sweet potatoes, keeping it in large chunks.

6 Spread about 1 tablespoon of the cilantro pesto on each tortilla. Spoon chunks of sweet potato, a bit of the bell pepper and onion mixture, and some of the roasted poblanos on top. Sprinkle 1/4 cup of the Gouda cheese on top of each tortilla. Tuck the top and bottom of the tortillas over the filling, roll them up, and serve.

The L.A. version.

A double-handed offering from Dogtown dogs.

How they do it in Boston.

Street scene, Tucson.

HOT DOGS

HOT DOGS

with a

BOW TO BURGERS

CHAPTER 6 →

Hot dogs are a street food of last resort,

priced cheap and made of cheap ingredients, from the cereal-stuffed dog itself to the flimsy bun in which it's too often served. That's the reigning perspective. And, sad to say, that's the reigning reality. I live for the exceptions. Like the knife-scored and charcoal-grilled dogs sold in the 1980s at the Barkers Red Hots cart in Woodruff Park in downtown Atlanta. Like the Sonoran-style hot dogs, wrapped in bacon and dressed with *salsa verde,* now sold in Tucson.

"Boston Speed's" Famous Hot Dog Wagon is a Massachusetts exception. It's an honest wagon, parked on a gravel concourse at the center of Newmarket Square in the industrial heart of Roxbury, surrounded by warehouses operated by the American Nut & Chocolate Company and Chang Ching Produce. Ezra "Speed" Anderson worked that trailer for more than thirty years. More recently his longtime apprentice Gregg Gale has taken up the tongs. Here's how he does it: First Gregg simmers natural casing dogs in apple juice and brown sugar. Then he smokes them on a closed charcoal grill installed inside the wagon. Then he slashes the casings lightly before griddling the weenies and basting them with a sweet, ketchup-based, barbecue sauce–like condiment.

Eating a Speed's dog while seated in a plastic chair, alongside a plastic table, is a singular experience. I recommend it to all who hold hope of exceptions. The recipes and stories that follow catalog exceptional hot dogs and hamburgers served by mobile vendors. From bacon-wrapped sausages to burgers bracketed by grilled cheese sandwiches, the recipes give lie to the belief that food served fast, from a cart or truck, need not reek of the scent of compromise.

Bacon-wrapped dogs on the grill in Tucson.

ON THE LEDGE AT DOGTOWN, ONION DOGS AND SLAW DOGS.

DOGTOWN DOGS

CLOSE YOUR EYES—REALLY SQUINT—and the red pepper slices tucked alongside the dogs resemble pipelines of ketchup. Yellow ballpark mustard gets Californicated, too, by way of a Dijon sub, in this homage to Mike Rosá and Ryan Bailey's baseline menu item.

Psychedelic dog stylings.

SERVES 2 TO 4

1 red bell pepper

4 all-natural beef hot dogs, with natural casings

1/4 cup Dijon mustard

4 hot dog buns, split and toasted

Fennel slaw (recipe follows)

10 fresh basil leaves, slivered

1 Roast the red bell pepper by placing it directly over the flame of a gas burner or under the broiler until evenly charred, 3 to 4 minutes per side, 12 to 16 minutes in all, turning with tongs. Once the skin is blistered, immediately put the pepper in a paper or plastic bag and seal it tightly so the pepper can steam (this will make the skin easier to remove). When the pepper is cool enough to handle, using a paring knife, peel away the charred skin. Core, seed, and cut the pepper into long narrow strips. Set the pepper strips aside.

2 Cook the hot dogs on a hot griddle or in a dry skillet (do not use a nonstick skillet for this) over medium heat until they are heated through and the skins begin to brown, turning them so that they brown evenly.

3 Spread some of the mustard on the inside of each hot dog bun, then place a hot dog inside. Line both sides of the dogs with strips of red pepper, then top them with some of the Fennel Slaw. Top the slaw with basil and serve to people who claim they don't really care for hot dogs.

Fennel Slaw

THERE ARE A NUMBER OF WAYS to make a simple slaw. Most recipes start with cabbage and a binding of mayonnaise. Better ones cut the cloy of the mayo with vinegar. In this recipe, inspired by Dogtown Dogs, the mayo gets ditched altogether, and fennel—with its pleasant licorice flavor—steps to the fore.

MAKES ABOUT 2 1/2 CUPS

1 1/2 tablespoons cider vinegar

2 teaspoons sugar

1 teaspoon extra-virgin olive oil

1/4 teaspoon freshly ground black pepper

1/4 teaspoon salt

2 cups very thinly sliced fennel

1/2 cup very thinly sliced onion

1 Combine the cider vinegar, sugar, olive oil, pepper, and salt in a blender and blend until well combined.

2 Place the fennel and onion in a mixing bowl, add the dressing, and toss to coat. Cover and refrigerate the slaw until ready to use.

MEXICAN COKES: The Search for Sugar

SOLD IN BOTTLES incised with the slogans *Hecho en Mexico* and *Refresco,* Mexican-made Cokes are often the most expensive drinks served from a taco truck. A quick look at one of the labels on the bottle tells you why: *azúcar.*

That's sugar. Cane sugar, more than likely. While American bottlers have, since the 1980s, sweetened their Coca-Cola with high fructose corn syrup, many, if not all, Mexican bottlers cleave to the old ways and, by extension, the old Coke recipe.

A thriving gray-market trade has developed. Mexican Coke is now sold across the United States, from border-focused towns like San Diego, California; Tucson, Arizona; and Houston, Texas; to Vicksburg, Mississippi, where Coke was first successfully bottled, and Atlanta, Georgia, the burbling heart of Coca-Cola country.

Mexican migrants were early adopters. They recognized the heavy, returnable bottles as totems of home. They argued that a proper Coke deserved more than a mere aluminum or plastic conveyance. That the thick glass bottles sustained a greater wallop of carbonation. They claimed the fizzy brown water within tasted somehow sweeter. But less saccharine. Somehow more caramely. Somehow better.

Consumers with a taste for cane sugar–sweetened Cokes now buy imported Cokes, trucked into the U.S. by the trailer load, to the consternation of American Coca-Cola bottlers who lament the loss in sales, but with the assent of the U.S. Customs office.

Coke has long built its brand around the notion that no matter where you travel a Coke is a Coke is a Coke. The diffusion of the brand, fueled by the introduction of New Coke in 1985, called such absolutes into question. So did the realization that individual bottlers have long held sway, oftentimes in opposition to corporate dictates.

When I was a boy, my friends and I were convinced that we could discern a difference between Coke bottled in Macon, Georgia, the closest facility, and Coke bottled in Atlanta. We reasoned that Atlanta Coke had more bite, that it was somehow stronger. Maybe we were right. Two different bottling lines supplied those cities. Then, as now, headquarters sold syrup to bottlers the world over. And headquarters devised the advertising campaigns. But individual bottlers carbonated and packaged the product.

Some Mexican bottlers never gave up on cane sugar. In the United States all bottlers adopted corn syrup as the standard. In that gap, between the real thing and the realer thing, cane sugar Coke bootleggers have, for the past decade, exploited a cross-border market.

More recently, as drinkers clue in to cane sugar, distribution has gone mainstream and small-time bootlegging is becoming a thing of the past. Meanwhile, some Mexican bottlers are adopting corn syrup, while others are striking deals with American colleagues who are intent upon importing their own supply of the good stuff.

Mexico's best in icy repose.

CALIFORNIA DOGS

THIS RECIPE, INSPIRED by the work of Mike Rosá and Ryan Bailey of Dogtown Dogs, reads like the punch line to a joke about California cuisine. Basil aioli, arugula, and avocado, indeed. But take a bite and you'll understand. It's not trite, it's fresh. Plus the fried onions pack a pleasantly greasy wallop of flavor.

Dogtown's short but sweet menu.

SERVES 2 TO 4

FOR THE BASIL AIOLI

1/2 cup mayonnaise

1/4 cup finely chopped fresh basil

1/2 teaspoon minced garlic

1 teaspoon freshly squeezed lemon juice

1/4 teaspoon salt

Freshly ground black pepper

FOR THE HOT DOGS

4 all-natural beef hot dogs, with natural casings

4 hot dog buns, split and toasted

1/2 cup baby arugula leaves

2 ripe plum tomatoes, cored, seeded, and cut into strips

1 ripe avocado, peeled, pitted, and cut into thin wedges

Crispy Fried Onions (recipe follows)

LAST SEEN: Outside The Brig, 1515 Abbot Kinney Boulevard, Venice, California

DOGTOWN DOGS

MIKE ROSA AND RYAN BAILEY vend nitrate-free, grass-fed, natural casing dogs that snap when you bite. That, Mike and Ryan told me, is what God intended. (Mike and Ryan source their dogs from a local wholesaler.)

Some nights Dogtown Dogs parks its starburst-painted truck on a street in Venice outside The Farmacy Global Organic Medicine store. (Upstairs is a consultancy, Urban Remedy Community Acupuncture.)

Some days, they work the office buildings along Wilshire Boulevard.

Aside from slaw—which is a thing of minimalist beauty—the only side they serve is Tater Tots. To drink, Mike and Ryan stock cans of Hawaiian Punch and bottles of cane sugar-sweetened Mexican Coke.

1 Make the basil aioli: Combine the mayonnaise, basil, garlic, lemon juice, and salt and

Note the website, a de rigueur marketing tool.

mix until very smooth. Season the basil aioli with pepper to taste. Refrigerate the aioli, covered, until ready to use.

2 Prepare the hot dogs: Cook the hot dogs on a hot griddle or in a dry skillet (do not use a nonstick skillet for this) over medium heat until they are heated through and the skins begin to brown, turning them so that they brown evenly.

3 Spread some of the basil aioli on the inside of each hot dog bun, then place a hot dog inside. Line both sides of the dogs with arugula leaves and tomato strips, then top them with a few slices of avocado. Blanket the dogs with the fried onions and serve.

Crispy Fried Onions

YOU KNOW THOSE French's brand fried onions—the ones sold in a can? The ones you top your Thanksgiving green bean casserole with? These, inspired by the Dogtown boys, are just like that. Only better.

MAKES ABOUT 2 CUPS

2 cups canola oil, for frying the onions

2 medium-size red onions, thinly sliced in half moon shapes (about 2 cups)

1/2 cup cornstarch

1 Heat the oil in a deep heavy pan over high heat until a deep fry thermometer attached to the side of the pan registers 350°F.

2 Dust the onion slices with the cornstarch. Working in batches and being careful not to overcrowd the pan, carefully add the onion slices to the hot oil and cook them until crisp and golden, about 3 minutes. Using a slotted spoon, transfer the fried onion slices to a rack covered with paper towels to drain. Serve the fried onions at once.

HOT DOGS:
A Short and New York City–Centric History

THE HISTORY OF THE AMERICAN HOT DOG is murky, like the hot water baths in which many New York street vendors warm their dogs. We know that the hot dog is a sausage, an encased meat product with likely roots in Austria (the wiener) or Germany (the frankfurter.)

And we know that German-born butcher Charles Feltman of Coney Island, in the borough of Brooklyn, in the city of New York, was a popularizer of the product. By 1867 Feltman was working a charcoal-fueled stove on wheels, peddling sausages in buns to the boardwalk promenade crowd. (The bun conveyance proved key, remaking a knife-and-fork dish into a portable snack.)

And we know that from the time of Feltman until now a long and unbroken chain of hot dog vendors has worked the New York streets, beneath pinwheel umbrellas, tonging sausages from steam baths,

New York City beginnings.

tucking those dogs in cottony buns, slathering on mustard and red onion sauce, while cracking wise, cursing the weather, and making change.

MEET ME IN THE MORNING DOGS

THE MAGIC BUS CAFE TWINS, Cathy and Chrissy, back up their shtick with good food. They use Boar's Head natural casing wieners, which they split and griddle fry. And they recognize that, like baloney and eggs, hot dogs and eggs are perfectly complementary. This recipe comes straight from the sisters. The reference, by the way, is to the Bob Dylan song "Meet Me in the Morning."

Breakfast of champions, as interpreted by Kesey acolytes.

LAST SEEN: East Lake Street and 22nd Avenue South, Minneapolis, Minnesota

MAGIC BUS CAFE

THE SHTICK IS more than a little over-the-top. Cathy Lockyear and her twin sister Chrissy Russell, who own the bus with Cathy's husband, Chris Lockyear, wear flowers in their hair, saris around their hips, and T-shirts that declare "You're either on the bus or off the bus."

The bus in question is a Ken Keseyian, thirty-one-foot 1978 Chevrolet, decoupaged with daisies and outfitted with red leatherette booths that seat a total of eight at white veneer-top tables. The menu includes the Give Beets a Chance dog, a natural casing wiener capped with garlic beet sauerkraut, the beets rendering the sauerkraut a thematically appropriate deep purple.

It will not surprise you to learn that the proprietors are Grateful Dead fans and that they provide, for partakers, salt shakers full of nutritional yeast for sprinkling on the dogs.

SERVES 3 TO 6

6 all-natural beef hot dogs, with natural casings

6 organic eggs

1/4 cup organic half-and-half

1 tablespoon butter

6 whole wheat hot dog buns

1/2 cup grated colby-Jack cheese

6 slices thick-cut bacon, cooked and chopped

1 Using a knife, split the hot dogs lengthwise, stopping just short of cutting all the way through. Open the hot dogs up like a book and place them, cut side down, on a hot griddle or dry skillet over medium heat to sear until heated through (do not use a nonstick skillet for this).

2 Crack the eggs into a bowl. Add the half-and-half and whisk to mix. Melt the butter in a skillet over medium heat. Add the egg mixture and cook, stirring often, until set to taste.

3 Place the hot dogs in the buns, top them with the scrambled eggs, then sprinkle the cheese and bacon over them. Serve quick like.

Cathy, Chris, and Chrissy on the bus.

RELISHES FOR YOUR GRATEFUL DOGS

TOO OFTEN COMMERCIAL PICKLE RELISH is saccharine stuff, tasting of corn syrup and little else. In the two recipes here, from the Magic Bus Cafe crew, wisely chosen additions enliven the standard pickle relish. I'm especially keen on the psychedelic version. Sure, it's great on hot dogs, but it's also fine stirred into tuna salad. If you can find it, Gedney organic sweet relish is a Magic Bus Cafe favorite.

The purple people mover.

Read about the Magic Bus Cafe on page 183.

Psychedelic Relish

MAKES ABOUT 2 CUPS

1 cup (from one 16-ounce jar) pickle relish

3/4 cup (from one 12-ounce jar) hot mango chutney, preferably Patak

1/2 yellow bell pepper, stemmed, seeded, and cut into small dice

1 teaspoon curry powder

Drain the pickle relish and place it in a large bowl. Pulse the chutney in a food processor or dice it by hand. Add the chutney, bell pepper, and curry powder to the pickle relish and stir to mix. The relish can be refrigerated, covered, for 1 month.

Fire Relish

MAKES ABOUT 2 CUPS

1 jar (16 ounces) pickle relish

1 red bell pepper, stemmed, seeded, and cut into small dice

2 medium-size jalapeño peppers, stemmed, seeded, and minced

3 tablespoons Sriracha chile sauce

Drain the pickle relish and place it in a large bowl. Add the bell pepper, jalapeños, and Sriracha and stir to mix well. The relish can be refrigerated, covered, for up to 1 month.

Garlic beet sauerkraut front and sort of center. See page 187 for the recipe.

ADZUKI CHILI

I'M NOT ONE FOR SUBSTITUTE FOODS—as in tofu pups. Or veggie burgers. (Yes, you'll find a vegan recipe in this book from The Dandelion cart in Madison, Wisconsin, but that seems to fit the gestalt of Madison.) That's all to say, I don't consider the chili from the Magic Bus Cafe girls to be a recipe that uses beans instead of meat. I consider this a chili recipe that happens to include nutty adzuki beans. Heap this chili liberally on natural casing all-beef dogs.

Hippy idealism, applied to hot dogs.

Peace, love, and wienies!

SERVES 4 TO 6

2 cans (14.5 ounces each) diced tomatoes in juice, preferably Muir Glen brand

1 1/2 tablespoons canola oil

1 cup diced yellow onions

1 red bell pepper, stemmed, seeded, and diced

3 cloves garlic, minced

2 teaspoons salt

1 teaspoon crushed red pepper flakes

1 teaspoon freshly ground black pepper

1 teaspoon ground cumin

1 bay leaf

1 tablespoon brown sugar

1 can (15 ounces) adzuki beans

1 can (15 ounces) navy beans

Read about the Magic Bus Cafe truck on page 183.

1 Puree 1 can of tomatoes in a blender or food processor. Set aside.

2 Heat the canola oil in a stockpot over medium-high heat. Add the onion, bell pepper, and garlic and cook until the onion is translucent, about 5 minutes. Add the salt, red pepper flakes, black pepper, cumin, bay leaf, and brown sugar and cook until the brown sugar has dissolved completely, about 5 minutes.

3 Drain and rinse the adzuki and navy beans well in a colander. Add the beans, pureed tomatoes, and the remaining can of tomatoes to the pot and let come to a burbling simmer. Reduce the heat to low and let the chili cook slowly until well blended, about 2 hours. Remove the bay leaf from the chili before serving.

GARLIC BEET SAUERKRAUT

THE COLOR OF THE MAGIC BUS CAFE'S sauerkraut is shocking in a good way. But it begs the question *Why not just use red cabbage?* The answer is the flavor, which speaks of beet but also of garlic and cries out to be served on a hot dog with a whole-grain mustard slather.

MAKES ABOUT 2½ CUPS

1 large red beet, peeled

2 cups sauerkraut, preferably Eden organic sauerkraut

1 medium-size yellow onion, sliced very thin

4 to 5 cloves garlic, minced

Grate the beet on a box grater or in a food processor. Combine the grated beet, sauerkraut, onion, and garlic in a mixing bowl. For best flavor, let the sauerkraut sit for several hours or overnight before serving. The sauerkraut can be refrigerated, covered, for up to 1 month.

The girls will do almost anything to sell their dogs.

TUCSON:
LAND OF THE *HOTDOGUEROS*

Tucson is a place of craggy peaks pocked with scrub and sandy lowlands steepled with saguaro, backlit by an unrelenting sun fixed in a preternaturally blue and cloudless sky.

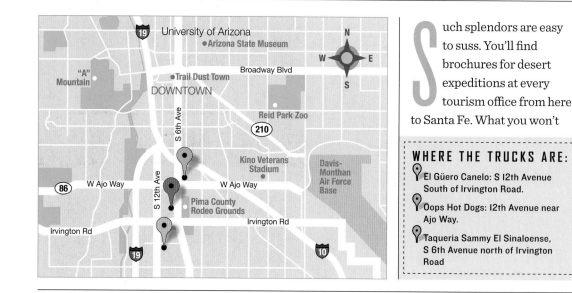

University of Arizona
• Arizona State Museum
"A" Mountain
• Trail Dust Town
Broadway Blvd
DOWNTOWN
Reid Park Zoo
210
Kino Veterans Stadium
S 6th Ave
Davis-Monthan Air Force Base
86
W Ajo Way
S 12th Ave
W Ajo Way
Pima County Rodeo Grounds
Irvington Rd
Irvington Rd
19
10
N W E S

Such splendors are easy to suss. You'll find brochures for desert expeditions at every tourism office from here to Santa Fe. What you won't find are brochures promoting honest food. You won't easily find the taco trucks and fry bread huts that Tucsonans love. And that means you may not avail yourself of the Tucsonan splendor that is the bacon-wrapped and mayonnaise-stippled Sonoran-style hot dog.

Sonora is the Mexican state immediately below the Arizona border, the place where, out in the desert beyond the capital city of Hermosillo, *carboneros* prune and harvest mesquite trees, slowly burn the wood in monstrous hole-in-the-ground kilns, and package the petrified remains as charcoal.

Sonora's greatest contribution to late-twentieth-century borderlands foodways is not, however, charcoal. It's the Sonoran-style hot dog. Yes, the borderlands are a place of contention that cultural critic Gloria E. Anzaldúa once described as *"una herida abierta"* (which translates as an open wound), where "the Third World grates against the first and bleeds." But the borderlands are also places of smooth

WHERE THE TRUCKS ARE:

El Güero Canelo: S 12th Avenue South of Irvington Road.

Oops Hot Dogs: 12th Avenue near Ajo Way.

Taqueria Sammy El Sinaloense, S 6th Avenue north of Irvington Road

and easy cultural exchange, where constituencies as various as accordion-driven Tejano bands, black velvet portraitists, and hot dog grill cooks have honed a modern Mexican-American aesthetic.

By the 1950s American hot dogs had more than likely jumped the gate into Sonora and Baja and elsewhere. The date at which bacon-wrapped hot dogs became known as Mexican hot dogs is unclear. The mystery deepens when you factor in that Sonora is a locus for cattle ranching, not pig farming.

From the southern side of the border, numerous tales of a Mexico City origin emanate, some tied to feeding crowds at wrestling matches in the 1950s, others to feeding skyscraper construction workers during the same decade. (Daniel Contreras, of El Güero Canelo in Tucson, cites a similar time frame and tells just as plausible a story, but sets the action in his home state of Sonora, where a man he knew as Don Pancho worked the streets.)

As is the case with most folk dishes, we may never pinpoint the true crucible of place and people that birthed the bacon-wrapped hot dog. Folkloric suppositions aside, the answer may be a simple matter of salesmanship. By 1953 Oscar Mayer was running print ads selling American consumers on the virtues of bacon-wrapped hot dogs. Perhaps Mexican consumers, inspired to emulate American dietary habits, took Oscar Mayer at its word, wrapping American-made hot dogs in American-made bacon and claiming the resulting construction as their own.

Drive south of downtown Tucson today and you spy a vendor every six or eight blocks. A typical dog cart shares a street corner pad with a stepside truck, where cooks prepare more labor-intensive foods like *tortas* and quesadillas. Between the two you'll find a tented eating area, referred to locally as a *ramada*. Beneath that tent is a condiment bar, stocked with salsas and limes, onions and radishes.

Eating my way through the city, I isolated a few favorites: El Güero Canelo, which began as a cart but has morphed into two brick-and-mortar restaurants, is the restaurant most likely to take the phenomenon nationwide. Taqueria Sammy El Sinaloense, on the other hand, is more humble, more evocative of the Sonoran dog's street food roots. (Never mind that the owners, the Perez family, are from the adjacent state of Sinaloa.)

And then there is Oop's Hot Dogs, one of Martin Lizarraga's stands. One afternoon, it appeared like an apparition, anchored on one end by a hot dog cart with a flattop grill and on the other end by a minivan, painted with a hip-hop hot dog character. I pulled over. Quickly. And as a tripod-mounted speaker blared *norteño* music into the street, Martin talked to me of the days when he worked as a liquor salesman in Hermosillo, frequenting the "table dancing club" for which he named his two hot dog stands.

- - - - - - - - - - - - - - - - - -

To: The original El Güero Canelo stand.

Middle: Oop's Hot Dogs.

Bottom: A sugary lineup of sodas.

BACON-BASTED DOGS.

HOW TO BUILD A
SONORAN HOT DOG

HERE'S A PRIMER on how to build a hot dog Sonoran style. If you happened to be at El Güero Canelo, you would, dog in hand, adjourn to the condiment bar where all manner of extras, from sliced mushrooms to griddled green onions, await. If you were at Taqueria Sammy El Sinaloense, you would find similar accompaniments. If, however, you eat these dogs at home, I suggest that you do so while perched over the sink.

MAKES 6

6 bolillo buns (see Note)

6 slices of cheap bacon

6 cheap hot dogs

I can (15 ounces) pinto beans, rinsed, drained, and heated through

I cup chopped onions

I cup diced tomatoes

Mayonnaise

Yellow mustard

Jalapeño Salsa (recipe follows)

1 Slit the top of each bun, cutting into the middle and leaving an inch on each end uncut. If the buns are especially doughy, make a pocket in each by pulling tufts of dough out of the centers. Toast the buns slightly or steam them; Tucson's hot dog vendors do both.

2 Take one end of a slice of bacon, hold it against one end of a hot dog, and wrap the bacon around the dog like the stripe on a candy cane. Repeat with the remaining slices of bacon and hot dogs.

3 Arrange the bacon-wrapped hot dogs in a small skillet, making sure that all of the dogs are touching. Cook the hot dogs over medium heat on one side until the bacon is crisp and fused to the dogs. Carefully turn all of the hot dogs over at once and cook the second side until all of the bacon is brown and fused to the hot dogs.

4 Place a hot dog in a bun. Add the beans, along with a scattering of onions and tomatoes. Using squirt bottles, if possible, pipe thin lines of mayonnaise across the dog, followed by mustard and the Jalapeño Salsa. Repeat with the remaining buns and hot dogs.

LAST SEEN: 5201 South 12th Avenue, Tucson, Arizona

EL GUERO CANELO

AT EL GUERO CANELO a sign advertises *Salchicha Envuelta en Tocino,* which translates as sausage wrapped in bacon. If you want to get technical about it, yes, a hot dog is a sausage. But in Tucson, it's much more. After spending an afternoon standing at the once-mobile cart around which the restaurant El Guero Canelo's south side location revolves, I think I have a handle on how they wrap their dogs with bacon.

Go heavy on the beans, like
El Güero does.

NOTE: The bun is all–important. What you want is a Mexican *bolillo,* the soft version, not the crusty one. Check a *panadería*—a Mexican bakery—or a bodega. At the bodega, look for an oversize plastic box near the register; that's where the breads are usually stashed. If you can't find *bolillos,* you can use regular hot dog buns that are already split.

Jalapeño Salsa

THIS STUFF IS KEY. Otherwise you're just dressing your hot dog with mayo and mustard. And what good is that going to do? That's better for a turkey on wheat than a bacon-wrapped weenie with Sonoran aspirations. If you want to cheat and sub, buy the hottest commercial *salsa verde* you can find and thin it a bit with a mix of water and lime juice.

MAKES ABOUT ¹/₂ CUP

¹/₄ cup coarsely chopped onion

2 cloves garlic, minced

4 tablespoons olive oil

10 jalapeño peppers, stemmed, seeded, and cut in half lengthwise

2 tablespoons freshly squeezed lime juice, or more as needed

1 tablespoon chopped fresh oregano, or 1 teaspoon dried oregano

1 teaspoon salt

1 Place the onion in a cast-iron skillet over high heat and cook until slightly charred, about 5 minutes, stirring often. Add the garlic and cook for 30 seconds longer, making sure the garlic does not burn. Remove from the skillet and set aside.

2 Add 2 tablespoons of the olive oil and the jalapeños to the hot skillet and cook until the jalapeños are slightly charred, then add the lime juice, the remaining 2 tablespoons of olive oil, and the oregano and salt and cook until the jalapeños are softened, 1 to 2 minutes.

3 Transfer the jalapeño mixture and the onions and garlic to a blender and puree until smooth. If you plan to apply the salsa with a squirt bottle, add a little more lime juice and some water to thin it.

TOP OF THE DOG

ALTHOUGH THE HOT DOGS ARE GOOD, Taqueria Sammy El Sinaloense defines its excellence by way of the salsa bar. Here are two salsas inspired by Sammy's to get you started.

Sammy credits both Sinaloa and Sonora for his dogs.

Sunset with hot dogs.

Guacamole Sauce

MAKES ABOUT 1/2 CUP

1 ripe avocado, peeled, pitted, and cut into chunks

1/4 cup chopped fresh cilantro

4 to 8 tablespoons water

1 tablespoon freshly squeezed lime juice

1/2 teaspoon salt

Place the avocado, cilantro, 4 tablespoons of water, lime juice, and salt in a blender and puree until smooth and thick. Add more water if necessary. Store the Guacamole Sauce in an airtight container in the refrigerator until ready to serve. The Guacamole Sauce can be refrigerated for 4 hours.

Red Onion in Vinegar

MAKES ABOUT 1 CUP

1 large red onion, cut into half-moon slices 1/4 inch thick

1/2 cup cider vinegar

1 clove garlic, peeled and crushed

1/2 teaspoon salt

1/2 teaspoon freshly ground black pepper

Combine the onion, cider vinegar, garlic, salt, and pepper in a bowl or jar, cover, and let sit for at least 6 hours. The onion mixture can be refrigerated, covered, for up to 2 weeks.

📍 **LAST SEEN:** 2425 South 6th Avenue, Tucson, Arizona

TAQUERIA SAMMY EL SINALOENSE

SET ON SOUTH 6TH AVENUE, across from the Tucson Rodeo Grounds, alongside a tire repair shop that is also operated by the Perez family, Taqueria Sammy El Sinaloense is the place to draw a bead on the Mexican dog vibe. I spent the better part of an afternoon watching the scene unfold.

On one end of the virtual restaurant was a white Grumman truck. On the other was a step-up hot dog wagon with a four-foot *plancha*. Between the two was a ramada, accessorized with a misting machine that fitfully cooled down the customers.

Flanking the two was a salsa trolley, stocked with everything from sliced radishes to searing *salsas rojas*.

DANTE'S CHICKEN DOGS

DANTE RIVERA GOT THE IDEA for his cream cheese caulk gun from a Taco Bell. He saw the device they use to shoot ersatz guacamole and sour cream into hard-shell taco cavities and figured he could employ a similar technology. As for following his lead at home, my suggestion is to spread whipped cream cheese inside the bun. This recipe comes straight from Dante.

LAST SEEN: Ballard Avenue and Northwest Vernon Place, Seattle, Washington

DANTE'S INFERNO DOGS

DANTE RIVERA was nineteen when he read *A Confederacy of Dunces,* John Kennedy Toole's absurdist novel of New Orleans. He fell for the protagonist, Ignatius J. Reilly, a lapsed medievalist-focused academic who to make ends meet takes a job selling hot dogs in the French Quarter.

In 2000, inspired by Ignatius, Dante opened a Seattle hot dog stand. His customers were, for the most part, drunks exiting bars. That proved a good fit. Dante was, by his own admission, a drunk, too. He did well with the cart, selling jalapeño cheddar sausages with sweet Korean chile paste and natural casing hot dogs smeared, in the Seattle style, with cream cheese. But Dante didn't do well with the drinking. Back in 2008, his friends staged an intervention. At their urging, he checked himself into the Betty Ford clinic. "I got a scholarship," Dante told me, his voice still tinged with wonder.

His term at the Betty Ford seems to have taken. When I last saw Dante, he was working a custom pneumatic gun, piping cream cheese onto a dog the way a tub-and-tile man lays in caulk. At the time he had four carts in his stable. And he was planning to open more, by way of a scenario that would put recovering alcoholics and other teetering folk to work dealing dogs.

MAKES 4

4 spicy chicken sausages
2 tablespoons vegetable oil
1/2 cup sliced onion
1/2 cup sliced green bell pepper
1/2 cup whipped cream cheese
4 hot dog buns, split and toasted
1/4 cup sliced pepperoncini

1 Using a knife, split the sausages lengthwise, stopping just short of cutting all the way through.

2 Heat the oil in a skillet over medium-high heat. Add the onion and bell pepper and cook until the onion is translucent, about 5 minutes. Remove them from the skillet and set them aside.

3 Open the sausages up like a book, place them, cut side down, in the skillet, increase the heat to high, and sear the sausages, turning once, until cooked through, about 15 minutes.

4 Smear some of the cream cheese onto each hot dog bun. Place a sausage in each bun and top it with the onion and bell pepper mixture and sliced pepperoncini.

A CAULK GUN FILLED WITH CREAM CHEESE IS KEY TO DANTE'S DOGS.

KALBI BEEF SLIDERS

KALBI-BEEF SHORT RIBS, marinated in a mix of soy sauce, garlic, sesame oil, and sugar (among other ingredients) is traditionally grilled over a charcoal flame and snipped into serving pieces with kitchen shears. Usually diners wrap *kalbi* inside lettuce leaves along with steamed rice, some garlic, and lengths of scallion. This slider riff was inspired by KOi fusion.

KOi Fusion preaches its gospel via Twitter.

MAKES ENOUGH FOR 6 SLIDERS

FOR THE BEEF

1 pound beef rib eye, thinly sliced

2 tablespoons brown sugar

2 tablespoons soy sauce

1 tablespoon mirin (sweet rice wine)

2 teaspoons Asian (dark) sesame oil

2 teaspoons minced garlic

1 scallion, both white and green parts, chopped

1/2 ripe kiwi, juiced in a blender

1/4 teaspoon freshly ground black pepper

FOR THE DRESSING AND SLAW

2 tablespoons soy sauce

4 tablespoons rice wine vinegar

1/2 teaspoon granulated sugar

1/2 teaspoon salt

1/2 teaspoon freshly ground black pepper

1/4 teaspoon crushed red pepper flakes

2 tablespoons canola oil

1 tablespoon Asian (dark) sesame oil

1/2 cup shredded cabbage

1/2 cup shredded romaine lettuce

2 tablespoons chopped scallion

2 tablespoons toasted sesame seeds (see Note)

6 slider buns

1 Prepare the beef: Sprinkle the beef with the brown sugar and let sit for a few minutes.

2 Place the soy sauce, mirin, sesame oil, garlic, chopped scallion, kiwi juice, and pepper in a mixing bowl and stir to mix. Add the beef, massaging the marinade into the meat. Let the beef marinate in the refrigerator, covered, for at least 2 hours.

3 Heat a griddle or cast-iron skillet over medium-high heat. Drain the beef, discarding the marinade, and pat the slices dry with paper towels. Add the beef to the griddle and cook, turning once, until cooked through, 3 to 5 minutes.

4 Make the dressing and slaw: Place the soy sauce, rice wine vinegar, granulated sugar, salt, black pepper, red pepper flakes, and canola and sesame oils in a blender and blend until well combined.

LAST SEEN: PGE Park, West Burnside Street and SW 20th Avenue, Portland, Oregon

KOI FUSION

MOST PORTLAND STREET FOOD VENDORS work stationary carts and hutches. But Bo Kwon and his partners do business from a sleek truck that looks like it rolled straight off the streets of LA. KOi fusion traces its lineage to the LA phenomenon called Kogi (you can read about it on page 212). "I called them up and asked about buying a franchise," Bo told me. "They told me that they didn't want to do that kind of thing. But they gave me their blessing. Said I was free to take the general idea and Portlandize it."

Korean-Mexican fusion, as filtered through the Portland experience, means that Bo Kwon's mother makes the various marinades that KOi fusion applies to its short ribs and chicken. And it means that, when you step up to the truck, the young man working the window says, "Hey, glad you're here. What's your name?" KOi fusion styles itself as the antihip answer to LA's Kogi. "This isn't about a scene," Bo said. "This is about good food. This is about the food I grew up on. When I was a little boy, they called me a 'Twinkie.' Yellow on the outside, white on the inside. This is that kind of food."

5 Place the cabbage and lettuce in a bowl, add the chopped scallion, toasted sesame seeds, and the dressing and toss to mix.

6 To assemble the sliders, shred the beef and place it in a hot skillet for a few seconds to reheat. Spoon the warm meat onto the slider buns, topping it with some of the slaw.

NOTE: To toast the sesame seeds, set a dry skillet over medium heat (do not use a nonstick skillet for this). Add the sesame seeds and heat them until lightly toasted and aromatic, 3 to 5 minutes. Keep an eye on the sesame seeds; you don't want them to burn. Transfer the toasted sesame seeds to a heatproof bowl to cool.

Sliders topped with slaw and—why not?—a slice of American cheese.

GRILLED CHEESE CHEESEBURGER

THE BRUNCH BOX does not have a lock on the grilled cheese cheeseburger market in Portland. Also working that schtick is The Grilled Cheese Grill, where the kitchen is set in a 1968 travel trailer and seating is in a school bus fitted with booths and a counter. Their grilled cheese cheeseburger is called the Cheesus. I prefer this recipe, which comes from the repertoire of Ryan and Ariana at the Brunch Box.

LAST SEEN: SW 5th Avenue and Stark Street, Portland, Oregon

BRUNCH BOX

IT'S A HUTCH, REALLY. A narrow rectangle with ninety-six square feet of workable kitchen space, owned by Ryan Incles and Ariana Berry. They built their business, which opened in March of 2009, on homemade English muffins, stuffed with ring-cooked eggs.

Burgers, stacked with Spam and God knows what else, came next. Of those, the cryptically named youcanhascheeseburger—a slab of beef, sandwiched between two grilled cheese sandwiches made from Texas toast—has emerged as Brunch Box's most popular. Originally known as the fatty melt, it's a paragon of textural complexity.

Out of a small space come big tastes.

MAKES 1 SANDWICH

1/4 pound ground beef

About 2 tablespoons canola oil

Salt and freshly ground black pepper

4 slices Texas toast (see Note)

3 slices American cheese, at room temperature

1 green lettuce leaf

1 slice ripe tomato

2 tablespoons yellow mustard

1 Shape the ground beef into a thin patty. Heat a small amount of oil in a griddle or skillet over high heat. Add the beef patty and, using the edge of a thin metal spatula, quickly score the top of the patty in a crisscross pattern. (Do this immediately, while the meat is still pink, or not at all.) Don't press down on the patty, or it will dry out.

2 Let the patty cook for a of couple minutes before seasoning it with salt and pepper. The goal as you cook is to flip the burger only once. Cook it for 2 to 3 minutes on one side; the edge should brown first. When it looks good, turn the patty over and place a slice of cheese on top to melt. Cook the patty on the second side until done to medium and slightly seared, 2 to 3 minutes.

3 While the patty is cooking, pour a small amount of oil in another skillet to heat or on a different area of the hot griddle. Add the

Grilled Texas toast bestows heft and texture.

second grilled cheese sandwich, mustard side down.

NOTE: Texas toast is white bread cut in slices that are double the thickness of regular bread slices. The "toast" part happens when both sides of the bread are smeared with butter or oil and toasted or griddled.

slices of Texas toast and put a slice of cheese on top of 2 of the 4 slices. Once the cheese has melted, place a plain slice of toast, toasted side up, on each cheese-covered slice to form 2 grilled cheese sandwiches. Remove the sandwiches from the grill and set them aside.

4 When the grilled cheese sandwiches have cooled a bit, arrange the lettuce leaf and tomato slice on top of one grilled cheese sandwich. Smear mustard on top of the second sandwich. Place the burger on top of the tomato slice and cover it with the

In Portland coffee is the drink of choice.

BURGER EMBELLISHMENTS

BOTH THE BACON KETCHUP and Nettle Butter are intended for burger toppings. Lisa Carlson and Carrie Summer serve bison burgers which they cook on a charcoal-fueled grill set behind the truck, in sight of the brown and lumbering Mississippi River below. But these condiments would be great on any sort of burger. For hot dogs the ladies offer a ramp mustard. Although they were happy to provide the ketchup and butter recipes here, you'll have to go to the Chef Shack to get a taste of that mustard.

BURGERS: A Story Told in Metal and Flat Screens

BURGERS have long been America's favorite portable food. Tucked into a bun and slipped into a paper sleeve, a burger is the perfect food to gobble between gear shifts, while weaving through heavy traffic.

In 2009 the portable burger began to realize its true potential. During the summer a burger truck from La Cense Beef began serving New Yorkers griddled beef from Black Angus cattle that graze on grass pastures. (By way of flat screens mounted to the truck, you can watch said cattle graze said pastures.)

On the other coast, the Grill 'Em All burger truck hit the Los Angeles streets in December of 2009, featuring heavy metal–inspired fare, like the Molly Hatchet burger, topped with fennel sausage gravy, bacon, and maple syrup. The proprietors put Twitter to good use. One early tweet, posted on a rainy day, proclaimed "the sky is about to open up! come crush a burg and some homemade tots before the rain!" The truck's name, in case you're wondering, references Metallica's 1983 debut album, *Kill 'Em All.*

Bacon Ketchup

THIS RECIPE CALLS for roasted bell peppers. You'll find instructions for roasting bell peppers in Step 1 of Dogtown Dogs on page 179.

MAKES ABOUT 2½ CUPS

1 tablespoon olive oil

½ medium-size onion, diced

5 cloves garlic, diced

¼ cup packed brown sugar

1 can (15 ounces) diced tomatoes, strained

2 large red bell peppers, roasted, peeled, stemmed, seeded, and chopped

½ teaspoon smoked paprika

1 small bay leaf

2 fresh thyme sprigs

1½ teaspoons balsamic vinegar

Salt and freshly ground black pepper

2 slices of thick-cut bacon

1 Heat the olive oil in a skillet over medium-low heat. Add the onion and garlic and cook until tender and caramelized, 10 to 15 minutes. Add the brown sugar and cook a couple of minutes longer. Add the tomatoes, bell peppers, paprika, bay leaf, and thyme and let simmer until the flavor develops, about 1 hour. Add the balsamic vinegar and season the ketchup with salt and black pepper to taste.

Read about the Chef Shack truck on page 141.

2 Cook the bacon until crisp, then drain it on paper towels. Remove the bay leaf and thyme sprigs from the ketchup. Crumble the bacon and fold it into the ketchup. The ketchup can be refrigerated, covered, for up to 2 weeks.

Nettle Butter

WILD NETTLES ARE a peppery fresh green similar to prickly dandelion greens, often harvested in the spring and consumed as a restorative. You can find them at farmers' markets.

MAKES ABOUT 1¹⁄₄ CUPS

A mighty menu wagon.

Better than your average salad bar.

Ice

¹⁄₂ cup wild nettles

I cup (2 sticks) best-quality unsalted butter, at room temperature

I¹⁄₂ teaspoons sherry vinegar

¹⁄₈ teaspoon Maldon (flaky) sea salt

1 Prepare a bowl of ice water. Bring 8 cups of water to a boil in a large saucepan. Add the nettles and let them boil for 1¹⁄₂ minutes. Immediately drain the nettles in a colander, then plunge them into the ice water to cool. Drain the nettles completely in the colander again. You'll need ¹⁄₄ cup prepared nettles for the butter.

2 Place the butter, sherry vinegar, and drained nettles in a food processor and pulse until the nettles are chopped into the butter. Add the salt and pulse a couple of times to incorporate it. Nettle Butter can be refrigerated, covered, for up to 2 weeks.

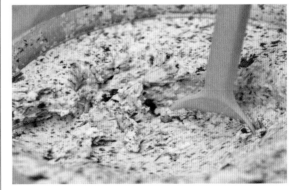

These nettles don't sting.

A WORKING MAN'S TOWN GETS A MAKEOVER:
DURHAM

"A veil of humility between two mountains of conceit." That's how Zebulon Baird Vance described antebellum North Carolina, back when neighboring South Carolina and Virginia were loci of plantation wealth and aristocratic mien.

could make a similar point about Durham, the longtime working-class enclave tucked between Chapel Hill, the academic citadel of North Carolina, and Raleigh, the capital city.

WHERE THE TRUCKS ARE:
📍 Durham Farmers' Market: Foster Street at Hunt Street

Durham has long been a great place to eat. Magnolia Grill, Karen and Ben Barker's temple of New South dining, has been setting standards and dishing sweet tea–brined pork chops and transcendent maple-bourbon sweet potato pies since the current crop of chefs were weed-hoppers.

But Durham has never been hip. Not in a way that made its neighbors jealous. Until now. While Chapel Hill and Raleigh debated the relative merits of street food, Durham served it forth. From battered taco trucks patronized by construction workers at midday to sleek stepsides that vend late-night Korean tacos to carousing Duke students, street vendors now charm and feed a wide range of Bull City folk.

The scene is diverse. Klausie's, a pizza truck, bakes cheese-smothered slices that, depending on whom you ask, are either Detroit inspired or a singular invention of a *pizzaiolo* who claims his crust owes its character to the forty-year-old pans he employs. Meanwhile, an Indian food truck, doing business in a bright red school bus, dishes *lengua* tacos at night and lamb-topped *paratha* bread during the day.

Farmhand Foods Sausage Wagon, from which Jennifer Curtis and Tina Prevatte serve fennel chowchow–topped sausages made from humanely raised North Carolina pigs, may be the best merchandiser of the bunch. Their slogan is "(m)eat local." (They got some of their startup funding from the W. K. Kellogg Foundation and the North Carolina Tobacco Trust Fund Commission.)

Talk to locals of long standing and they'll tell you that those chowchow–topped sausages—not to mention sweet potato muffins and morning burgers topped with pimento cheese, fried green tomatoes, and eggs—are all newfangled additions to a street food scene that has long employed and fed Hispanic immigrants.

In Durham, *horchata* is now as popular as Pepsi. Cow head *barbacoa* rivals pork shoulder barbecue. And *salsa verde* graces as many dining room tables as sawmill gravy.

With that in mind, you might make an argument that Durham, rife with multicultural influences and thriving African American communities, has always been hip.

It's just that few outside the city knew it until now.

- - - - - - - - - - - - - - - - - - - -

Left to Right:
Top Row: Morning burger, Only Burger. Curbside sweets.

Middle Row: Tanya Catolos, cupcakes supreme. Farmhouse—honest food.

Bottom Row: Only Burger delivers. Konrad and Tanya of DaisyCakes.

MORNING BURGER

THE FOLKS AT ONLY BURGER use hormone-free beef, ground daily at Cliff's Meat Market. Good beef is key. But what makes this burger great is their talent for synthesizing traditions and tastes. Pimento cheese-capped burgers are usually found in the American South. Egg-topped burgers are more popular in South America. Maybe there's some province where the two traditions are commonly combined at breakfast. But I doubt it. To my palate, this morning burger—inspired by their work—tastes singular.

The fluid dynamics of pimento cheese.

This truck is plain but the burgers are baroque.

MAKES 4 BURGERS

4 hamburger buns

1 cup pimento cheese (recipe follows)

1 pound ground chuck

1 teaspoon salt

1 teaspoon freshly ground black pepper

4 large eggs

8 slices Fried Green Tomatoes (recipe follows)

1 Toast the hamburger buns. Spread pimento cheese on the top and bottom halves of the buns. Set the buns aside.

2 Place the ground chuck, salt, and pepper in a bowl and knead them gently with your hands until blended. Divide the meat mixture into 4 even portions and form each portion into a patty.

3 Heat a heavy skillet or griddle pan over medium-high heat for 1 to 2 minutes. Place the patties in the skillet and cook for 3 to 4 minutes per side for medium-rare.

4 While the burgers are cooking, crack the eggs into a separate nonstick skillet and cook them sunny-side up over medium heat until all of the egg whites are cooked but the yolks are still runny, about 3 minutes.

5 To assemble the burgers, place a burger on the bottom half of each bun. Top each with a fried egg, 2 slices of Fried Green Tomato, and the top half of the bun.

Pimento Cheese

IF YOU MAKE the pimento cheese in advance and refrigerate it, remove it about 10 minutes before using.

MAKES ABOUT 1 1/2 CUPS

1 1/2 pounds extra-sharp cheddar cheese, shredded

1 jar (4 ounces) pimentos, drained and diced

1 small serrano pepper, seeded and diced (about 1 tablespoon or more to taste)

1/3 cup mayonnaise, or more if you like a creamier consistency

1 tablespoon freshly ground black pepper

1 teaspoon salt

Place the cheese, pimentos, serrano pepper, mayonnaise, black pepper, and salt in a large mixing bowl and stir them together using a large spoon until a spreadable paste forms. If you are not going to use the pimento cheese immediately, place it in an airtight container in the refrigerator. It will keep for up to 1 week.

Fried Green Tomatoes

DON'T RESERVE THESE just for burgers.

MAKES 8 TO 10 TOMATO SLICES

2 large or medium-size firm green tomatoes

1 large egg

1 tablespoon milk

2 cups panko (Japanese bread crumbs)

1/2 teaspoon salt

3 cups canola or peanut oil, for frying

1 Cut the tomatoes into slices about 1/4 inch thick. Place the egg and milk in a small bowl and whisk until well blended. Combine the *panko* and salt in a separate shallow bowl or on a plate.

2 Heat the oil in a cast-iron skillet or deep sauté pan over medium-high heat until it pops loudly when a few drops of water are tossed in.

3 Dip the tomato slices into the egg mixture and then in the *panko,* turning to coat them all over. Being careful not to crowd the skillet, carefully add the tomato slices to the hot oil and cook, turning once, until golden brown, about 3 minutes. Using a slotted spoon, transfer the tomato slices to paper towels to drain.

LAST SEEN: Durham Farmers' Market, Durham, North Carolina

ONLY BURGER

THIS WHITE TRUCK, with its conservative maroon script and retro slogan, "when only the best will do," has been rolling on the streets of Durham since 2008. Sam Poley, a former restaurateur who now works with the Durham Convention & Visitors Bureau, was an original owner. So was Tom Ferguson, a local caterer, who has more recently been joined by Brian Bottger.

Like so many of the successful first-generation truckers, Only Burger now has a brick-and-mortar location. But the truck, with its rumbling generator, is still the draw, especially when it's parked for a morning gig at the Durham Farmers' Market.

Step to the window and you'll walk away with a brown paper bag of crisp and twiggy hand-cut fries and a foil-wrapped pouch of burger goodness that evokes the backyard cookouts of your youth—if you were lucky enough to attend backyard cookouts during which burgers emerged from the grill with a pink core and earned caps of homemade pimento cheese.

Ladle of chili for a Frito pie, Houston.

High Noon quesadilla, Los Angeles.

Pickled onions add brightness.

Calexico tortillas on the griddle, New York City.

TACO
palooga

CHAPTER 7

Tacos are nothing more, and nothing less, than sandwiches made from Mexican flatbread,

sometimes folded, sometimes open-faced. Over the last three decades, tacos—and the soft corn and flour tortillas on which the best are built—have escaped from the American fast–food ghetto. Tortillas have become the next best thing to white bread for huge swaths of our wrap-obsessed population.

Having traveled the country eating tortilla-wrapped hot gut sausages in Texas and lacquered duck-topped tortillas in San Francisco, I've come to realize that tacos have been deracinated. Like hot dogs and hamburgers—once associated to varying degrees with Germany—tacos, formerly pegged to Mexico, are now unimpeachably American.

Take Indianapolis, for example. Korean food, still considered exotic by many Americans, has begun to gain widespread acceptance in this Midwestern city when served on a tortilla, with taco truck embellishments.

That's just what happened when West Coast Tacos opened in 2010. John Ban, who was raised in Indiana by Korean parents, and Arnold Park, a native of Seoul, South

Korea, quickly earned a city-wide reputation selling Indianapolis club kids corn tortilla tacos, piled with nubs of beef, chopped onions, cilantro leaves, and red jalapeño salsa.

"First we were going to move to Korea and open a regular taco truck," Ban told me. "Then we thought we'd do a Korean taco truck in Korea. We settled on doing a Korean taco truck in Indianapolis.

"The meat makes it Korean," continued Ban, who marinates chuck roll in a soy and garlic sauce traditionally used with Korean barbecue dishes. Then he got to the point: "The tortilla and the toppings are a way to tell our customers that this food is okay, that this food is American."

An avocado finish from a squirt bottle.

SHORT RIBS AND SALSA VERDE.

EAST L.A. TACOS

A FEW YEARS BACK fusion got a bad rap. Traditionalists decried the forced mixing of flavors as a sign of the coming culinary apocalypse. And they were, to a certain degree, right. But honest mixing and marrying of peoples and traditions is a different matter altogether. That's what Kogi preaches, that's what this Kogi-adapted recipe delivers.

A commissary stock–up for a Kogi truck.

MAKES 8 SMALL TACOS

- 1/4 cup finely diced yellow onion
- 1/4 cup chopped fresh cilantro
- 2 tablespoons freshly squeezed lime juice
- 1/2 cup shredded green cabbage
- 1/2 cup shredded romaine lettuce
- 1/4 cup chopped scallions, both white and green parts
- 1/4 cup Chile Vinaigrette (recipe follows)
- 4 teaspoons canola oil
- 8 small (4 to 6 inches each) corn tortillas, store-bought or homemade (page 87)
- 2 cups chopped short ribs (page 99), or spicy pork al pastor (page 241)
- 1/4 cup Salsa Verde (page 243)
- 1 teaspoon sesame seeds, toasted and crushed (see Note)

1 Combine the onion, cilantro, and lime juice in a small bowl and set aside.

2 Toss the cabbage, romaine lettuce, and scallions with the chile vinaigrette in another small bowl and set aside.

3 Heat the canola oil in a cast-iron skillet over high heat. Heat the tortillas on each side just before assembling the tacos.

4 To assemble the tacos, put equal amounts of meat on each tortilla, add a tablespoon of *salsa verde,* then put some of the onion and cilantro mixture on top, followed by the cabbage, romaine, and scallion mixture. Sprinkle the tacos with the toasted sesame seeds.

N O T E : To toast the sesame seeds, set a dry skillet over medium heat (do not use a nonstick skillet for this). Add the sesame seeds and heat them until lightly toasted and aromatic, 3 to 5 minutes. Keep an eye on the sesame seeds; you don't want them to burn. Transfer the toasted sesame seeds to a heatproof bowl to cool.

Chile Vinaigrette

KOREAN CHILE FLAKES—*KOCHUKARU*— DELIVER the heat that powers kimchi and a host of other Korean dishes. Good quality *kochukaru* should be bright red and smell

KOGI

WHILE RESEARCHING THIS BOOK I took three trips through Los Angeles. One trip coincided with the opening of the LA Auto Show. All the buzz that week seemed to focus on hybrid this and electric that—and on the brand Scion, which was showing a custom Kogi-inspired car. The designers had removed the Scion rear seats and tucked in a refrigerator. They had installed a sink in the passenger side rear door and a slide-out grill in the back hatch. In essence they had fused a taco truck with a subcompact.

When asked what he planned to do with such a vehicle, Roy Choi, the chef and face man for the Kogi food trucks, said that he planned to cook *amuse-bouche* from the car and serve them to patrons waiting in line for service at one of his trucks. And he said those words with a straight face.

The year 2009 was the Year of Kogi. Choi and his crew reinvented the American concept of street food in a dozen different ways, developments that, in total, managed to prove that a truck food vendor could produce food that was high-concept and high-quality, while retaining street credibility. "Everything you get in that taco is what we live in LA," Roy told a writer back in the early days. "It's the 720 bus on Wilshire, it's the 3rd Street Juanita's Tacos, the Korean supermarket, and all those things that we live every day in one bite. That was our goal. To take everything about LA and put it into one bite."

Since the first Kogi truck hit the streets in late 2008 selling *kalbi* tacos to late-night club goers, a devotion to the democracy of street life has informed the Kogi approach. "I cook food for the guy fixing your house, the guy in the tow truck," Roy told me. "I'm feeding everybody, from Nancy Silverton to nine-year-old girls and five-year-old boys."

Born in Seoul, South Korea, Roy immigrated to America when he was not quite two. He grew up in East Los Angeles. He graduated from the Culinary Institute of America. He has cooked at Le Bernardin in New York City and The Beverly Hilton in Los Angeles. One of the reasons that Kogi has become so successful is that Roy gives good quotes, observations that offer glimmers of how honest fusion actually happens in modern America. Among my favorites, both overheard and second-hand: "If Dean & Deluca is a gourmet store, we're a thrift store." And, "Street food can be served in a stationary place, but your heart and your spirit has to be moving." And, "I don't want to go to other cities to conquer them. But I would like to go to other cities to spread the love."

Inevitably, the success of Kogi has spawned imitators. In the Los Angeles area alone, there's Calbi, a franchise-ready truck concept, selling kimchi quesadillas. And Don Chow Tacos, serving kung pao chicken tacos. And Bool BBQ, dishing Korean-inflected tacos as well as Puerto Rican–inspired *pasteles* (savory meat pies wrapped in banana leaves).

sweet. In better-stocked stores you can find three grades: a fine grind for cooking, a coarse grind for pickles, and the crushed flakes called for here, which are frequently used for garnish.

MAKES ABOUT 1½ CUPS

- 1 tablespoon kochukaru (see Note)
- ¼ cup soy sauce
- 2 tablespoons Asian (dark) sesame oil
- ½ tablespoon diced peeled fresh ginger
- 2 scallions, coarsely chopped (use the whites and 2 inches of the green parts)
- 3 cloves garlic, minced
- 2 tablespoons granulated sugar
- 1 tablespoon kosher salt
- 1½ teaspoons freshly ground black pepper
- 1 cup rice wine vinegar
- ½ cup canola oil

Place the *kochukaru,* soy sauce, sesame oil, ginger, scallions, garlic, sugar, salt, pepper, rice wine vinegar, and canola oil in a blender and puree. The vinaigrette can be refrigerated, covered, for up to 1 week.

N O T E : *Kochukaru* is available at Asian groceries.

CARNE ASADA TACOS EL GALUZO

TACOS EL GALUZO stocks a feedlot full of various animal parts. There's *lengua,* cow tongue. And *tripa,* the lining of a pig's stomach. And *buche,* the muscular part of the pig's stomach. Depending upon your taste, you may order any of those meats, simmered el Galuzo style in a cauldron of broth and whole onions, then crisped on the flattop grill. Or you can drop the machismo posturing and go for *carne asada* tacos and chorizo tacos.

Most trucks, including Tacos el Galuzo, buy their tortillas. But they buy in volume and can demand freshness. If you want to go that route, stake out a bodega and look for stacks of tortillas wrapped in paper or in plastic bags. You want the small tortillas, four to six inches in diameter. You also want the freshest ones. When you poke the package, the tortillas will feel pliable—slightly moist, the result of condensation. If you can't find good-quality corn tortillas, you can craft your own. Easily. You'll find a recipe on page 87.

MAKES 10 TO 12 SMALL TACOS

FOR THE CARNE ASADA

1 scant teaspoon salt

1 scant teaspoon MSG

1/2 cup freshly squeezed lemon juice

2 pounds thin beef steak (see Note)

FOR THE TACOS

1 medium-size onion, chopped

1 bunch fresh cilantro, chopped

1 cup of lard, melted

10 to 12 small (4 to 6 inches each) corn tortillas, store-bought or homemade (page 87)

Salsa Roja (recipe follows), or Salsa Verde (page 216)

6 lime wedges, for serving

12 radishes, trimmed and cut in half, for serving

1 Prepare the *carne asada:* Combine the salt, MSG, and lemon juice in a large resealable plastic bag, add the beef, and massage the marinade into the meat. Press any air out of the bag and seal it, then let the beef marinate in the refrigerator for 1 to 3 hours. Turn the bag occasionally to distribute the marinade evenly over the meat.

2 Set up a charcoal grill for direct grilling and preheat it to medium-high. Or heat a stovetop grill pan over medium-high heat.

THE LARD DIP

BEFORE THEY HIT the flattop grill at Tacos el Galuzo, Juan Torres dips his tortillas in melted lard. That's right, lard. Pig fat gets a bad rap, especially the hydrogenated stuff that Torres uses. But we're not talking much lard here, just enough to wet the griddle, to refresh the tortillas, to make them taste *comal*-fresh again.

Torres stores his lard bucket on the hot griddle, so the stuff stays liquid. You can keep a small jar of *manteca*, which is the Spanish word for lard, sealed in the fridge. Pop it in the microwave when you're ready to cook. You'll find hydrogenated *manteca* in many grocery stores. Alternately, if you're into rendering your own lard, a process that yields a joyously nonhydrogenated and unsaturated fat, you know to store it the same way.

A rolling billboard.

3 Remove the beef from the marinade and discard the marinade. Pat the steak dry with paper towels. Cook the beef until the exterior is nicely charred on both sides and the interior is cooked through but not beginning to dry out, about 3 minutes per side. Transfer the beef to a cutting board to rest for a few minutes, then slice the steak into thin strips across the grain on the diagonal. Coarsely chop the strips of beef into chunks.

4 Make the tacos: Combine the onion and cilantro and set aside.

5 Heat a griddle or cast-iron skillet over high heat. Pour the lard into a shallow bowl or pan. Briefly dip the tortillas into the lard on each side, just enough to make them shiny and refresh them. Place the tortillas on the hot griddle or skillet and cook them for about 30 seconds on each side.

6 Pile about 1/3 cup beef chunks on each tortilla. Drizzle salsa over the meat and top it with some of the onion and cilantro mixture. Serve the tacos immediately with lime wedges and radish halves.

NOTE: Grilled meat—that's how the two word conjunction *carne asada* translates from the Spanish. In reality *carne asada,* as understood in Los Angeles, is grilled beef. Often the beef in question is *espaldilla,* boneless beef clod steaks, or *diesmillo,* boneless beef chuck steaks.

Stainless steel ledges serve as taco truck tables.

TACOS EL GALUZO

JUAN TORRES works the night shift at Tacos el Galuzo, a white truck blazoned with a mural of his hometown, Arandas, in the state of Jalisco in Mexico. Each evening around five Torres pulls to a curb just off Whittier Boulevard, in East Los Angeles. Most nights Juan Jr., his high school age son, rides shotgun.

Torres's taco truck may not be the best in Los Angeles, but it's good—very good. Which means that when you take a step toward the order window, when you crane your neck upward and speak, in the best Spanish you can mangle, you will receive, in return, a textbook take on the minimalist taco form.

What's more, you'll get a lesson in taco truck economics for, in addition to piloting a truck, Torres serves as president of the *Asociación de Loncheros L.A. Familia Unida de California*, an alliance that lobbies and organizes on behalf of the taco truck drivers who work the Los Angeles streets.

When, a couple of years back, the City of Los Angeles proposed onerous regulations that would have virtually criminalized roving taco trucks, Torres, speaking on behalf of vendors and consumers alike, fought the law. And he won. (He enjoyed an unconventional boost from a loose association of friends and smart-asses who printed T-shirts reading "Carne Asada Is Not a Crime.")

The promise of fresh-shaved pork.

Chances are if you have a Mexican grocery close by, it will stock one or both of those cuts, sliced very thinly into steaks. If it doesn't, skirt steak or flank steak will do, but they'll set you back more money. No matter which cut you choose, you'll need a marinade.

Salsa Roja

THIS RECIPE, ADAPTED FROM TACOS EL GALUZO, is one to make in a double batch and stash in the fridge. The color should be dusky. And, owing to the oregano and cumin, so should the taste.

MAKES ABOUT 1 CUP

12 medium-size ripe tomatoes, cut in half

2 medium-size onions, peeled and quartered

2 cloves garlic, peeled

2 dried chiles de árbol, cayenne peppers, or similar hot dried red peppers, stemmed

1 teaspoon dried oregano

1 teaspoon ground cumin

1/2 cup freshly squeezed lime juice, or more to taste

1 teaspoon salt, or more to taste

1 Preheat the oven to 375°F.

2 Place the tomatoes and onions on a rimmed baking sheet lined with aluminum foil. Bake the tomatoes and onions for 5 minutes, then add the garlic and bake until the tomatoes collapse and begin to blacken, about 10 minutes, turning them occasionally. Watch the garlic; if the cloves start to brown slightly, remove them and set them aside. Let the vegetables cool.

3 Toast the chiles, oregano, and cumin in a dry skillet over medium-high heat until fragrant, 1 to 2 minutes (do not use a nonstick skillet for this).

4 Place the toasted chile mixture and the tomatoes, onions, and garlic in a blender or food processor and pulse until just pureed. Add the lime juice and salt. Taste for seasoning, adding more lime juice and/or salt as necessary.

THE TACO PLATE

WHEN POSED by a taco truck cook, simple questions sound existential. "For here or to go?" Absent interior dining space, and taking into account the axles and wheels on which these almost-restaurants rest, isn't every taco truck order to go?

Well, no. Order tacos to go at Tacos el Galuzo and you'll get a brace of corn tortillas folded over some sort of chopped meat, the tacos wrapped in aluminum foil and stuffed in a paper sack, with plastic bullets of salsa thrown on top.

But order your tacos for here and Juan Torres will pass a paper plate through the service window. That plate will be lined with open-faced tortillas, each piled with meat and capped with onion-cilantro confetti, each ready to drizzle with red or green salsa. Flanking the tortillas will be radish halves and emerald green lime wedges.

As for portion control, when served by better trucks, tacos are not overly stuffed. They do not overflow. They're comparatively restrained, respectful of the equilibrium of filling and garniture. Torres uses a tortilla to measure his filling. He clasps a warm tortilla in one hand and reaches for a pile of meat. What he grasps is what he lays flat on a plate, atop the tortilla.

At a taco truck it's customary to eat while leaning over the fold-down shelf that cantilevers from the side of the truck. At home, your kitchen counter will suffice.

Paper plates are common taco conveyances.

Salsa Verde

ANGULAR. AND CLEAN. And pleasantly vegetal. That's the way to describe the taste of this *salsa verde,* adapted from Tacos el Galuzo.

MAKES ABOUT 1 CUP

20 tomatillos, husks removed

3 jalapeño peppers, stemmed and seeded

1/2 bunch fresh cilantro, chopped

3 cloves garlic, peeled

Salt

1 Place 3 quarts of water in a large pot and let come to a boil. Add the tomatillos, jalapeños, cilantro, and garlic, reduce the heat, and let simmer until softened, about 10 minutes. Remove the tomatillo mixture from the heat and drain it, setting aside 1 cup of the cooking liquid. Let the tomatillo mixture and the reserved cooking liquid cool.

2 Put the cooled tomatillo mixture in a blender and puree until smooth, adding small amounts of the reserved cooking liquid as necessary to achieve the right consistency. Season the salsa with salt to taste.

WHAT TO DRINK:
CHEATER'S HORCHATA

MEET *HORCHATA,* THE NONALCOHOLIC THIRST QUENCHER, traditionally made with rice water, cinnamon, and other flavorings. While traditional recipes call for soaking rice in water for two to three hours and then pureeing the mix to make a base, Juan Torres at Tacos el Galuzo begins with evaporated milk.

N.B.: *Horchata* makes a great cocktail base. Just add two fingers of bourbon to a collins glass full of ice, top it with chilled *horchata,* stir, and serve.

Horchata is ready for American prime time.

Note the mural of Juan Torres's hometown.

Read about the Tacos el Galuzo truck on page 215.

MAKES ABOUT ¹/₂ GALLON

I can (12 ounces) evaporated milk

2 tablespoons powdered rice (see Note)

2 tablespoons granulated sugar

I tablespoon ground cinnamon

I tablespoon unsweetened cocoa powder

Place the evaporated milk, powdered rice, sugar, cinnamon, and cocoa in a ¹/₂-gallon jar. Close the lid and shake to combine. Add 3 pints of water and shake the jar again. Refrigerate the *horchata* until chilled before serving over ice, if desired.

NOTE: You can use either rice flour, found in the "alternative flours" section of the supermarket, or "rice protein," sold at health food stores, to make the *horchata.*

CARNE ASADA MULITAS

MULITA IS SPANISH for little mule. I see a parallel with the words *burro,* which translates as the donkey, and *burrito,* or little donkey. All of these animals are beasts of burden, and the dishes describe means of wrapping and conveying food from cook to eater. This recipe was inspired by Taqueria El Carreton.

MAKES 6 SMALL *MULITAS*

1 jalapeño pepper, stemmed, seeded, and minced

1 bunch fresh cilantro, chopped

2 tablespoons minced garlic

1/4 cup freshly squeezed lime juice

2 tablespoons cider vinegar

1/2 teaspoon ground cumin

1/2 teaspoon granulated sugar

1/2 cup plus 2 tablespoons olive oil

2 pounds beef skirt steak or flank steak

1 teaspoon salt

1 teaspoon freshly ground black pepper

12 small (4 to 6 inches each) corn tortillas, store-bought or homemade (page 87)

1 cup shredded Jack cheese

1 avocado, peeled, pitted, and sliced

Lime wedges

TACO TRUCKS AND THE DOCUMENTARY IMPULSE: A Report from Columbus, Ohio, and Elsewhere

WEBSITES ACROSS THE COUNTRY provide blow by blow, bite by bite coverage of street food. As of this writing, no one has built a website with national reach. But VendrTV, a fledgling series hosted by Daniel Delaney, has since early 2009 been filming short webisodes that play like street reports from an aspirational Al Roker.

There are now downtown and midtown editions of Midtown Lunch, the culinary seeker website founded by Zach Brooks and focused, at least initially, on New York City. Now there's a Philadelphia edition, too. That one will have some stiff competition, especially among the eaters near the University of Pennsylvania and Drexel University campuses, ably covered by the website pennfoodtrucks.com.

In Portland, Oregon, foodcartsportland.com is the source that comes closest to definitive. The roster of carts is encyclopedic and searchable by type of cuisine, hours, and location. You'll find embedded videos, glossy pics of both carts and their specialties, and field reports that play across the screen like virtual love letters to the possibility of street eats.

But you kind of expect that sort of coverage for Portland, a progenitor of the American street food scene. More surprising—and, when looking to the future, more hopeful—is the extensive coverage at tacotruckscolumbus.com, where in addition to viewing reviews of the various Columbus, Ohio, vendors, you can peruse essays on taco truck etiquette, taco truck regulations, and taco truck terminology.

---

1 Place the jalapeño, cilantro, garlic, lime juice, cider vinegar, cumin, sugar, and 1/2 cup of olive oil in a mixing bowl and stir to mix well. Pour the marinade into a large resealable plastic bag, add the beef, and massage the marinade into it. Press any air out of the bag and seal it, then let the beef marinate in the refrigerator for at least 2 hours. Turn the bag occasionally to distribute the marinade evenly over the meat.

2 Heat a griddle or cast-iron skillet over high heat. Remove the beef from the marinade and discard the marinade. Pat dry with

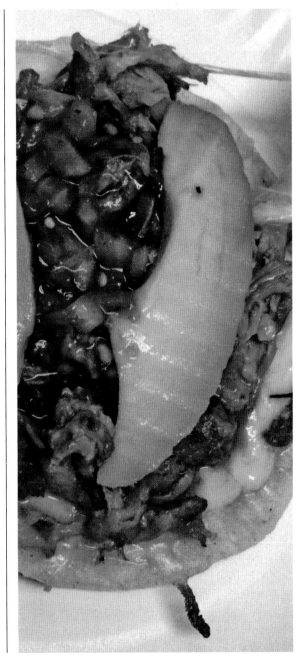

LAST SEEN: Aurora Avenue North and 152nd Street, Seattle, Washington

TAQUERIA EL CARRETON

SET IN A PARKING LOT that includes a dentist and a karaoke bar, the Taqueria El Carreton bus serves *buche* (pig stomach muscle) and *sopitos*, which the menu describes as "wet chipotle burritos." No matter, I'm keen on the *mulitas,* oozing with cheese that turns crisp on the griddle. In true Seattle form, a trash can occupies the driver's seat. Alongside, mounted on the transmission hump, a television blares Mexican soap operas.

paper towels. Season the meat with the salt and pepper. Cook the beef until the exterior is nicely charred on both sides and the interior is done to taste, about 5 minutes per side. Transfer the beef to a cutting board to rest for a few minutes, then slice the steak into thin strips across the grain on the diagonal.

3 Working in batches if necessary, place the tortillas on the hot griddle or skillet. Sprinkle some cheese on top of 6 of the tortillas, dividing it evenly among them. Let the cheese melt a little, then arrange the strips of meat on top of the cheese. Arrange avocado slices on top of the meat and squeeze lime juice over the avocado and meat. Top each *mulita* with another warm tortilla, carefully flip them, and toast until the cheese is melted and the bottom tortillas are beginning to brown, 3 to 5 minutes.

A crescent of creamy avocado is customary.

CALEXICO CARNE ASADA TACOS

TRADITIONALLY *CARNE ASADA* is made with beef variety cuts like shoulder clod and the lesser sirloins. This recipe, based on one made by Jesse and the boys at Calexico Carne Asada, relies on hanger steak, known among clever chefs and informed eaters as butcher's fillet. The implication is that a butcher knows this cut to be the equal of a tenderloin. That's a bit of an overstatement, but it does make a fine taco.

Calexico claimed its street perch early.

MAKES 8 SMALL TACOS

2 tablespoons freshly squeezed lime juice

2 tablespoons freshly squeezed lemon juice

1/4 cup vegetable or canola oil

3 cloves garlic, minced

I small onion, thinly sliced

1/2 teaspoon ground cumin

1/2 teaspoon ground coriander

1/2 teaspoon hot paprika or sweet paprika

1/2 teaspoon kosher salt

I1/2 pounds hanger steak, trimmed

8 small (4 to 6 inches each) corn tortillas, store-bought or homemade (page 87)

Avocado Crema (recipe follows)

Calexico Pico de Gallo (page 222)

I small head cabbage, cored and shredded

1 Place the lime juice, lemon juice, oil, garlic, onion, cumin, coriander, paprika, and salt in a mixing bowl and stir to mix well. Pour the marinade into a large resealable plastic bag, add the steak, and massage the marinade into the meat. Press any air out of the bag and seal it, then let the beef marinate in the refrigerator for no less than 6 hours and preferably for 24 hours. Turn the bag occasionally to distribute the marinade evenly over the meat.

2 Set up a charcoal or gas grill for direct grilling and preheat it to high. Or heat a stovetop grill pan over high heat.

3 Remove the beef from the marinade and discard the marinade. Pat the steak dry with paper towels. Grill the steak until done to taste, about 5 minutes per side for medium-rare. Transfer the beef to a cutting board and let it rest for 5 to 10 minutes, then slice the steak into thin strips across the grain.

4 Heat a skillet over medium heat and warm the tortillas one at a time in the skillet until pliable, about 30 seconds on each side. As you work, wrap the tortillas in a clean kitchen towel to keep them warm.

5 To serve, place a few slices of meat on a tortilla and garnish it with Avocado Crema, Calexico Pico de Gallo, and shredded cabbage.

Avocado Crema

AT FIRST BLUSH the pairing of buttermilk and avocado seems unlikely, but the interplay of acidic buttermilk and fat, rich avocado is a natural. Inspired by Calexico Carne Asada, this recipe is just the thing to keep in a squeeze bottle in your fridge.

MAKES ABOUT 1 CUP

1 avocado, peeled, pitted, and cut into chunks

3/4 cup sour cream

1/4 cup buttermilk

2 tablespoons freshly squeezed lime juice

1/2 teaspoon salt

Put the avocado, sour cream, buttermilk, lime juice, and salt in a food processor or blender and puree until smooth. The *crema* can be refrigerated, tightly sealed, for 2 to 3 days; it must be sealed airtight or the sauce will turn brown.

A rainbow of salsas.

Calexico Pico de Gallo

THIS *PICO DE GALLO,* from Calexico Carne Asada, could become your summer table sauce—the stuff you make when the July heat bears down. The stuff you pull from the fridge every afternoon. If you make it in the winter, look for plum tomatoes.

MAKES ABOUT I CUP

3/4 cup chopped ripe tomatoes (about 2 medium-size tomatoes or 6 plum tomatoes)

2 tablespoons finely chopped onion

Juice of 1/2 lime

2 tablespoons chopped fresh cilantro leaves

I teaspoon salt, or more to taste

1/2 teaspoon freshly ground black pepper, or more to taste

Place the tomatoes, onion, lime juice, cilantro, salt, and pepper in a small bowl and stir to mix. Taste for seasoning, adding more salt and/or pepper as necessary.

Weighing down tortillas while they grill keeps them flat and helps to give them a pliable texture.

LAST SEEN: At the corner of Wooster Street and Prince Street, New York, New York

CALEXICO CARNE ASADA

JESSE VENDLEY, originally from Calexico, California—across the border from Mexicali, Mexico—once worked as an advertising copywriter in New York City. He considered himself an ace *carne asada* cook. He tried to raise money to open a restaurant. Jesse failed.

In 2005 Jesse attended the inaugural Vendy Awards. Watching New York City's best street food vendors duke it out for the Vendy Cup, he came away inspired. And he came away with an alternate vision for a *carne asada–*fueled business, which he executed in 2006. (Read about the Vendy Awards on page 264.)

What Jesse has honed, with his two brothers Brian and Dave Vendley, is a ragged riff on Cal-Mex tradition. Last time I stopped by Calexico Carne Asada, the stereo speakers were blaring Johnny Cash's *At Folsom Prison,* as the brothers slung hanger steak quesadillas and bullets of chipotle "crack" sauce to a line of addicts that unspooled down the Soho block.

CHIPOTLE SAUCE
FOR ROLLED QUESADILLAS

WHILE A TRADITIONAL quesadilla is half-moon shaped, Calexico Carne Asada serves rolled quesadillas. A configuration like that is easier to stuff in a bag for a customer on the go. What's more, the blunt edge of a rolled quesadilla calls out for a dipping sauce. The Calexico boys call their dip "crack" sauce.

Calexico's fans crowd the sidewalk.

MAKES ABOUT I CUP

2 canned chipotle peppers with I teaspoon of their juices (see Note)

1/2 cup mayonnaise

1/4 cup sour cream

If there are any stems or seeds in the chipotle peppers, remove them. Put the chipotles with 1 teaspoon of their juices and the mayonnaise and sour cream in a blender or food processor and puree until very smooth. The sauce can be refrigerated, covered, for up to 2 weeks.

NOTE: You'll find small cans of chipotle peppers in the Mexican section of the supermarket.

At the ready—plastic crocks of "crack."

SUADERO TACOS

SUADERO IS PROBABLY a slim cut from the beef brisket. Unless it's flank steak. I've studied the Spanish language butcher charts and I'm still not sure. What I am sure of is that at Jarro Cafe *suadero* reaches its potential by way of a deep citrus marinade. I suggest using flank steak for this recipe inspired by Jarro because brisket is a tough cut—even if you start off with thin slices.

Citrus is key in taco cookery—a choice of salsas doesn't hurt, either.

Jarro is a Houston standard-bearer.

MAKES 12 SMALL TACOS

1/2 cup freshly squeezed lemon juice

1 teaspoon dried Mexican oregano

2 teaspoons minced garlic

1/4 cup plus 2 tablespoons vegetable oil

1 teaspoon salt

1 teaspoon freshly ground black pepper

2 pounds beef flank steak, sliced 1/4-inch thick

12 small (4 to 6 inches each) corn tortillas, store-bought or homemade (page 87)

1/2 cup chopped white onion

1/2 cup chopped fresh cilantro

Serrano-Cilantro Salsa (recipe follows), or salsa of your choice

Lime wedges, for serving

1 Place the lemon juice, oregano, garlic, 1/4 cup of the oil, and the salt and pepper in a mixing bowl and whisk to combine well. Pour the marinade into a large resealable plastic bag, add the beef, and massage the marinade into the meat. Press any air out of the bag and seal it, then let the beef marinate in the refrigerator for at least 2 hours or overnight. Turn the bag occasionally to distribute the marinade evenly over the meat.

2 Heat the remaining 2 tablespoons of oil in a skillet over medium-high heat. Remove the beef from the marinade and discard

the marinade. Pat dry with paper towels. Add the beef to the skillet and sear it on both sides. Reduce the heat to medium and cook the beef until it is no longer pink, 5 to 8 minutes. Transfer the beef to a cutting board and let it rest for about 10 minutes, then chop it.

3 Heat another skillet over medium heat and warm the tortillas one at a time in the skillet until pliable, about 30 seconds on each side. As you work, wrap the tortillas in a clean kitchen towel to keep them warm.

4 To assemble the tacos, put equal amounts of beef on each tortilla and top it with some chopped onion and cilantro. Serve the tacos with the salsa and lime wedges.

LAST SEEN: 1521 Gessner Road, Houston, Texas

JARRO CAFE

MEMO PINEDA, born in Mexico City, made his name stateside by building a better taco. When he opened his first cart in 2001 he sourced superior ingredients like sirloin for his *carne asada*, instead of the more common flank steak, and developed a rainbow of salsas, which he displayed in *molcajetes* stationed on the bar that folded down from the side of the trailer. (Now the salsas are poured from plastic bottles stationed on the same shelf.)

Memo takes his cues from the fast casual end of the American restaurant business. He dresses his employees in uniforms. And he painted his truck a glossy black, eschewing the typical folksy murals and cartoon characters. He now owns a restaurant, too, set in a former Pizza Inn. The walls are covered with Beatles posters. A Little Red Wagon hangs from the ceiling, in the manner of a T.G.I. Friday's. But he keeps the trailer out front. He calls it his "drive-thru window."

Serrano-Cilantro Salsa

THE SALSAS served by the Jarro Cafe require a tolerance for heat. They can be searing. And this recipe, inspired by the work of Memo Pineda and his wife, Claudia, is no exception. That said, in addition to heat, this sauce shows a fine balance of sweet and sharp flavors.

MAKES ABOUT 1 CUP

1 tablespoon vegetable oil

10 serrano peppers, stemmed and seeded

$1/2$ cup diced onion

3 cloves garlic minced

$1/2$ cup chopped fresh cilantro

1 teaspoon distilled white vinegar

$1/2$ teaspoon salt

$1/4$ teaspoon ground cumin

Heat the oil in a small skillet over medium-high heat. Add the serrano peppers, onion, and garlic and cook until the peppers begin to brown and blister, about 10 minutes. Let the pepper mixture cool, then transfer it to a blender. Add the cilantro, vinegar, salt, cumin, and 3/4 cup of water and puree until smooth. The salsa can be refrigerated, covered, for up to 1 week.

HOUSTON:
THE THRILL OF THE OLD SCHOOL

Pandemonium erupts daily at the rear of the Mexican Consulate, set on the edge of downtown underneath an interstate overpass.

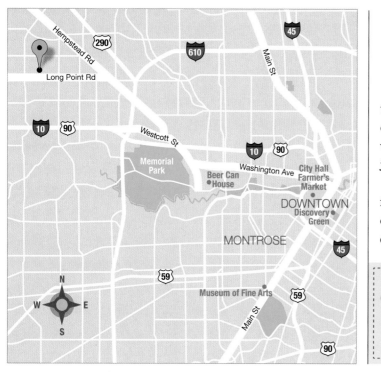

WHERE THE TRUCKS ARE:

📍 Drive Long Point Road for a sampling of Houston old-guard truck food.

For new guard trucks check roaminghunger.com.

Cars throng Caroline Street, angling for parking places. Attendants hustle the traffic, waving flags toward their lots, trying to collect money from drivers who could park free curbside, just two blocks away.

A long line snakes from the back door of the consulate. New immigrants clutch documentation papers as they inch up the sidewalk toward the entrance. Many look glum, apprehensive. Walking away, some—at least the ones clutching the forms necessary to establish legal residence—look joyful.

A number of businesses focus on this back-door crowd. To the right is a white bunker of a building where petitioners get passport pictures taken, buy auto insurance, fax documents, copy documents, and draw money from a bank machine. To the left, there's an ice cream stand, selling, among other sweets, *horchata*-flavored Mexican Popsicles. At the center of this scrum two taco trucks face off. They're diner-style trucks, by which I mean they're the sort of trucks that are, in actuality, short-order restaurants tucked into too-small boxes.

Taqueria Atotonilco is a battered white jalopy, dishing sandwiches *al gusto,* which look like country club–style club sandwiches, along with fried fish platters and *tortas cubanas* stuffed with, among other meats, flattop-fried hot dogs. Across the way, Taqueria Torres vends quesadillas *al pastor* and *hamburguesas,* the latter lacquered with avocado slices in the way slices of cheddar cover burgers.

Neither of those establishments are paragons of the Houston form. But given the milieu in which they work and the customers they serve, both are worthy of attention. These trucks—and the dozens of other working-class eating conveyances on wheels I've visited while wandering around Houston—dish everyday indulgences. They serve the sustenance of daily life as lived in America by émigrés of Mexican birth. They are not faddish. They are not fey. And they matter.

Until very recently, Houston did not support a large cadre of New Wave food trucks. There were, of course, exceptions, like Haute Texan Tacos, brainchild of Jason Jones, where the specialty is an avocado half, stuffed with seasoned ground beef and *pico de gallo,* battered, and

then deep-fried. And then there's Oh my! Pocket Pies, which opened in December of 2009, selling the love child of freezer case Hot Pockets and South American empanadas, which engird everything from Salisbury steak to the constituent ingredients in a chile relleno. Both hold promise. Both have honed good shticks. In Houston, however, traditional trucks continue to hold sway.

The curious eaters of Texas appear to be more focused on digging into the diversity of their taco truck offerings—on seeking out the sweetbread tacos dished up by the truck that parks near the produce mart, on tracking down the mythical *barbacoa* vendor who still smokes cow heads in subterranean chambers—than playing tag with the next new thing.

- - - - - - - - - - - - - - - - - - -

Left to Right:

Top: Porky loves a taco. *Elotes en vaso.*

Middle: Frito pie in the making. A lineup of liquid refreshment.

Bottom: Spoonful of sweets. *Elotes* will likely make you sing.

TACOS ADOBADO

LIKE MOST SEATTLE BUSES, Tacos El Asadero focuses on *mulitas*. Tacos prepared *adobado* style are also a common component of the local repertoire. These are comparable to tacos prepared in the "pasture style," known as *al pastor*.

Bus space is tight.

MAKES 15 TO 20 SMALL TACOS

2 cups diced onion

2 tablespoons minced garlic

1 teaspoon ground cinnamon

2 teaspoons ground cumin

2 teaspoons dried coriander

2 teaspoons dried oregano

2 tablespoons chili powder

1 teaspoon salt

1 tablespoon honey

2 tablespoons red wine vinegar

3 pounds pork butt or loin, cut into chunks

3 cups chicken broth or water

15 to 20 small (4 to 6 inches each) corn tortillas, store-bought or homemade (page 87)

Salsa of your choice

6 radishes, trimmed and thinly sliced, for serving

LAST SEEN: 3517 Ranier Avenue South, Seattle, Washington

TACOS EL ASADERO

THIS IS UTILITARIAN DESIGN at its best: A trash can occupies the driver's seat in Tacos El Asadero's teardrop-shaped white bus. A neon sign flashes from the passenger side of the windshield. Ten stools line the front of the bus. A kitchen, dominated by a flattop grill, occupies the rear. On a metal shelf by the kitchen entrance, pickled carrots and jalapeños bob in a jar.

Chicken benefits from the taco truck treatment, too.

TACO TRUCK PRIMER

YOU'VE GRADUATED from hard-shell tacos, overstuffed with pebbled beef and counterfeit salsa. Left them behind along with other childish things, like aerosol cheese and clip-on bow ties. Now, you're ready to begin a lifelong study of honest Mexican food. You've done the groundwork. You're a vet of the bodega circuit. With a working knowledge of piñata iconography. And a taste for Mexican *queso*. And an appreciation for Mexican Coca-Cola, sweetened with sugar, not corn syrup.

Taco trucks are the next step. Forget "roach coach" talk. That's for incurious eaters. And xenophobes. Your palate knows better. You recognize taco trucks for what they are: Rolling exhibitions of provincial Mexican cookery. Quick-service restaurants on wheels that charge a pittance and brook no compromise. Delivery systems for diminutive corn tortillas.

Soft, still warm from the *comal,* those tortillas taste like minor masterpieces. With griddled beef nestled inside, a splash of *salsa roja,* and chopped sharp white onions and cool green cilantro, taco truck tacos taste like your future. Heaped with crumbled chorizo, sluiced with *salsa verde,* served with a side of radishes and a spritz of lime, they're also reproducible in your home kitchen.

A flattop is key to taco truck cookery.

1 Place the onions, garlic, cinnamon, cumin, coriander, oregano, chili powder, salt, honey, and vinegar in a large mixing bowl and stir to mix. Add the pork to the marinade and massage it well into the meat. Cover the bowl and let the pork marinate in the refrigerator overnight.

2 Preheat the oven to 350°F.

3 Place the pork with its marinating liquid in a baking dish. Add 1 cup of chicken broth or water and bake until very tender, 1 to 2 hours (pork loin will cook faster than pork butt). Check the pork every 30 minutes and if it seems too dry, add more broth or water to the baking dish. Remove the pork from the liquid, discarding the liquid. Let the pork rest for about 30 minutes, then chop or shred it.

4 Heat a skillet over medium heat and warm the tortillas one at a time in the skillet until pliable, about 30 seconds on each side. As you work, wrap the tortillas in a clean kitchen towel to keep them warm.

5 To assemble the tacos, put some of the meat on each tortilla. Serve the tacos with salsa and radishes as desired.

PICKLED CARROTS AND JALAPENOS

YOU'LL NOTICE A JUG of pickled carrots and jalapeños on the counter of many a taco truck. Use the tongs to reach in and grab a few carrot coins and a couple of jalapeños. They're free for the taking, a Mexican analog to the pickle that comes with a deli pastrami on rye. This recipe was inspired by the counter treats at Tacos El Asadero.

A teardrop rear.

Read about the Tacos El Asadero truck on page 228.

MAKES ABOUT 3 CUPS

3/4 pound carrots, peeled and sliced diagonally

3/4 pound jalapeño peppers, stemmed, seeded, and sliced

4 scallions, both white and green parts, trimmed and chopped

I tablespoon kosher salt

I cup distilled white vinegar

1/2 teaspoon black peppercorns

1/2 teaspoon cumin seeds

3 bay leaves

2 whole cloves

1/2 teaspoon dried thyme

1/2 teaspoon dried oregano

1/2 teaspoon brown sugar

1/4 cup canola oil

5 cloves garlic, peeled

1 Place the carrots, jalapeños, scallions, and salt in a large mixing bowl and toss to mix, making sure the salt is well distributed. Let the mixture sit for 1 hour.

2 Put the vinegar, peppercorns, cumin seeds, bay leaves, whole cloves, thyme, oregano, brown sugar, and 1/4 cup of water in a blender and pulse until pureed. Set the vinegar mixture aside.

3 Heat the oil in a large skillet over medium-high heat until hot but not smoking. Drain the carrot and jalapeño mixture, setting aside the juices in a separate bowl. Add the carrot and jalapeño mixture to the skillet and cook until slightly softened, about 2 minutes. Add the garlic cloves and cook for a couple of minutes longer. Add the vinegar mixture and the reserved juices from the carrot and jalapeño mixture and cook until well blended, about 5 minutes. The vegetables should still be slightly firm.

4 Let the carrots and jalapeños cool in the liquid, then place them in a large glass container with a lid and let pickle in the refrigerator for at least 24 hours. The carrot and jalapeño pickles can be refrigerated, covered, for up to 3 months.

MULITAS CARNITAS

THE WORD *CARNITAS* translates from the Spanish as little meats. And the meat here is pork. In Mexico, traditional cooks prepare *carnitas* in giant copper pots. In America, Crock-Pots are commonly used. In this recipe, inspired by El Camión, a hint of citrus cuts what little greasiness lingers. And, in case you're wondering, *mulitas* might best be understood as sandwich-style tacos.

You might also like to add sauteed onions to your *carnitas*.

LAST SEEN: 2918 1st Avenue South, Seattle, Washington

EL CAMION

"I WAS AT THE HOME DEPOT when I made the connection," El Camión proprietor Scott McGinnis told me. "Working as a builder, I was making a lot of Home Depot runs. And I got to thinking, 'Why am I eating those roller hot dogs three days in a row? I can do better.'"

Scott's response was an homage to traditional Mexican cookery, tucked into a jet-black trailer. "I wanted to make taco truck food more approachable," he said. At the time of this writing, Scott has three locations, one next door to the Home Depot north of town, another in the emerging Seattle SoDo district, a third in Ballard in the northwest part of Seattle.

At the SoDo location, in sight of the Starbucks headquarters, he has installed a foosball table for idling cubicle dwellers. At both locations, he follows the lead of chief cook Anna Osoro, a native of Oaxaca. She's an expert in *moles* and banana leaf–wrapped tamales and also, by the way, makes a peerless chorizo.

Another kind of Mexican folk art.

MAKES 6 SMALL MULITAS

2 tablespoons vegetable oil

2 pounds pork shoulder, cut into large chunks

1 quart beef broth

2 cups chunky tomato salsa

1 tablespoon salt

1 tablespoon freshly ground black pepper

12 small (4 to 6 inches each) corn tortillas, store-bought or homemade (page 87)

1 cup shredded Jack cheese

1 avocado, peeled, pitted, and sliced

Lime wedges

1 Heat the oil in a large saucepan over medium-high heat. Add the pork and cook, turning once, until browned, 4 to 5 minutes. Add the beef broth, salsa, salt, and pepper, and enough water to cover the meat. Bring to a boil and then cover the pan, reduce the heat, and let simmer until the meat is falling apart, 3 to 4 hours. Let cool a little bit, remove the meat from the pan, and discard the cooking liquid.

2 Heat a skillet over medium heat and warm the tortillas one at a time in the skillet until pliable, about 30 seconds on each side. As you work, wrap the tortillas in a clean kitchen towel to keep them warm. Coarsely chop the meat, then add it to the skillet and cook it until the meat is heated through and the edges caramelize.

3 Working in batches if necessary, assemble the *mulitas:* Place a tortilla on a hot griddle or skillet and sprinkle some cheese over it. Let the cheese melt a little, then put some meat on top of it. Arrange avocado slices on top of the meat and squeeze lime juice over the avocado and meat. Top each *mulita* with another tortilla, carefully flip them, and toast until the cheese is melted and the bottom tortillas are beginning to brown, 3 to 5 minutes. Repeat with the remaining tortillas, cheese, meat, and avocado slices.

URBANIZATION AND THE TACO TRUCK DIET: Eating in Proximity

IN 1900 one of every eight people in the world lived in a city. By 2000 the ratio was one of every two. That rapid-paced urbanization has been one of the driving forces behind the American street food phenomenon, too. As American cities have expanded in both population and surface girth, workers have had a harder time returning home for lunch. And they're more inclined to stop off on their way from work and haul dinner home for all.

In years past that reality drove the lunch wagon and diner trade in the northeastern United States. More recently urbanization has been a driving force in areas of the U.S. where Hispanic laborers now provide most of the muscle, as both soccer moms and Jalisco-born landscaping crews alike embrace the taco truck diet.

FRIED AVOCADO TACOS

AVOCADOS DON'T HOLD up well to the heat of cooking. That's the proverbial wisdom, disproved by Michael Rypka, from whom this recipe was adapted. Wander around Austin and you'll note that a number of New Wave taco wagons try this fried avocado trick. None is as successful as Torchy's Tacos.

Look for the little devil.

MAKES 6 SMALL TACOS

I cup all-purpose flour

I teaspoon salt

I teaspoon freshly ground black pepper

1/2 teaspoon cayenne pepper

2 large eggs, lightly beaten

1/4 cup milk

2 cups panko (Japanese bread crumbs)

2 ripe but firm Hass avocados

I quart vegetable oil, for frying

6 small (4 to 6 inches each) corn tortillas, store-bought or homemade (page 87)

I can (15 ounces) vegetarian refried beans, heated

2 cups shredded iceberg lettuce

I cup Calexico Pico de Gallo (page 222)

I cup shredded cheddar or Jack cheese

Poblano Ranch Sauce (recipe follows)

Torchy's menu of neo-traditional tacos.

1 Mix the flour, salt, black pepper, and cayenne in a small, shallow bowl and set aside.

2 Place the eggs and milk in another bowl and whisk to mix. Set the egg wash aside. Place the *panko* in a third shallow bowl and set it aside.

TORCHY'S TACOS

MICHAEL RYPKA, a cofounder of Torchy's Tacos, likes to talk about the divide between the east side and the west side of Austin. He told me that there have always been great tacos in east Austin, especially along Cesar Chavez Street, which threads through the Hispanic heart of the city. And he told me that he has long made early morning and late night runs to the east side, for *tacos al pastor* and *tacos barbacoa.* "What we're doing," Rypka told me, is "paying tribute to the east side style in a west side kind of way."

Set on the dirt and gravel grounds of a onetime auto repair shop, flanked by a horseshoe pit, a fire pit, and picnic tables, and cordoned off by a chicken wire fence, Torchy's Tacos is the anchor tenant of the self-styled and ironically named South Austin Trailer Park & Eatery.

3 Heat the oil in a deep fryer or Dutch oven over high heat until a deep fry thermometer attached to the side of the pot registers 350°F.

4 Peel and pit the avocados. Cut each half lengthwise into 6 slices. Dredge the avocado slices in the seasoned flour, dip them in the egg wash, and then in the *panko.* Working in batches and being careful not to overcrowd the pot, carefully add the avocado slices to the hot oil and cook until golden brown, about 1 minute. Using a slotted spoon, transfer the cooked avocado slices to paper towels to drain.

5 Heat a skillet over medium heat and warm the tortillas one at a time in the skillet until pliable, about 30 seconds on each side. As you work, wrap the tortillas in a clean kitchen towel to keep them warm.

6 To assemble the tacos, put 1 tablespoon of warm beans, 2 slices of fried avocado, and then some lettuce, *pico de gallo,* and cheese on each tortilla. Drizzle the Poblano Ranch Sauce over the tacos before serving.

Poblano Ranch Sauce

MUCH OF THE FOOD of Austin falls under the loose rubric of Tex-Mex. This dipping sauce and salad dressing, adapted from Mike Rypka, tastes decidedly more Tex than Mex.

MAKES ABOUT 1 CUP

1 poblano pepper

1 cup store-bought ranch dressing

1 serrano pepper, chopped

1 Roast the poblano pepper over the open flame of a gas burner or place it under the broiler until evenly charred, 3 to 4 minutes per side, 9 to 12 minutes in all, turning with tongs. Let the poblano cool, then remove the charred skin and stem and coarsely chop the pepper.

2 Place the ranch dressing, the chopped poblano, and the serrano pepper in a blender and puree until smooth. The sauce can be refrigerated, covered, for up to 1 month.

FRUITVALE PLATING SCHEMES:
Thoughts on Taco Composition

WALKING ALONG International Boulevard in the Fruitvale neighborhood of Oakland, drinking from a foam cup full of *champurrado,* a hot, chocolate-flavored, masa-thickened, cane sugar–sweetened drink, I first began to notice the careful composition of taco plates. I'm not saying these were the first artfully composed tacos I had eaten. I'm saying that Tacos El Grullo, at the corner of International and 26th Avenue, served the first plate of tacos I ever really noticed.

The palette was a fluted white paper plate. An *al pastor* taco was placed at six o'clock, a *cabeza* taco at three. A wedge of lime and a white packet of salt marked the twelve o'clock position. Radish slices, red at their edges, snowy at their cores, were shingled between the tacos. Overlapping were coins of pickled carrot and ropes of sliced and pickled onion. A pickled jalapeño, emerald green with a corkscrew stem, anchored the plate alongside a stewed onion, relieved of its husk.

That composition came together in haste, arriving through the window of the truck parked opposite a radiator repair shop. But it was presented with care, an awareness for spatial relationships, and an eye for color. It was an ephemeral work of art, consumed in six bites.

BENEATH CHOPPED LETTUCE AND TOMATOES LURK CRESCENTS OF FRIED AVOCADO.

HOISIN SAUCE AMPLIFIES THE NATURAL SWEETNESS OF ROASTED DUCK.

ROAST DUCK TACOS

THE INSPIRATION IS *MU SHU* DUCK, a hoisin-swabbed staple of Chinese-American restaurants. Jonathan Ward, whose recipe you will find here, buys his duck each morning at a restaurant in Chinatown. Back at the kitchen, he picks the carcass clean of meat. If you don't have access to the sort of Chinese restaurant that displays lacquered ducks in the window, go ahead and roast your own.

Jonathan Ward, duck fiend.

Bold design benefits a bold idea.

MAKES 12 SMALL TACOS

I whole roast duck (about 2 pounds)

I bunch scallions

Ice water

12 small (4 to 6 inches each) corn tortillas, store-bought or homemade (page 87; see Note)

2 cups Mango Salsa (recipe follows)

3/4 cup Spicy Hoisin Sauce (page 239)

1 Pull all of the duck meat off of the bones and discard the bones. Shred the duck meat and set it aside.

2 Cut the green parts off the scallions, setting the white parts aside for another use. Cut the scallion greens into 3-inch pieces, then slice them lengthwise into very thin strips. If desired, place the scallion slivers in a small bowl of ice water and set them aside. The ice water will curl the scallion slivers in a lovely way.

3 Heat a skillet over medium heat and warm the tortillas one at a time in the skillet until pliable, about 30 seconds on each side. As you work, wrap the tortillas in a clean kitchen towel to keep them warm.

4 Place a small amount of the shredded

Roasted ducks on display.

duck on each of the warm tortillas, spoon on some Mango Salsa, then drizzle about a tablespoon of the Spicy Hoisin Sauce on top. Garnish each tortilla with a few of the scallion slivers.

NOTE: You can substitute flour tortillas for the corn ones.

Mango Salsa

THIS SALSA PLAYS WELL off the duck. Of course, the pairing of sweet and gamy flavors is traditional. Come to think of it, that may be the only traditional taste that comes off Kung Fu Tacos' bright yellow truck.

MAKES ABOUT 2 CUPS

2 firm red mangoes, peeled, pitted, and diced
I cucumber, peeled and diced
I red onion, diced
I jalapeño pepper, stemmed, seeded, and diced
I bunch fresh cilantro, leaves only, chopped
2 tablespoons freshly squeezed lime juice
I teaspoon kosher salt
1/4 teaspoon freshly ground black pepper

Combine the mangoes, cucumber, red onion, and jalapeño in a mixing bowl. Add the cilantro, lime juice, salt, and black pepper and mix gently to incorporate. The salsa can be refrigerated, covered, for up to 2 days.

LAST SEEN: At the corner of Sacramento and Montgomery Streets, San Francisco, California

KUNG FU TACOS

ONE SUMMER DAY IN 2009 Jonathan Ward, a dot-com bust survivor, and Tan Truong, proprietor of the Candybar, a dessert and cocktail lounge in the San Francisco neighborhood known as the Western Addition, planned a road trip to Los Angeles to feed at the Kogi food truck altar. But they pulled up short, Jonathan told me, when they realized they already had their own formula.

"My wife is Chinese," Jonathan said. "But I was thinking about Korean tacos.

Why would I try Korean tacos when I could try Chinese tacos? So I texted Tan. I wrote 'char siu taco.' And he wrote back 'brilliant.'" By August, the partners had purchased a twenty-five-year-old taco truck, refurbished it, coined the name Kung Fu Tacos, and hit the streets, selling *Nun Chuk Chicken* and *Wu Shu Char Siu.*

Spicy Hoisin Sauce

HOISIN SAUCE IS DARK BROWN, almost black, in color and sweet on the tongue. Soy is a primary flavoring. And so is sugar. Taking into account the sweetness, some call this stuff Chinese barbecue sauce. Jonathan Ward of Kung Fu Tacos uses Lee Kum Kee brand hoisin. But he wisely cuts the sugar with a searing hit of Sriracha.

MAKES 1½ CUPS

1 cup hoisin sauce
1/2 cup Sriracha hot sauce

Place the hoisin sauce and the Sriracha in a small mixing bowl and mix well. The sauce can be refrigerated, covered, for up to 1 week.

A duck gets cut up by well-placed whacks with a cleaver.

A HIGH NOON BEAUTY SHOT.

HIGH NOON QUESADILLAS

I ATE QUESADILLAS like these a couple of times. Once at eleven in the evening, while standing outside a downtown Los Angeles bar, another time at high noon, sitting on a curb in Santa Monica. I saw Roy Choi of Kogi cook this dish only once, though—at a CIA conference in Napa, where the Culinary Institute has its California headquarters. Roy wowed an industry crowd with both forethought and technique.

You could argue that pork *al pastor*, which translates from the Spanish as shepherd's style, is a fusion dish of long heritage in Mexico. One prevailing theory of origin is that Lebanese migrants brought spit-roasted meat with them to Mexico. From there, it was a hop and a skip to Roy Choi's East Los Angeles truck.

Read about the Kogi truck on page 212.

MAKES 4 QUESADILLAS

FOR THE PORK AL PASTOR

6 cups Kalbi Marinade (page 99)

2 cups kochojang (see Notes)

$1/2$ cup kochukaru (see Notes)

3 jalapeño peppers, stemmed and cut in half

$1/2$ cup whole cloves garlic, peeled

$1/2$ cup granulated sugar

$2 1/2$ pounds pork butt, sliced $1/8$-inch thick

$1 1/2$ pounds pork belly, sliced $1/8$-inch thick

FOR THE QUESADILLAS

2 tablespoons canola oil

4 cups diced onions

4 large (12 inches each) flour tortillas

4 cups grated cheddar Jack cheese

2 cups chopped fresh cilantro

Salsa Verde (recipe follows)

4 teaspoons sesame seeds, toasted (see Notes)

4 lime wedges, for serving

1 Make the pork *al pastor*: Combine the *kalbi* marinade, *kochojang*, *kochukaru*, jalapeños, garlic, and sugar in a blender and puree until smooth.

2 Place the pork butt and belly in a large bowl and pour the marinade over it. Massage the marinade into the pork, as Roy says, "with heart and soul" until fully covered. Let the pork marinate in the refrigerator, covered, for at least 2 hours.

3 Make the quesadillas: Heat the oil in a cast-iron skillet or on a griddle over medium-high heat. Remove the pork from the marinade, discarding the marinade. Pat dry with paper towels. Cook the pork and onions, turning several times, until the meat is cooked through

and the onions are browned, about 8 minutes. Transfer the pork and onion mixture to a bowl.

4 Place a tortilla in the skillet or on the griddle and arrange 1 cup of cheese on top of the tortilla. Place one quarter of the pork and onions on the cheese and top it with 1/2 cup of the cilantro. Fold the tortilla in half to cover the filling. Cook the quesadilla over medium heat, turning once, until both sides are browned and the cheese is melted, about 2 minutes per side. Repeat with the remaining tortillas, cheese, pork mixture, and cilantro.

5 Transfer the quesadilla to a plate and cut into 4 wedges. Drizzle some *salsa verde* over the top of each. Garnish the quesadillas with the sesame seeds and serve them with the lime wedges.

NOTES: *Kochojang,* a thick Korean chile paste, is often used as a soup base. *Kochukaru,* Korean crushed red chile flakes, are used when making kimchi. Both are available at Asian groceries.

To toast the sesame seeds, set a dry skillet over medium heat (do not use a nonstick skillet for this). Add the sesame seeds and heat them, tossing occasionally, until lightly toasted and aromatic, 3 to 5 minutes. Keep an eye on the sesame seeds; you don't want them to burn. Transfer the toasted sesame seeds to a heatproof bowl to cool.

ROADSTOVES: Outfitter to the Truck Food Stars

AT FIVE IN the morning the parking lot behind the Cater Craft, located underneath the Santa Monica Freeway, was jammed with food trucks. Nom Nom Truck, Dogtown Dogs, Asian Soul Kitchen, Yum Yum Bowls, and Baby's Badass Burgers were all there—along with a dozen or so regular old taco trucks and a dozen or more other nouveau trucks.

Parked near the entrance, in the ogle-friendly manner that the valet man at Ma Maison used to park the Rolls-Royces, was the fleet of Kogi food trucks. (Deeper in was the Calbi truck, one of the Kogi imitators, and the Kabob truck, which claims "Mexi-terranean fusion flair.") On the opposite end of the lot was the Cater Craft commissary, where trucks stock up on everything from ten-pound coils of chorizo, to quart bags of udon noodles, to pouches of instant *atole*, used to make that masa and chocolate drink.

Cater Craft, founded in 1956, built its business sending food trucks to construction sites. "It used to go like this," proprietor Herman Appel told me. "There would be a construction site in the middle of nowhere with a thousand men working. We'd put three trucks out there, serving burgers, whatever. And we'd make a killing."

A few years back, when construction catering slowed and some of their trucks began to sit idle, Josh Hiller, an attorney, and Morris Appel, son of Herman, conceived RoadStoves. "What we did was flip the trucks," Josh said. "We just rebranded them and sold them to a new audience." In the wake of the Kogi phenomenon, the truck food business had gotten a bit more glamorous, Herman said. "But in the end, it still reminds me of how when two hookers fight for a corner, the stronger one survives."

RoadStoves is now a one-stop shop for the new class of so-called gourmet food trucks. They will lease you a truck. They will gussy up said truck, adding your custom wrap. They will also secure permits and licenses and teach you viral marketing tricks. When your truck breaks down they'll repair it. When you clip a car while taking a tight turn, they'll bend out your bumper.

RoadStoves is quite good at what they do. Based on their work with Kogi, momentum is building. When last I saw Josh, he was plotting expansion of the Roadstoves concept to other markets. Atlanta was tops on his list. And Washington, D.C. was close behind.

An uncharacteristically short Kogi line.

Salsa Verde

KOGI WAS VERY GENEROUS with techniques and recipes. They refused few requests. "I can't say what's in our *salsa roja,*" Roy Choi told me. "I got to keep something in my pocket." I didn't have the heart to tell him that I like the green stuff better, anyway.

MAKES ABOUT 2 CUPS

I cup canola oil

I cup peeled whole garlic cloves

1/4 cup coarsely chopped yellow onion

2 jalapeño peppers, stemmed, seeded, and cut in half

6 bunches fresh cilantro, chopped

1/4 cup sesame seeds, toasted (see Note)

1/2 cup kosher salt

2/3 cup freshly squeezed lime juice

2/3 cup freshly squeezed orange juice

1 Heat the oil in a small saucepan over medium-low heat. Add the garlic and cook, stirring constantly, until deep brown, 2 to 3 minutes. Set the garlic oil aside and let cool.

2 Char the onion and jalapeños in a dry cast-iron skillet over medium-high heat until nearly black, 5 to 7 minutes. Remove the onion and jalapeños from the heat and let cool.

3 When the garlic oil and the onion and jalapeños are cool enough to handle, put them and the cilantro, sesame seeds, salt, lime juice, and orange juice in a blender and puree until smooth. The salsa can be refrigerated, covered, for 1 week.

N O T E : To toast the sesame seeds, see Notes on the facing page.

LOS ANGELES:
WHERE TACO TRUCKS BUILD THEIR BRANDS

There are two ways to tell this story. And both are true. Tell the tale one way and Los Angeles emerges as the epicenter of working-class taco truck culture, a city where a spring drive down a boulevard smells of night-blooming jasmine and chorizo grease.

A city where a night on the town in the fall ends with a squeal of tires on La Cienega Boulevard and the promise of *tlayudas* for ballast and the masa-thickened drink *atole* for warmth.

That story heralds recent immigrants, who decorate the backs of their trucks with murals of the town squares around which their hometowns sprawl. That story brings into focus the Mexican men and women who are rendered on the hoods of those trucks, in color-saturated silhouettes, butchering pigs for slaughter, slicing *puerco al pastor* from spits, and kneading masa for tortillas.

In working-class Los Angeles tacos are not objects of fetishization. They're *mulitas* stuffed with *cabeza* for lunch. They're *tacos al pastor* for dinner. They're a taste of home for a forlorn native of Michoacán—a landscape contractor who would otherwise have had to settle for a cheeseburger.

Tell the tale another way, and you meet Brook Howell and Erik Cho, the young married couple behind the relatively new Frysmith truck. Both are graduates of UC Berkeley. Brook previously worked for a magazine and Erik worked in the film industry.

In modern LA opening a food truck that builds its brand around carefully composed french-fry dishes was a logical next step for a young and hip couple. And so was developing a repertoire that includes vegan chili fries with soyrizo (soy "chorizo"),

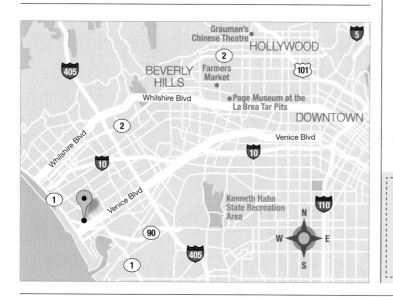

WHERE THE TRUCKS ARE:

Outside The Brig: Abbot Kinney Boulevard near the intersection of Venice Boulevard.

Other locations vary wildly. Check roaminghunger.com.

fries with *shawarma,* and kimchi fries with pork belly, cheddar, and well, kimchi.

Tell the tale that hipster way and you're soon standing on line for a *bánh mì* at the Nom Nom Truck, parked in Santa Monica at the back door of MTV Studios. A moment ago, a Mercedes S-Class Coupe parked behind the truck.

Now, two men, wearing black T-shirts and pressed jeans, are eating an impromptu lunch on the trunk lid, swapping bites of grilled pork *bánh mì* for bites of lemongrass chicken *bánh mì.* As they eat, David Strankunas, one of the three young entrepreneurs behind Nom Nom Truck, talks inspiration and business strategy.

David is half Vietnamese. So is one of his partners. The third is half Chinese. They met at the UCLA Hapa club. (Hapa is the Hawaiian word for half, used to describe anyone of mixed heritage with partial Asian ancestry.)

Like many New Guard trucks, David and his cohorts looked to the Kogi fleet for inspiration. These are social media hounds. They give good Twitter. They make a good sandwich. But they are even better marketers, an observation that David does not reject. "I'm all about building the brand," David told me. "That's what we're doing with this truck, building the Nom Nom brand. If we wanted to open a brick and mortar now, we'd get buzz. But if we had gone with a brick and mortar first and then tried to open a truck, nothing."

And so it goes in Los Angeles, where some new immigrants carry forward the taco truck tradition. And other new immigrants forge an edible revolution, trackable by all who follow Twitter.

- - - - - - - - - - - - - - - - - -

Left to Right:
Top Row: Kogi, window view. Bánh on wheels.

Middle Row: Dogtown at the ready. The Mexican standard.

Bottom Row: Buttermilk—it's not just for cornbread.

KIMCHI QUESADILLAS

THIS COMBO IS NOT THAT ODD. In Hawaii, where Kamala Saxton grew up, cooks have long garnished cheeseburgers with kimchi. From there, it's a quick hop to kimchi quesadillas. Of course, Marination Mobile is not the sole kimchi quesadilla vendor roaming America's streets. Kogi in LA does one, too. So does KOi fusion in Seattle. But I prefer the Marination Mobile style, with crescents of jalapeño atop. Their good work inspired this recipe.

Marination with overhanging fall foliage.

MAKES 4 QUESADILLAS

4 tablespoons (1/2 stick) unsalted butter

2 cups store-bought kimchi, drained and chopped

2 cups grated cheddar cheese

2 cups grated Jack cheese

4 medium-size (8 inches each) flour tortillas

1/4 cup sesame seeds, toasted (see Note)

Vegetable oil

1 Melt the butter in a large skillet over medium-high heat. Add the kimchi and cook until heated through and slightly softened, about 5 minutes. Let the kimchi cool.

Read about the Marination Mobile truck on page 103.

2 Mix the cheddar and Jack cheeses together. Spoon about 1/2 cup of the kimchi on one half of a tortilla. Sprinkle some of the sesame seeds over the kimchi and top this with 1 cup of the cheese mixture. Fold the tortilla in half to cover the filling. Repeat with the remaining tortillas, kimchi, sesame seeds, and cheese.

3 Put a little oil in the bottom of a nonstick skillet and heat over medium heat. Place the quesadillas one at a time in the hot skillet and cook, turning once, until both sides are browned and the cheese is melted, about 2 minutes per side. Transfer each quesadilla to a plate and cut each into 4 wedges.

N O T E : To toast the sesame seeds, set a dry skillet over medium heat (do not use a nonstick skillet for this). Add the sesame seeds and heat them until lightly toasted and aromatic, tossing occasionally, 3 to 5 minutes. Keep an eye on the sesame seeds; you don't want them to burn. Transfer the toasted sesame seeds to a heatproof bowl to cool.

FRITO PIE

ROBB WALSH SCHOOLED ME in the ways of Frito pie. This recipe, inspired by one in his *The Tex-Mex Cookbook: A History in Recipes and Photos,* recalls the Frito pie we ate one afternoon at Refresqueria Rio Verde. While we ate, Robb traced the history of the Frito pie back to Daisy Dean Doolin. She was the mother of C. E. "Elmer" Doolin, the man from Texas who introduced America to Fritos in 1932.

Smothering a generous amount of cheese with a heavy ladle full of chili.

MAKES I FRITO PIE

I single-serving bag (2 ounces) original flavor Fritos

1/2 cup chile con queso, or 1/2 cup grated cheddar cheese

1/2 cup Rio Verde Chili con Carne (recipe follows)

I tablespoon chopped onion

5 pickled jalapeño slices, chopped

Cut open the bag of Fritos lengthwise down the side. Ladle in the cheese, then the chili. Top with the onion and jalapeño slices. Dig the good stuff out of the bag with a plastic spoon, occasionally wiping your hands on your jeans.

📍 **LAST SEEN**: 8315 Long Point Road, Houston, Texas

REFRESQUERIA RIO VERDE

PICTURE A COUNTY FAIR TRAILER, the kind that peddles kettle-popped corn and lemonade to middle America. Now move that county fair from the middle of America to the middle of Mexico. That's the vibe at Victoria Galven's Long Point Road snack truck. She sells *raspas,* which are the Mexican equivalent of snow cones. And baked potatoes accessorized with taco truck garnishes. And Frito pies, a dish of Tex-Mex parentage now being adopted by Mexican-born vendors like Victoria.

Rio Verde Chili con Carne

YOU COULD CRACK OPEN A CAN of Wolf's chili, the kind with no beans, but are you really that lazy? The Frito pie is already trashy enough. Ladle on real chili, inspired by Refresqueria Rio Verde.

MAKES 6 SERVINGS

2 pounds beef chuck or blade, chopped

4 tablespoons chili powder

1¹/2 teaspoons ground cumin

1 teaspoon cayenne pepper

1 teaspoon salt

¹/2 teaspoon freshly ground black pepper

1 can (15 ounces) tomato sauce

1 cup beef broth

Brown the beef on all sides in a large skillet over medium-high heat, about 10 minutes. Add the chili powder, cumin, cayenne, salt, and black pepper and stir to coat the beef. Add the tomato sauce and beef broth, reduce the heat, and let simmer, stirring occasionally, until the desired thickness is obtained, about 30 minutes. For a Frito pie, you want a viscous chili. The flavors will improve if the chili is made 1 day ahead. Store the chili, covered, in the refrigerator, but you already know that. Reheat slowly over low heat.

DORILOCOS, NOT TO BE CONFUSED WITH TOSTILOCOS

TACOS MAYRA on Beechnut Street in the Houston exurbs serves *elotes en vasos* in stubby foam cups. The corn tastes canned but the truck boasts great art; painted down the back side is a cartoon menu mural dominated by a feral rendition of Bugs Bunny holding a fruit cocktail. And the proprietors serve a take on dorilocos, a twenty-first-century Mexican food now showing up stateside.

The dorilocos formula is comparable to Frito pie (see page 247), only the bag in question customizes nacho cheese Doritos. In Mexico, a vendor might shovel in chopped cucumbers, roasted peanuts, pickled pig skin, tomato salsa, and a tangle of shredded lettuce. In Houston, dorilocos have devolved. At Tacos Mayra the standard is ground beef chili, sliced jalapeños, and cheese goo. Meanwhile, I'm still on the lookout for a Houston take on the *tostiloco,* based on a bag of Tostitos.

TEAR OPEN A FRITO BAG AND YOU HAVE A MAKESHIFT CHILI BOWL.

A well-frosted red velvet cupcake.

The Choinkwich, Big Gay Ice Cream Truck, New York City.

Your heart's desire.

One of the boys from Merlindia by way of D.C.

ROLLING
IN
Sweets

CHAPTER 8

Cupcakes are overexposed.
Cupcakes are overwrought.
Cupcakes are too much with us.

That's the prevailing wisdom among the food cognoscenti. They're right, of course. Cupcakes went around the cute bend a long while back.

The popularity of cupcakes in truck food circles is of relatively long note. Way back in June of 2009, when this trend was just a pup, Lev Ekster—who says cupcakes were his bread and butter while he was studying at New York Law School—began parking the CupcakeStop, a traveling cupcake truck, on Park Avenue in the 20s. His opening repertoire included red velvet, as well as chocolate peanut butter swirl.

Later that same year, the Cupcake Truck began making the rounds in Philadelphia. Kate Carrara, the proprietor, quit the family law firm to follow her bliss. At about the same time, Sprinkles Cupcakes of Beverly Hills began dispatching a Sprinklesmobile to sell banana-chocolate baubles. And Curbside Cupcakes in D.C. hit the streets in a pink van, dishing key lime–frosted and tie-dye–frosted cupcakes. In their wake have come multitudes.

As more and more young entrepreneurs have opted to do their work in fluted paper cups, a very crowded cupcake field has gotten far more crowded. And a whole lot goofier. All that said, this is not the time to give up on cupcakes. Truth is, they are probably the dessert best suited for walking about.

In the recipes that follow, you'll find just one cupcake recipe. Cheater soft-serve ice cream gets more copy. So do campfire-cooked s'mores. I don't mean to slight cupcakes and cupcake bakers. My intent is to sidestep the trend, not the food.

Tanya Catolos from DaisyCakes in Durham, North Carolina, works the color wheel as well as the pastry bag.

OATMEAL JAMMY COOKIES

TOO MANY STREET VENDORS aspire to grandeur. Of late there's been too much crème brûlée and not enough brownies. This recipe, from The Treats Truck, rights those wrongs. Oatmeal jam cookies are elemental. They're satisfying. And they're eminently portable.

The silver bullet at rest.

MAKES ABOUT 3 DOZEN COOKIES

2 cups (4 sticks) butter

1 3/4 cups firmly packed brown sugar

1/4 cup granulated sugar

4 large eggs

1 tablespoon plus 1 teaspoon pure vanilla extract

2 cups all-purpose flour

2 teaspoons baking soda

2 teaspoons ground cinnamon

2 teaspoons salt

6 cups old-fashioned oats

1 cup thick jam of any flavor (raspberry and apricot are especially good)

1 Using an electric mixer on medium speed, cream the butter with the brown and granulated sugars. Add the eggs and vanilla and mix until smooth.

Cookies for the people on the streets of Manhattan.

2 In a separate bowl, combine the flour, baking soda, cinnamon, and salt. Gradually add the flour mixture to the butter mixture followed by the oats and mix until well combined. Refrigerate the cookie dough for 15 to 20 minutes to firm up.

3 Preheat the oven to 350°F.

4 When ready to bake, place tablespoon-size scoops of cookie dough on ungreased baking sheets about ½ inch apart. Make a little indentation in the middle of each and spoon a dollop of jam in the center. Bake the cookies until golden brown, 8 to 10 minutes.

5 Let the cookies cool on the baking sheets for 5 minutes, then transfer them to wire racks to cool completely. Repeat the process until you've baked all of the cookie dough. The cookies can be stored in an airtight container for up to 1 week.

Kim Ima at The Treats Truck window.

LAST SEEN: Fifth Avenue and 22nd Street, New York, New York

THE TREATS TRUCK

IN 2007 KIM IMA, an actress and director, drove a compressed natural gas–fueled truck nicknamed Sugar from a bakery and commissary in Red Hook, Brooklyn, onto the streets of Midtown Manhattan. "A few years back I was baking for the theaters I worked with," she told the *New York Sun*. "I'd bake for the cast of a show and then for a benefit. And then The Treats Truck idea hit me."

"Not too fancy, always delicious!" was the motto Kim chose. "How's my baking?" was her tagline, a rhetorical bumper sticker affixed to the rear of the truck. Her menu boasted middle school bake sale credibility: Rice Krispies treats bound with homemade marshmallow fluff. Peanut butter cookies slathered with jam.

In an effort to make her business accessible to children, Kim cut a small window in the truck and stashed cookie samples at an eye level comfortable for six-year-olds. To secure the devotion of their parents, she began donating 10 percent of the profits from her daily specials to a rotating list of charities.

PEANUT BUTTER SANDWICH COOKIES

VENDORS OF HONEY-ROASTED PEANUTS work Manhattan streets, trailing cirrus clouds of honey-scented steam. I've purchased perfectly good *churros* from subway platform vendors, too. But, on the whole, good street sweets are hard to come by. That's why in just a few short years Kim Ima's Treats Truck has become a de facto institution. Here's her recipe for peanut butter sandwich cookies. These are flourless—you know, gluten free.

An idealized New York street scene.

Read about The Treats Truck on page 255.

MAKES I DOZEN SANDWICH COOKIES

FOR THE COOKIES

2 cups peanut butter (smooth is best)

I cup granulated sugar

2 large eggs

2 teaspoons pure vanilla extract

1/2 teaspoon salt

FOR THE PEANUT BUTTER FILLING

I cup peanut butter

I cup firmly packed brown sugar

Jam of your choice (optional)

1 Preheat the oven to 350°F.

2 Make the cookies: Place the 2 cups of peanut butter and the sugar, eggs, vanilla, and salt in a large mixing bowl and stir to mix. Form the cookie dough into small balls and arrange them on ungreased baking sheets about 1 inch apart. Pat the balls of dough to flatten them, then using a fork, make crisscross marks on top of each. Bake the cookies until lightly browned, 7 to 9 minutes. Let the cookies cool on the baking sheets for 5 minutes, then transfer them to wire racks to cool completely before making the cookie sandwiches.

3 Meanwhile, make the peanut butter filling: Place the 1 cup peanut butter and the brown sugar in a medium-size mixing bowl and stir to mix.

4 To assemble the cookie sandwiches, spread some of the peanut butter filling on the bottom side of a cookie. Top it with the bottom side of another cookie to make a sandwich. You can add a smear of your favorite jam in between, if you're feeling kooky. Repeat with the remaining cookies and filling. The cookies can be stored in an airtight container for up to 1 week.

SWEET POTATO CUPCAKES

WITH TOASTED MERINGUE

CUPCAKES TOO OFTEN TASTE LIKE icing delivery systems posing as credible pastry. Tanya Catolos of DaisyCakes doesn't make that sort of mistake. Her diminutive little beauties are balanced. Nuanced even. Instead of white crumb, her cakes glow golden and boast a mellow sweetness. And that puff of meringue on top trumps a buttercream icing. Trust me.

Tanya and her husband, Konrad, ready to serve.

A bright beacon on the streets of Durham.

MAKES 24 CUPCAKES

FOR THE SWEET POTATO CUPCAKES

2 pounds sweet potatoes

2 cups all-purpose flour

2 teaspoons baking powder

1 teaspoon kosher salt

2 teaspoons ground cinnamon

1/2 teaspoon ground nutmeg

2 cups firmly packed light brown sugar

8 tablespoons (1 stick) unsalted butter, at room temperature

4 large eggs, at room temperature

2 teaspoons pure vanilla extract

Zest of 1 orange

FOR THE TOASTED MERINGUE FROSTING

8 large egg whites

2 cups granulated sugar

2 teaspoons pure vanilla extract

YOU'LL ALSO NEED

Piping bag fitted with a large round or star tip (optional)

Kitchen blowtorch

1 Preheat the oven to 350°F. Line two 12-cup cupcake tins with paper liners.

2 Make the sweet potato cupcakes: Prick each sweet potato several times with a fork. Place the sweet potatoes on an aluminum foil-lined baking sheet and bake until soft, 50 minutes to 1 hour.

3 When the sweet potatoes are cool enough to handle, remove and discard the skins. Place the sweet potatoes in a blender or food processor and puree until smooth. You should have about 2 cups of sweet potato puree.

4 Sift the flour, baking powder, salt, cinnamon, and nutmeg together in a mixing bowl and set aside. Place the brown sugar and butter in a large mixing bowl and, using an electric mixer fitted with a paddle attachment, beat them on medium speed until light and fluffy, about 5 minutes. Add the eggs, one at a time, beating well after each addition. Add the puree, vanilla, and orange zest and beat until incorporated.

5 With the mixer on low speed, add the flour mixture to the sweet potato mixture in 3 batches. After each addition, stop the machine and scrape down the side of the bowl with a rubber spatula. Mix the batter only until the flour is just incorporated.

6 Scoop the batter into the prepared cupcake tins, filling each well about three quarters full. Bake the cupcakes until a toothpick inserted in the center of one comes out with a few crumbs, about 20 minutes. Transfer the cupcakes still in the tins to wire racks to cool.

7 Make the toasted meringue frosting: Place the egg whites and granulated sugar in the top of a double boiler or in a stainless steel bowl set over hot water and heat, stirring, until the sugar crystals dissolve and the egg whites are very warm to the touch, about 5 minutes.

8 Transfer the egg white mixture to a large mixing bowl and beat with an electric mixer on high speed until stiff and glossy, about 10 minutes. Add the vanilla and mix until incorporated.

9 Scoop the meringue into a piping bag fitted with a large round or star tip and pipe swirls of meringue on top of the cupcakes or simply top them with the meringue using a spatula to create swirls and peaks. Use the kitchen blowtorch to "toast" the meringue.

LAST SEEN: Foster and Geer Streets
Durham, North Carolina

DAISYCAKES

IN THIS NEW WORLD order of street food, where thirty-year-old hipsters with three years' experience are elders, Tanya Catolos is a graybeard. Tanya learned her way around the kitchen at, among other restaurants, Bacchanalia in Atlanta. Along with her husband, Konrad Catolos, who is also a chef at the restaurant Piedmont in Durham, Tanya rolled out DaisyCakes, a business built around cupcakes, set in a shiny aluminum Airstream Sovereign.

Cupcakes are her calling card. But she also serves seasonal bread puddings. On the winter day I visited, she served pumpkin bread pudding with vanilla bean custard. She bakes what she calls Pop't Arts, too—postmodern takes on Pop-Tarts filled with orange-cardamom marmalade, strawberry conserves, or Nutella.

In Portland, Oregon, carts telegraph how serious they are about coffee by serving Stumptown, a well-respected hometown roaster. In Durham, Counter Culture Coffee is the tell. And DaisyCakes serves their strong, black stuff with aplomb.

VELVET BALLS

AT HOLY CACAO, Ellen Kinsey and John Spillyards make red velvet cake and cream cheese frosting from scratch. When they began learning to make cake balls they practiced with Duncan Hines red velvet cake mix, cream cheese frosting, and Wilton Candy Melts. Now, they dip the homemade ball-shaped cakes in something called couverture chocolate, sold to the trade by baking supply houses. With their original recipe in hand, you too can make Velvet Balls.

Everything tastes better on a stick.

Shiva likes chocolate, too.

MAKES 50 CAKE BALLS

FOR THE RED VELVET CAKE

3/4 cup (1 1/2 sticks) unsalted butter, at room temperature, plus butter for greasing the cake pan

2 cups granulated sugar

3 large eggs, at room temperature

1 jar (1 ounce) red food coloring

3 tablespoons unsweetened cocoa powder

1 3/4 teaspoons Madagascar vanilla bean paste (see Notes)

1 1/2 teaspoons salt

3 1/2 cups cake flour, sifted

1 1/2 cups buttermilk

1 1/2 teaspoons distilled white vinegar

1 1/2 teaspoons baking soda

FOR THE CREAM CHEESE FROSTING

1 cup (one 8-ounce package) cream cheese, at room temperature

1/3 cup confectioners' sugar, sifted

4 1/2 teaspoons freshly squeezed lemon juice

FOR DIPPING THE CAKE BALLS

1 package (14 ounces) white, dark, or milk chocolate Wilton Candy Melts (see Notes)

50 Popsicle sticks

Sugar crystals (optional), for garnish

1 Preheat the oven to 350°F. Grease a 9 by 13–inch metal baking pan.

2 Make the red velvet cake: Place the sugar and butter in a large mixing bowl and beat with an electric mixer on medium speed until light and fluffy, about 5 minutes. Add the eggs, one at a time, beating well after each addition.

3 Place the red food coloring, cocoa powder, vanilla bean paste, and salt in a small bowl and whisk to mix. Add the cocoa mixture to the butter mixture and beat well.

4 Beat the cake flour and buttermilk into the butter mixture. In a small bowl, stir the vinegar and baking soda together and add this to the batter, beating well to incorporate. Pour the batter into the prepared pan and bake until a cake tester inserted in the center of the cake

Cakes and drinks on special at Holy Cacao.

comes out clean, 30 to 35 minutes. Transfer the cake still in the pan to a wire rack and let it cool completely.

5 Meanwhile, make the cream cheese frosting: Place the cream cheese in a food processor and process until smooth. Add the confectioners' sugar and lemon juice and process until smooth.

LAST SEEN: At the South Austin Trailer Park & Eatery, 1311 South First Street, Austin, Texas

HOLY CACAO

"WE'RE A RESTAURANT that happens to be in a trailer." That's what the woman standing inside a trailer dealing stick-mounted orbs of carrot cake called "rabbit balls" and orbs of icing-shellacked red velvet cake said to me.

Holy Cacao is a smart concept. Ellen Kinsey and John Spillyards are the entrepreneurs behind the concept. In addition to the cake balls, they peddle hot chocolate spiked with ancho chiles and s'mores kits. A fire pit in the gravel lot out front provides the ideal place to dangle a hanger capped with a homemade marshmallow (see page 263).

6 Now comes the messy part: Once the cake has cooled completely, crumble it into a large mixing bowl. If using cake crumbs rather than sugar crystals as garnish, set aside a couple of handfuls of cake crumbs to toast for the topping. Add the cream cheese frosting, 1 tablespoon at a time, to the remaining crumbled cake, pressing it into the cake crumbs and adding enough to produce a mudlike consistency. There will be some frosting left over. Refrigerate the cake crumb mixture, covered, for at least 1 hour.

7 To make the cake balls, use a small scoop or a tablespoon to portion the cake crumb mixture into approximately 1-inch balls, rolling them between your hands to make them as evenly round as possible. Place the cake balls on a baking sheet lined with parchment paper and put them in the freezer for at least 1 hour.

8 Meanwhile, toast the reserved cake crumbs, if using. Preheat the oven to 350°F.

9 Spread the cake crumbs out on a rimmed baking sheet and bake them until crumbly in texture, 5 to 10 minutes.

10 When you're ready to assemble the cake balls, make the dipping mix: Melt the Candy Melts in a microwave oven following the directions on the package.

11 Dip a Popsicle stick halfway into the melted chocolate and then stick the chocolate half into a cake ball. Return the cake ball to the baking sheet, placing it so the Popsicle stick is pointing up. Repeat with the remaining balls of cake. Return the cake balls to the freezer for a few minutes. Then submerge a cake ball in the melted chocolate, shaking off the excess. Dip the very top of the ball in the toasted cake crumbs or the sugar crystals, if desired. Repeat with the remaining cake balls. After the melted chocolate has set, the cake balls are ready to serve.

NOTES: Madagascar vanilla bean paste, which has flecks of the vanilla bean seeds in it, is available online from www.williams-sonoma.com.

Wilton Candy Melts are easy-to-melt candy wafers that are used for cake and candy coatings. They come in a variety of flavors and are sold in Michaels and specialty cake and kitchenware stores. If you can't find them, check out the Wilton website at www.wilton.com.

THE DRAMATIC FIRE PIT AT HOLY CACAO. MARSHMALLOWS, IT SEEMS, ARE COMBUSTIBLE.

S'MORES

BENEATH STRINGS OF WHITE LIGHTS evening customers at Holy Cacao squat alongside a fire pit and toast home-made marshmallows. When those caramelized blobs of gelatin and corn syrup achieve the proper hue, customers of all ages do what kids have done for generations: They top the goo with a slab of chocolate, sandwich the whole between graham crackers, and drip a Rorschach pattern onto the dirt as they eagerly bite into the molten concoction. Here's the game plan for making your own marshmallows, straight from the Holy Cacao folks. The key is having an accurate candy thermometer, preferably one that attaches to the side of the pan.

Holy Cacao takes its s'mores seriously, but manages to be a bit goofball, too.

MAKES ABOUT 24 S'MORES

FOR THE MARSHMALLOWS

Vegetable oil, for coating the baking pan and knife

4 envelopes unflavored gelatin

3 cups granulated sugar

1¼ cups light corn syrup

¼ teaspoon salt

2¼ teaspoons Madagascar vanilla bean paste (see the Notes on page 261)

2 cups confectioners' sugar

FOR THE S'MORES

8 chocolate bars (1.55 ounces each), preferably Hershey's, broken into approximately 2-inch squares

48 graham crackers

1 Make the marshmallows: Lightly coat a 7 by 11–inch metal nonstick baking pan with the oil.

2 Pour ¾ cup of cold water into the mixing bowl of an electric stand mixer. Sprinkle the gelatin over the water and set the bowl aside.

3 Combine the granulated sugar, corn syrup, salt, and ¾ cup of water in a medium-size saucepan and attach a candy thermometer to the side of the pan. Let the mixture come to a boil over high heat, stirring until the sugar dissolves. Cook the sugar syrup without stirring until it registers exactly 238°F on the candy thermometer, about 10 minutes.

4 Attach the mixing bowl with the gelatin mixture to the stand mixer fitted with a paddle attachment. With the mixer running on low speed, pour the hot sugar syrup into the gelatin mixture in a slow, steady stream. Gradually increase the mixer speed to high. Beat the sugar syrup mixture until it is very stiff, about 12 minutes, then beat in the vanilla paste. Pour the mixture into the prepared baking pan and smooth the top with an offset spatula.

Read about the Holy Cacao truck on page 260.

A boatload of s'mores fixings.

VENDY AWARDS:
Fighting for the Right to Vend

STAGED ANNUALLY SINCE 2005, the Vendy Awards celebrate the best street food served in the five boroughs of New York City. It's a fall ceremony that has become a kind of populist alternative to the spring gala at which the James Beard Awards are announced.

As throngs of eaters ping from booth to booth, eating the food of the finalists, a panel of judges confers and anoints winners of, among other awards, the Vendy Cup and the Rookie Vendor of the Year. Compared to other food world awards ceremonies, the Vendy Award winners are more diverse.

Drill down into the literature and you realize that the Vendy Awards are actually a front for the Street Vendor Project, part of the Urban Justice Center, a feisty not-for-profit that organizes vendors, lobbies for their rights, and litigates to change onerous regulations, arguing all the while that the informal economy of street vending is a vital cog in the machine of New York commerce.

On the day I visited the Urban Justice Center, Michael Wells, a staff member and onetime street vendor, was sorting through a box of pink tickets, many of which set a vendor back one thousand dollars. Above him on the wall were two banners. One read "New York Street Vendors Unite," the other "Vendor Power."

Much of the work of Wells and of director Sean Basinski is consumed with disputing wrongfully awarded tickets. But there are also longer-term projects to tackle and big-picture responses to craft. An example of the latter is the Vendor Power! pamphlet, developed with the Center for Urban Pedagogy, a legalese-free how-to that details the regulations under which New York City street vendors must operate.

Set the marshmallow aside, uncovered and at room temperature, until firm, for 3 hours or overnight.

5 Sift 1 cup of confectioners' sugar onto a work surface. Run the tip of a paring knife around the edge of the baking pan to loosen the marshmallow. Unmold the marshmallow onto the work surface. Lightly brush a sharp knife with oil, then cut the marshmallow into 1½-inch squares. Sift the remaining 1 cup of confectioners' sugar into a small, shallow bowl and roll each marshmallow in the sugar to coat. The marshmallows can be stored in an airtight cookie tin with pieces of plastic wrap between each layer. They will keep in the refrigerator for up to 2 weeks.

6 Make the s'mores: Light a campfire (or a backyard grill). Stick a marshmallow on a pronged skewer or the end of a metal hanger that has been straightened out. Toast the marshmallow over the fire until it is softened and browned to taste.

7 Place a square of chocolate on a graham cracker. Place the toasted marshmallow over the chocolate and place a second graham cracker on top. The s'more is now ready to eat. Want s'more? Repeat with the remaining marshmallows, graham crackers, and chocolate.

CARDAMOM-SPICED DOUGHNUTS

THE CHEF SHACK LADIES, Lisa Carlson and Carrie Summer, built their business on doughnuts. Urban Donut was the name of their original enterprise at the Mill City Farmers Market. As Lisa added savory dishes to Carrie's menu of deep-fried sweets, Chef Shack evolved. This recipe, adapted from Chef Shack, produces doughnuts that are creamy at their core, in the manner of old-fashioned cinnamon buns.

The Shack's roster of good tastes.

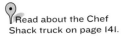

Read about the Chef Shack truck on page 141.

MAKES ABOUT 12 DOUGHNUTS

FOR THE SPICE MIXTURE

1 cup granulated sugar, preferably organic

1 tablespoon ground cinnamon

1 teaspoon ground nutmeg

1 teaspoon ground cardamom

1 teaspoon sea salt

FOR THE DOUGHNUTS

2 cups all-purpose flour, preferably organic, plus flour for cutting out the doughnuts

1/2 cup granulated sugar, preferably organic

1 tablespoon baking powder

1 teaspoon sea salt

2 tablespoons (1/4 stick) butter, melted

1/2 cup milk

1 large egg, lightly beaten

2 quarts vegetable oil, for frying the doughnuts

YOU'LL ALSO NEED

Doughnut cutter

1 Make the spice mixture: Mix the sugar, cinnamon, nutmeg, cardamom, and salt in a large, wide bowl. Set the spice mixture aside.

Diminutive doughnuts, direct from the fryer.

Sugar and spice—that's where you start.

2 Make the doughnuts: Sift the flour, sugar, baking powder, and salt into a large mixing bowl. Stir in the melted butter until just incorporated. Stir in the milk and egg very gently.

3 Lightly flour a work space and a baking sheet. Flour your hands, then lightly knead the doughnut dough in the bowl. Turn the dough out onto the lightly floured work surface and pat the dough into a ¼-inch thickness. Dip a doughnut cutter into flour, cut out doughnut shapes, and transfer them to the floured baking sheet. As you work, gather the scraps of dough together, pat them out again, and cut out more doughnut shapes.

4 Heat the oil in a deep fryer or Dutch oven over high heat until a deep fry thermometer attached to the side of the pot registers 375°F. Working in batches and being careful not to overcrowd the pot, carefully add the doughnuts to the hot oil. Cook the doughnuts until golden brown, about 3 minutes, turning them once. Using a slotted spoon, transfer the doughnuts to paper towels to drain, then toss them in the spice mixture.

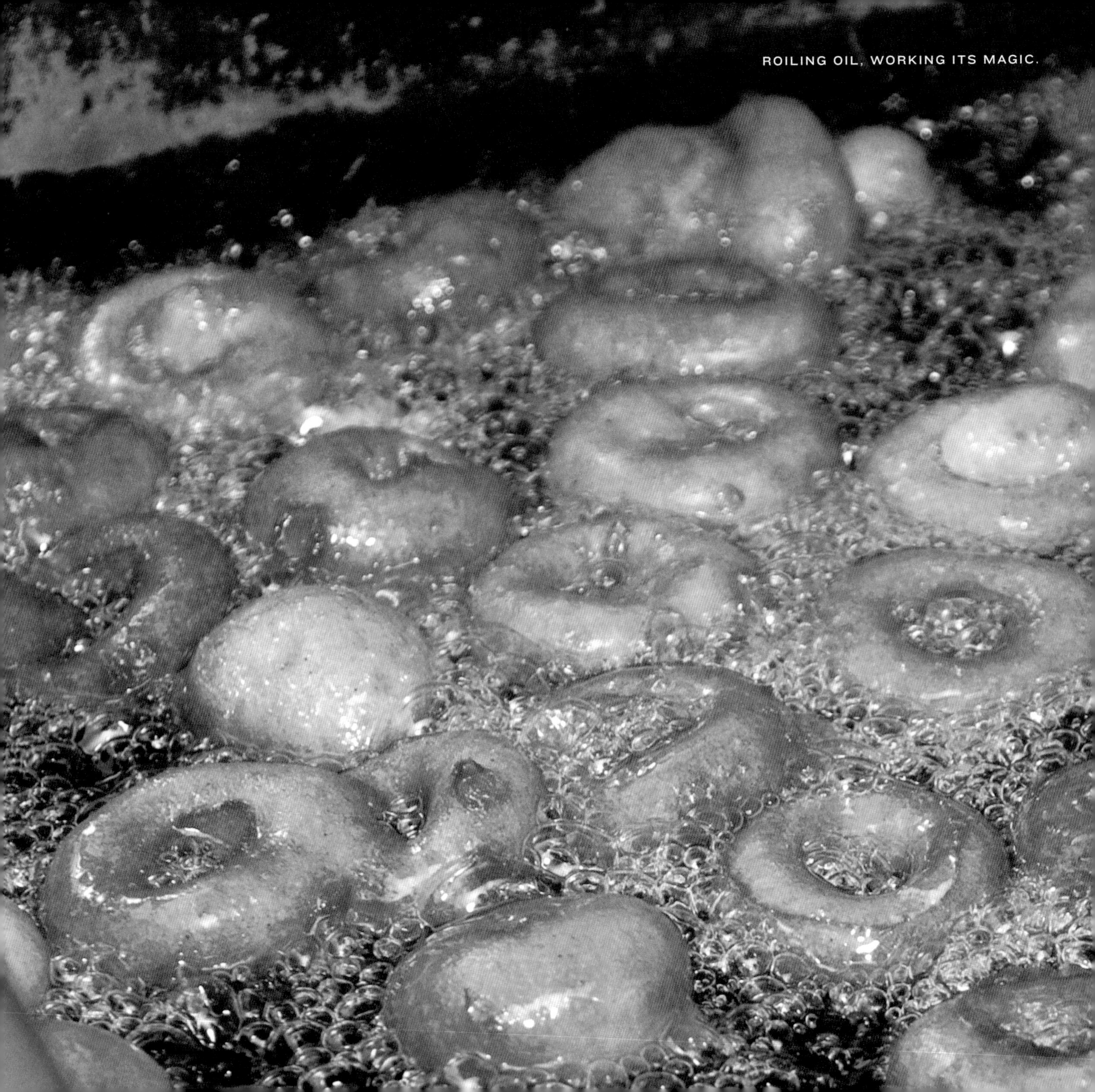

ROILING OIL, WORKING ITS MAGIC.

MINNEAPOLIS:
ASPIRATIONS OF WORLD-CLASS STREET FOOD

Minneapolis and, to a lesser degree, neighboring St. Paul, represent a certain kind of American city. Such a city aims to be world-class, a designation that usually translates as urbane, prosperous, and purposefully multicultural.

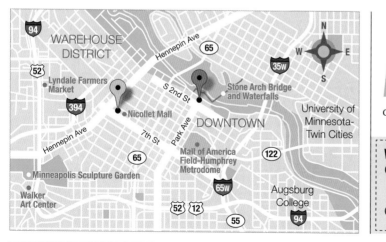

WHERE THE TRUCKS ARE:

⚲ Look for trucks at the Mill City farmers' market: S 2nd Street near Park Avenue.

⚲ Also check Nicollet Mall

A spirational folk apply a number of measures to determine whether a city makes the world-class cut: Airport take-offs and landings. Number of international cities the airport serves. Fortune 500 companies with local headquarters. And, the big banana, the Olympics.

Of late, other measures have come to the fore. Like street food. As in, "Does your world-class city have a diverse and thriving street food scene?" As in, "Can you walk out the door of your office, bypass the corner *pho* truck, and grab a world-class *dosa* from a bicycle-propelled cart?"

If the answer is no, then in the world-class city competition your city has failed. Online message boards are choked with plaints from Seattle residents who compare that city's street food scene to Portland, their sibling to the south, and come away with the sagging realization that Seattle may not be a world-class city.

In Atlanta, Georgia, a city long obsessed with its status on the world stage, my friend and colleague Christiane Lauterbach has been working to catalyze a street food scene by way of an effort she calls, simply, Atlanta Food Carts. Meanwhile, in Canada in early 2009, Toronto made a play to become a world-class city when it introduced a pilot program, Toronto A La Cart. The plan was to place carts selling a diversity of foods at different locations around the city. By the close of 2009 the program had been declared a failure and was being retooled. "It was embarrassing," Toronto chef Roger Mooking wrote in an editorial. "In a city where half of the population was born in a different country and 30 percent of our 2.6 million citizens do not speak either English or French as a first language, one would hope that Toronto's street food would reflect that cultural diversity; and in abundance."

The Twin Cities of Minneapolis and St. Paul labor under the same burden. They aspire to be world class. Truth is, by many measures, they are already world class. But not as measured by street food. The problems are long established.

While researching a story for the magazine *The Heavy Table,* Andy Sturdevant discovered that in 1902, St. Paul virtually outlawed street food. The "Pharisees of the St. Paul Council" have driven

the sandwich and hot tamale vendors from the street corners, *Minneapolis Tribune* columnist Ralph Wheelock wrote at the time. "Just how the odor of fried ham could contaminate the highly moral atmosphere of the capital city does not appear in the ordinance." (A few years before, Minneapolis had taken similar steps.)

Over the ensuing century, the laws have loosened a bit—especially in St. Paul, where Curbside, an Airstream food trailer plastered with the slogan "don't make me pull this kitchen over" sometimes plies the streets, dishing short rib sandwiches and garlic fries.

The answer to the street food woes of the Twin Cities may come from farmers. Or, more accurately, from farmers' markets. One day, at the Mill City Farmers' Market, I took my place in a long line that snaked from a polka-dotted red-and-white trailer known as the Chef Shack.

Surrounding me were market vendors selling green-hued wild rice that smelled like sassafras, and pleasantly stinky raw milk cheese known

as fish bait. (In the world of the food geek, you can't get much sexier than that.) But the biggest commotion was coming from that trailer with the red polka dots, where Minneapolis citizens, starved for street food, clamored for French toast and Indian-spiced doughnuts, pulled pork nachos, and bison burgers capped with nettle butter.

The scene was hopeful. It reminded me of the market in San Francisco where I first came upon the RoliRoti truck peddling rotisserie-cooked *porchetta.* It reminded me of the scene at the Brooklyn Flea, in New York City, where I jockeyed back and forth between a lobster roll guy and the kimchi hot dog chick.

And then I reached the front of the line. The food that emerged from the window of the trailer looked like world-class food. And it tasted like world-class food. Call me an optimist, but I'm thinking that Chef Shack will, prove a catalyst for Minneapolis's world-class street food revival.

From top to bottom: **The Magic Bus Cafe. Cardamom doughnut delights. Street theater.**

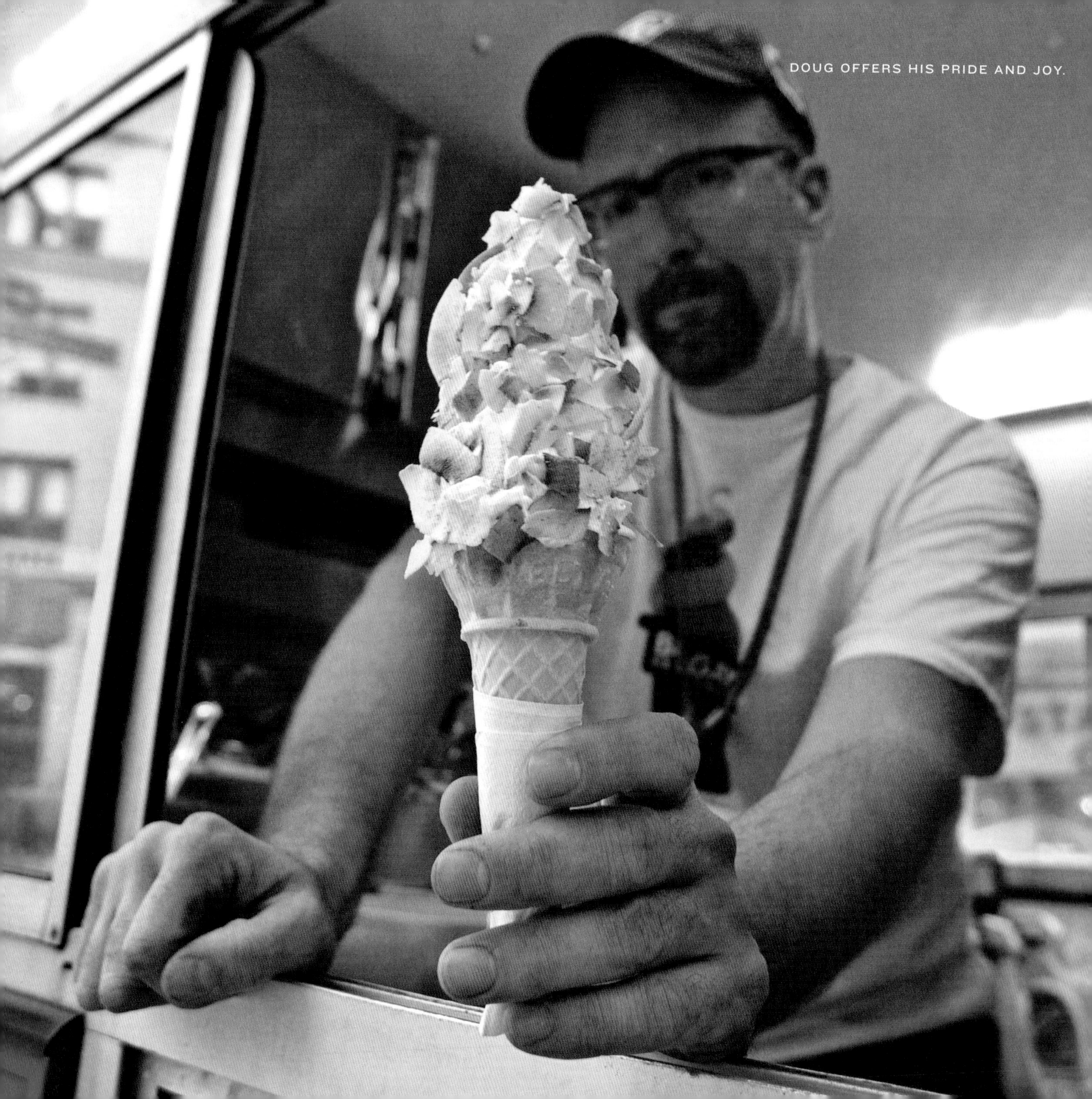

DOUG OFFERS HIS PRIDE AND JOY.

CHEATER SOFT-SERVE ICE CREAM

WHEN DOUG QUINT AND BRYAN PETROFF of the Big Gay Ice Cream Truck were developing their toppings, they tested recipes with a kind of homemade soft-serve ice cream, which they made in their apartment kitchen. Inspired by their efforts, I made some, too.

Rainbow signage defines both the ethic and the eats.

MAKES 4 CUPS

FOR THE ICE CREAM

3 cups vanilla ice cream, slightly softened

I cup whipped cream (see Note)

2 to 4 tablespoons chocolate syrup (optional)

FOR THE TOPPINGS (OPTIONAL)

Toasted Curried Coconut (recipe follows)

Wasabi Pea Dust Topping (page 272)

Olive Oil and Sea Salt Topping (page 273)

Scoop the ice cream into the bowl of an electric stand mixer. Add the whipped cream and, if you like, the chocolate syrup and beat until thoroughly blended. Cover the ice cream tightly, either by placing it in a container with a lid or by wrapping the bowl several times in plastic wrap. Place the ice cream in the freezer for at least 12 hours; it will still be slightly soft after that time. Then, it's ready to eat, with or without toppings.

NOTE: To make 1 cup of whipped cream, pour 1/2 cup cold, heavy (whipping) cream into a bowl. Add 1 tablespoon sugar and 1/4 teaspoon vanilla. Beat with an electric mixer on high until stiff peaks form, about 2 minutes.

Toasted Curried Coconut

HERE THE INSPIRATION is Southeast Asia. Doug and Bryan prefer large flakes of coconut over the shredded kind. They say the big flakes have more visual impact, plus you get a stronger, chewier coconut taste. For the recipe, they use a slightly sweet curry powder (Doug and Bryan like Whole Foods house blend muchi curry).

MAKES 2 CUPS

2 cups large-flake coconut

I tablespoon curry powder, or more to taste

Heat a dry skillet over medium-low heat (do not use a nonstick skillet for this). Add the coconut, then shake the curry powder on top and stir to coat. Taste for seasoning, adding more curry powder, if desired. Cook the coconut until it takes on a golden brown hue, about 2 minutes,

Wasabi pea dust is both vibrant and spicy.

stirring often to avoid burning the coconut. Transfer the curried coconut to a pan or heat-proof bowl to cool before using it as a topping for ice cream. The curried coconut can be stored in an airtight container for about 2 weeks.

Wasabi Pea Dust Topping

BELIEVE IT OR NOT, this topping from Doug and Bryan isn't as spicy as you would think. The wasabi's heat, combined with a little bit of salt and crunch, makes a great complement to smooth, cold ice cream.

MAKES ABOUT I CUP

I cup wasabi peas

Pulverize the wasabi peas in a coffee mill, spice grinder, or food processor. (This will be loud, says Doug—so loud that your cat will go into hiding.) Bryan likes to make the consistency as close to powder as possible. Doug leaves a little texture and crunch. Use a sifter to sprinkle the wasabi topping on ice cream. The topping can be stored indefinitely in an airtight container.

SONGS FOR ICE CREAM TRUCKS: Mister Softee Steps Down

WHEN I LISTEN to *Songs for Ice Cream Trucks,* the album by Michael Hearst, I hear carnival music. I hear gypsy dirges. I hear a theremin, maybe a tuba. I hear the summertime rattle and trill of a thousand ice cream trucks circling the suburbs of America, selling orange Creamsicles. Hearst's band, One Ring Zero, entered my consciousness when they cut an album, *As Smart as We Are,* featuring lyrics from novelists like Margaret Atwood, Jonathan Lethem, and Rick Moody. The songs were playful. And they were smart.

Soon Michael—who honed this sort of approach in college when, for his senior recital, he wrote a choral piece that relied upon a recitation of grocery store names—was casting about for his next opus. An ode to ice cream trucks made good sense, he told me, because "Who isn't damn sick of hearing the Mister Softee truck play that one song?"

Out of that simple question came an album of thirteen songs, from the upbeat "The Popsicle Parade" to the ponderous "What's Your Favorite Flavor?" to the downbeat "Where Do Ice Cream Trucks Go in the Winter?" Consider it the official soundtrack to the book you now hold in your hands.

Turns out Michael is not alone. Queen Frostine, a vampy New York City collective of female ice cream peddlers, cut some music, too. Not a whole album, but a single. Playing flute on "Ice Cream Girl," a rap, is Andrea Fisher, known to Queen Frostine fans as Fluterscooter. (Like Michael, she's an honest musician whose résumé includes collaborations with 50 Cent and Ian Anderson of Jethro Tull fame.) Genevieve Belleveau, known in the Frostine world as Punky B, contributed the lyrics.

BIG GAY ICE CREAM TRUCK

DOUG QUINT AND BRYAN PETROFF are the men behind the Big Gay Ice Cream Truck. Bryan works a corporate job. Doug is a professional musician in the process of completing his Ph.D. in bassoon performance.

It all began this way: On spring, summer, and fall days, Doug checked out a truck from an ice cream truck depot in Greenpoint, Brooklyn. The depot assigned him a parking place in Manhattan. And he fixed a Big Gay Ice Cream Truck banner to the side of the truck.

The boys vend soft-serve ice cream accessorized with a range of flavors concocted in their apartment kitchen. Toasted coconut, ground wasabi peas—that sort of thing. On the day I tried their olive oil cone, Doug was pouring La Belle Excuse, a Greek green olive oil, over their soft serves.

He was also offering instructions on how to eat a Choinkwich, the flagship BGICT creation. "Treat it like a delicate flower," Doug told me, as I bit into the sandwich of chocolate pinwheel cookies, chocolate ice cream, and bacon chips. "Be gentle, you heathen, be gentle," he said as I savored the lovely interplay of sweet pork and sweeter cream.

Olive Oil and Sea Salt Topping

SOFT-SERVE ICE CREAM is a blank slate, the BGICT boys say: "Since the olive oil and sea salt topping is the star, the thing to keep in mind is quality. On the truck we only use high-quality oil and salt. It will cost more, but you don't need to use much, and remember you are trying to spotlight the taste of the toppings."

For the salt, they recommend Maldon sea salt, a flaky salt that is relatively easy to find. They taste tested different olive oils and realized the best for ice cream are not the earthier oils but the grassy, green finishing ones. Their favorite brand is Bariani, from a small, family-run business near Sacramento, California. Other oils they recommend are La Belle Excuse, from Greece, and Ranieri, from Italy. Add some crunch with a topping of toasted pine nuts.

MAKES 1 SERVING

1 tablespoon high-quality olive oil

Pinch of Maldon sea salt, or another flaky salt

1 cup vanilla soft-serve ice cream (page 271)

2 tablespoons toasted pine nuts (optional; see Note)

Drizzle the olive oil and crush the salt between your fingers as you sprinkle it over the ice cream. To distribute the flavorings, stir them into the ice cream before eating.

NOTE: To toast the nuts, heat a dry pan over medium-low heat (do not use a nonstick skillet for this). Add the pine nuts and heat them until lightly toasted, fragrant, and golden brown, 3 to 5 minutes. Shake the pan often to avoid burning the pine nuts. Do not overcook them or you'll have a mouthful of cinders. Let the pine nuts cool before sprinkling them over the ice cream.

WHIFFIES FRIED PIE PASTRY

WITH COCONUT CREAM PIE FILLING

IN TEXTURE, the dough of Whiffies Fried Pies recalls an elephant ear served straight from a trailer at an idealized county fair. To get the best results with this recipe, inspired by Gregg Abbott's work, keep your eye on the oil temperature.

The masked pie bandit cavorts in Portland.

MAKES 12 FRIED PIES

3 cups all-purpose flour, plus flour for dusting the work surface

2 teaspoons baking powder

I teaspoon salt

I teaspoon granulated sugar

3/4 cup lard or vegetable shortening

3/4 cup milk

Coconut Cream Pie Filling (recipe follows)

2 quarts vegetable oil, for frying the pies

1 Combine the flour, baking powder, salt, and sugar in a large mixing bowl. Add the lard or shortening and, using a pastry blender or fork, cut the fat into the flour mixture until it resembles coarse crumbs. Sprinkle the milk over the flour mixture, gently incorporating it with your hands just until the dough comes together to form a ball. Divide the dough in half, wrap each half with plastic wrap, and refrigerate it for about 1 hour.

2 Roll out one piece of the dough on a lightly floured work surface to a thickness of 1/4 inch. Using a small plate or saucer, trace circles to cut out disks 4 to 5 inches in diameter. Repeat with the second piece of dough.

3 Place 2 tablespoons of coconut cream filling in the center of one half of a circle of dough. Wet the inside edge of the dough with a little water and fold the other half of the dough over the filling to make a half-moon shape. Crimp the edge of the dough together with a fork to seal it well. Repeat with the remaining circles of dough and filling.

4 Heat the oil in a deep fryer or Dutch oven over high heat until a deep fry thermometer attached to the side of the pot registers 375°F. Working in batches and being careful not to overcrowd the pot, carefully add the pies to the hot oil. Cook the pies for 2 to 3 minutes, turn them over and continue cooking them until golden brown, about 2 minutes longer. Using a slotted spoon, transfer the pies to paper towels to drain.

Coconut Cream Pie Filling

THIS RECIPE, from Gregg, is unapologetically low-rent, by which I mean it's an honest reflection of how cooks across America often adapt traditional recipes to suit the constraints of time and commitment.

MAKES ENOUGH FILLING FOR 12 FRIED PIES

1/2 cup canned coconut cream

1 quart nondairy whipped topping

4 packages (3.4 ounces each) instant vanilla pudding

8 ounces shredded unsweetened coconut

In a large bowl, fold the coconut cream into the whipped topping. Add the instant pudding and whip until thick, about 3 minutes. Add the shredded coconut and stir to incorporate.

Those are crescents of coconut and pastry—not feet with way too many toes.

LAST SEEN: Hawthorne Boulevard and SE 12th Avenue, Portland, Oregon

WHIFFIES FRIED PIES

GREGG ABBOTT, the young man who stands tall by the fryer well in this trailer each night, traces the origins of deep-fried pocket pies to Oklahoma and Texas. He also mentions Argentina and Colombia, where empanadas are beloved. And he factors in the influence of his adopted hometown of Portland, too. (A hand-drawn sign tacked to the cart reads "Let us know if you want your pie cooked in the vegan fryer.")

Gregg's trailer is a repurposed model that looks like it was serving the state fair circuit until recently. Plastered on the side is his logo, an anthropomorphic pie person wearing a Zorro-style mask. Crescent-shaped pies stuffed with coconut cream or marionberries define the sweet end of the spectrum, with chicken pot pie and franks and beans on the savory end.

SHAKER LEMON PIE

IT'S IMPORTANT TO SLICE the lemons as thinly as you can when making these pies. If you have a mandoline, use it. And since lemon is front and center in Natalie Galatzer's recipe, source the best fruit you can get your hands on. Natalie specifies Meyer lemons, but hey, they grow in her neighborhood. You could get away with ordinary grocery store lemons.

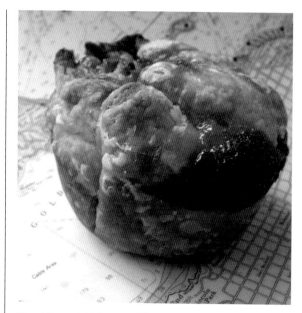
Three bites and this beauty will be gone.

Natalie plus bike, about to hit the streets.

Read about Bike Basket Pies on page 31.

MAKES 12 CUPCAKE-SIZE PIES

2 lemons, preferably Meyer

2 cups extra-fine sugar, plus 2 tablespoons sugar, for sprinkling over the pies

4 large eggs

1 teaspoon salt

Natalie's Pie Dough (page 31; see Note)

Flour, for rolling out the pie dough

1 Rinse and pat the lemons dry with paper towels. Cut the ends off of the lemons, quarter them lengthwise, and remove the seeds. Slice the lemon quarters crosswise into paper-thin slices. Place the lemon slices in a nonmetallic mixing bowl, toss them with the 2 cups of sugar, and let macerate, covered with plastic wrap, for at least 1 hour, possibly overnight, until the sugar liquefies.

2 Beat the eggs in a mixing bowl with the salt and add them to the lemon and sugar mixture. Set aside.

3 Preheat the oven to 425°F.

4 Divide the 2 disks of dough into 6 equal pieces each. Using a floured rolling pin, roll out each on a lightly floured work surface to a thickness of ¼ inch. Add a little flour if necessary to prevent the dough from sticking. Gently press the rounds of dough into the wells of one 12-cupcake, or two 6-cupcake, dark-surfaced cupcake tins. The dough rounds will extend up the side and over the edge of the wells. Place

the cupcake tin in the refrigerator for 5 to 10 minutes for the dough to chill.

5 Spoon the filling into the cupcake wells, dividing it evenly among them. Place a cup of water close by, wet your fingers, and fold the dough over the top of each pie, pinching the edges together to prevent the dough from sinking into the lemon filling. Wet your fingers frequently. Sprinkle the top of each pie with some of the 2 tablespoons of sugar. Refrigerate the pies for about 15 minutes.

6 Bake the pies for 15 minutes, then lower the temperature to 350°F and bake the pies 20 to 30 minutes longer. The pies are done when the crust is a deep golden brown.

7 Remove the pies from the oven and immediately slide a knife between the edge of the tin and the crust and twist the pies to loosen any sugar that would cause them to stick. Place the tin on a wire rack to cool for 5 minutes. Remove the pies from the tin and transfer them to parchment paper to cool completely. The pies should sit for an hour or so at room temperature before you put your paws on them.

NOTE: Remove the pie dough from the refrigerator about 15 minutes before you plan to roll it out. If the dough has been frozen, transfer it from the freezer to the refrigerator 4 to 5 hours before making the pies.

THEATER OF THE STREET:
Burlesque Tacos and Bollywood Paneer

STREET FOOD AT ITS BEST is street theater. It's a diversion, a quick bite, delivered with panache. I'm thinking of Flair Taco in the Fremont neighborhood of Seattle, Washington, where I first glimpsed the burlesque taco phenomenon, complete with sword swallowers. I'm thinking of the ladies who run Chef Shack in Minneapolis, who for very special events book hula hoopers to work their roof.

I'm thinking, too, of I Dream of Weenie in Nashville, Tennessee, where Alisa Martin has been known to wear a hot dog tiara while vamping to the 1930s song "Frankfurter Sandwiches." But mostly I'm thinking about the Fojol Bros. of the Merlindia truck, doing business, for the moment, on the streets of Washington, D.C., in a deliriously accessorized 1965 Chevy stepside van.

The Fojols' food—chicken curry over basmati rice, potatoes and cauliflower, spinach, and cheese—comes from a D.C. area restaurant that the brothers won't disclose. Their shtick is a queer mashup of Bollywood and vaudeville. Wearing bright yellow, orange, and blue jumpsuits, scooting down the sidewalks in roller skates, hip shaking to a hurdy-gurdy of carnival music that sounds like it's been channeled through a disco synthesizer, the Fojols, two of whom are real brothers, work the truck under their adopted Merlindian names of Ababa Du, Dingo, Dewpee, and Kipoto.

To lick a mango lassipop and watch the brothers work as potential customers reel and then get reeled in, is to glimpse the transformative possibilities of life on the street.

MY LIFE AS A LUCKY DOG

IF, AFTER READING THESE PAGES and cooking some of these recipes, you get the notion to run your own food cart, truck, or caboose, allow me to challenge that notion. Street eating is an enjoyable activity. (So is cooking at home, inspired by the street.) But cooking and serving on the street is tough. Regulations are onerous. Profit margins are ridiculously thin. Consumers—and not a few officers of the law—too often treat street vendors like criminals instead of small-business people. Work the street and you get a new perspective on the concept of personal space. Work the street and you realize that the weather packs wallops, no matter the season.

- -

I know a bit about street life. A very little bit. I've tried to live it myself. In the introduction of this book, I detailed a failed effort to run a hot dog cart on the courthouse square in my hometown of Oxford, Mississippi. In the story that closes this book, I lay bare my inspiration. Read it as a diary of three hot dog-fueled days in New Orleans. Or think of it as a glimpse at the sometimes absurd reality of a life lived on the street. The choice is yours.

Lucky Dog Dalliance

"ANYBODY CAN BE A LUCKY DOGS VENDOR," Jerry Strahan promised me. "We've had transvestites, transsexuals, homosexuals, and just plain old eccentrics. You name it. We've employed them all. And as long as they stay somewhat sober, they work out fine. Almost anybody can sell hot dogs down in the French Quarter." But, as a pall crossed his jowly face, Jerry, who manages the crew who vend for Lucky Dogs, reconsidered. "Well, okay, anybody but mimes—mimes just won't work out! Anybody else, we'll take them. Hell, we could even put you to work."

Standing amid the clutter and clamor of the dank, New Orleans offices of Lucky Dogs, I did not take the offer of employment seriously. I had come not in search of a place to work, but to see the workplace of Ignatius J. Reilly, the corpulent, flatulent, and overeducated antihero of *A Confederacy of Dunces,* John Kennedy Toole's Pulizer Prize-winning novel. Like Dante Rivera of Dante's Inferno Dogs (page 194), who read the book when he was nineteen, and who, inspired, went on to open his own fleet of hot dog stands in Seattle, I had come to get a handle on the life of Ignatius, the character who, when forced by his mother to find a job, sought solace in the employ of "Paradise Vendors," Toole's fictional equivalent of Lucky Dogs.

With that in mind, Jerry offered to put me to work for two or three nights around New Year's Eve. That's how I came to stand in the heart of the French Quarter at the corner of Bourbon and St. Louis Streets, wearing a red-and-white striped shirt and an official-issue Lucky Dogs cap, listening to a vendor's harangue: "Drink up, you slobs! You know the routine. Drink. Stumble. Dance. Eat a Lucky Dog. Go home...."

"LUCKY DOGS. GET YOUR LUCKY DOGS HERE. BUY ONE AT THE REGULAR PRICE, GET A SECOND ONE AT THE SAME PRICE!"

Hot Dog Intern

IT WAS A LITTLE after 9 o'clock on a frigid Tuesday night and a vendor named Adolf was upset. With New Year's Eve only a day away, he had hoped to be raking in big commissions on the sale of quarter-pound Lucky Dogs. Instead, business was down. According to Adolf, the crowd was too sober. Lucky Dogs vendors pray for drunks like farmers pray for rain. Drunks do not normally debate the relative merits of paying $4.25 for a turgid tube of offal meat, fished from the steamy depths of a hot dog-shaped cart and cradled in a gummy bun that threatens to collapse under a molten mountain of mustard, ketchup, chili, relish, and onions. For drunks, Lucky Dogs are not so much food as fuel, and drunks need fuel if they are to survive a night of debauchery in the French Quarter, an area that Ignatius, perhaps the most famous vendor ever to peddle a dog, claimed "houses every vice that man has ever conceived in his wildest aberrations, including, I would imagine, several modern variants made possible through the wonders of science."

With business still at a crawl, Adolf asked me to look after things as he went in search of a bar that would let him use its bathroom. I began poking around inside the cart. Self-contained restaurants of a sort, Lucky Dogs carts are equipped with sinks, steamer compartments, iceboxes, propane tanks, and prep tables—all enclosed within a 7-foot-long, 650-pound metal wienie on wheels. As I peered into the inner workings, I began to understand Ignatius's befuddlement when he exclaimed, "These carts are like Chinese puzzles. I suspect that I will continually be pulling at the wrong opening."

When Adolf returned, I wandered up the street in search of a bit more on-the-job training. At the corner of Bourbon and St. Peter, I found Rick. Pleasant and well spoken, Rick was the antithesis of Adolf. As drunks stumbled out of the Krazy Korner bar, Rick jingled the change in his pocket and called out: "Lucky Dogs. Get your Lucky Dogs here. Buy one at the regular price, get a second one at the same price!" While we were talking, a black man in a white satin jumpsuit stopped in front of us and screamed out, apropos of nothing, "That Tom Jones is a bad white mother!" His attempt at doing a split in the middle of the street was unsuccessful. When he toppled, I walked on.

At the corner of Bourbon and Orleans, David was sporting a soiled Santa hat and barking like a carny. "I don't want your first born!" he shouted. "I certainly don't want your ex-wife! And I probably don't want your college grades! But I do want your tips!" Like many of the twenty-odd vendors working Bourbon Street on a typical night, David saw Lucky Dogs as a way station, not an occupation. "I'm a commercial fisherman by trade," he said. "But I've done my share of street vending. Worked the carnival circuit, too. I love it out here.... Out here I'm just David. No past, no future—just passing through."

It was now about eleven o'clock. I was enjoying the spectacle, but not doing much work. Most carts were already fully staffed by two vendors. Fortunately, soon after I left the corner of Bourbon and Orleans, I met up with Jerry. He told me that Alice was in need of help and was willing to share her cart with me for the next few nights.

Alice Rules

WHEN I FIRST SAW ALICE, a woman of great girth and

great enthusiasms, she was standing at the corner of Bourbon and Conti, opening and closing the cart's steamer compartment, fanning wiener fumes across the street in hopes of luring passersby. She was having little luck. "It's still a little too early. They're drinking now, but they're not quite drunk enough. They'll come around; they've got to. . . . I only cleared sixty-five dollars yesterday," she said, a touch of desperation in her voice. "We've been waiting too long for this—suffering through December, waiting for New Year's and then Mardi Gras."

After more than fifteen years on the job, Alice knows the street. Over the course of the next few hours she showed me the ropes and mentally prepared me for what would happen the next night. "It's going to be hell on New Year's Eve," she warned. "This isn't a party; this is a job. And you damn well better treat it that way."

Alice ran a well-stocked cart. In addition to the company-issued condiments like mustard, ketchup, chili, onions, and relish, Alice offered pickled jalapeño peppers. And, for those in search of still more heat, Alice would douse a Lucky Dog with her own blend of hot sauce. During the lulls between customers Alice and I gazed at the slovenly promenade. The few customers we served retreated just a few feet before trying to stuff the oversize dogs in their mouths. I watched as chili and relish plopped from the back end of their buns and onto the sidewalk like dung from the business end of a horse. But, as one o'clock passed, the lulls became shorter. Soon a line had formed and the rush was on.

By two in the morning Alice and I were working as one. I made the dogs. She made the change. And when she flailed away at a gawky drunk who cursed me for being too slow, I tried to hold her back. Fortunately for the drunk, the crowd parted and he vanished into the lurch. Meanwhile, with the horde pressing down upon us, Alice and I scrambled to keep up with the orders. In a rush of syllables and slobber, two college freshmen, down to their last dollar, pleaded for a bun full of chili, and then, as if by divine intervention, scrounged together the $3.25 needed for a regular dog.

With my back to the crowd, I leaned into the cart, reached for the tub of relish, and began spooning it on their dog. I grabbed a pair of tongs and began to pile on a mess of onions. When the soberer of the two leaned in and mumbled "Gimme more chili on it, will ya?" I felt the spray of spittle and liquor on my nape. Rather than break the rhythm of work to wipe away his request, I ladled on the chili and turned to take the next order. Alice collected the clump of bills that he shoved in her face.

By half past two, our pockets were bulging from the night's take. When the pizza place across the street closed at three o'clock, we suddenly had six customers in line. "They've got no choice now!" Alice cried. "Now we've got them." We may well have had them, but thirty minutes later the street was starting to clear. At a quarter before four, Alice decided to call it a night. Ketchup splattered and bone tired, I headed on.

New Year's Eve

WHEN I ARRIVED at the corner of Bourbon and Conti, Alice was already on the job. Standing at the prow of the cart, she surveyed the crowd.

> I WATCHED AS CHILI AND RELISH PLOPPED FROM THE BACK END OF THEIR BUNS AND ONTO THE SIDEWALK LIKE DUNG FROM THE BUSINESS END OF A HORSE.

"It's coming," she warned. "I can just tell it's coming. Some little creep is going to piss me off and I'm going to have to whale on them. I've got too much at stake to put up with anything tonight!"

Though it was only eight, foot traffic on Bourbon Street was heavy. Friends locked arms and swayed down the street, sloshing their way through extinguished cigarettes, spilled daiquiris, discarded beers. Above it all rode mounted police patrols, searching the crowd for prone bodies, pickpockets, bare breasts.

Alice and I began laying in supplies for the night ahead. "No regular dogs tonight, honey.... They'll take what we give them," she said, dumping bag after bag of Lucky Dogs in the steamer. As I worked to stuff the packs of Evangeline Maid buns in the cart, Alice ran down the street for a half pint of bourbon.

In the five minutes that Alice was gone, I sold five hot dogs—three alone to a pack of barely postpubescent kids. Alice returned and a dapper, seemingly sober young man wearing a black turtleneck and blue sunglasses approached the cart. When I asked for his order, he struck a match, then lit his entire pack with it and stood back to admire the flame. It flared and then fizzled. He stood transfixed. I asked again for his order, and he tried to hand me the blackened book of matches. When I let them fall to the street, he screamed, "Damn, that was pretty! Wasn't that pretty, hot dog man?" He walked off.

As the clock heaved toward midnight, we enjoyed a breather, although Alice took time to do business with a pack of young tap dancers who had been working the street for tips. After an evening of performance, their pockets were heavy with quarters and Alice cashed in a couple of twenty dollar bills with the smallest of the four, a cute, brown-eyed girl who looked like she should know more about Sesame Street than Bourbon Street.

I knocked back a finger or four of bourbon and began

cleaning up around our cart. With neither a trash can nor a cop in sight, I swept everything—half-eaten hot dogs, broken beer bottles, sticky plastic drink cups, and gaudy plastic necklaces—under a police car parked hard on our bumper.

At the stroke of midnight I dropped my broom and joined the drunken revelry in the center of Bourbon Street. As the sky above the French Quarter blossomed with fireworks, I searched for someone to kiss. But no one wanted to kiss the wienie man. My red-and-white striped uniform, smeared with mustard and ketchup had, in the words of Ignatius, "stamped me as a vendor, an untouchable." Before I had a chance to feel sorry for myself, Alice called me back to the cart. "They're coming now," she promised. "And if anybody messes with me, they're going to get it. I'm going to whale on them!"

In drunken droves, they came. Screaming, yelling, banging their fists on the cart, their mouths sticky and stained purple, orange, and blue, they crowded around us, shouting orders and demanding our attention. "Get your butts in line or you get no dogs," I screeched, my voice tinged with panic.

For the next four hours Alice and I crammed Lucky Dogs into buns and slapped change into palms. But no matter how fast we worked, they just kept coming. By two in the morning we were out of relish. And still they came. At three o'clock we tossed out the warming rack where the dogs usually rest and plunged a few more bags of meat directly into the steamer.

As the line backed up, tempers grew short. When a smarmy kid reached into the cart to grab a napkin, Alice bellowed, "Keep your hands out of my cart or I'll kick your ass!" When a bullnecked drunk with a sneer on his face spilled beer on my feet and questioned whether the Lucky Dog I made for him was worth the price, profanity spewed from my mouth like water from a fire hose. He took the dog. I pocketed the money. And the night rolled on.

Over and Out

BY FOUR THE LINE was gone. By half past four, we were out of ketchup and down to three dogs in the steamer. Alice said she had had enough. Though some of the other vendors would stay on the street until past dawn, we packed up and began the long slog back to the shop.

Across Bourbon, down Royal, and out of the French Quarter I pushed the top-heavy cart down a one-way street and into oncoming traffic, swerving to avoid open car doors and potholes. With Alice at my side, shouting directions, we crossed six lanes of speeding taxicabs at Canal Street. Halfway through the intersection, the cart fishtailed and I almost lost control. Two blocks later we took a hard left onto Gravier Street and gathered speed to push the cart up the ramp and into the shop.

My first attempt at making it up the slight incline failed when the seven-foot-long metal wienie careened to the left and gouged yet another hole in the narrow doorframe. By the time I stopped its recoil, the cart had rolled into the middle of the street. Exhausted, agitated, and close to quitting, I began the second push just as Alice leaned over and whispered in my ear. "You were great out there. You didn't take anything from anybody. You're just like the rest of us. You can come back and work a cart with me any time."

And the cart cleared the door.

CONVERSION TABLES

PLEASE NOTE that all conversions are approximate but close enough to be useful when converting from one system to another.

OVEN TEMPERATURES

FAHRENHEIT	GAS MARK	CELSIUS
250	1/2	120
275	1	140
300	2	150
325	3	160
350	4	180
375	5	190
400	6	200
425	7	220
450	8	230
475	9	240
500	10	260

NOTE: Reduce the temperature by 20°C (68°F) for fan-assisted ovens.

WEIGHT CONVERSIONS

US/UK	METRIC	US/UK	METRIC
1/2 oz	15 g	7 oz	200 g
1 oz	30 g	8 oz	250 g
1 1/2 oz	45 g	9 oz	275 g
2 oz	60 g	10 oz	300 g
2 1/2 oz	75 g	11 oz	325 g
3 oz	90 g	12 oz	350 g
3 1/2 oz	100 g	13 oz	375 g
4 oz	125 g	14 oz	400 g
5 oz	150 g	15 oz	450 g
6 oz	175 g	1 lb	500 g

LIQUID CONVERSIONS

U.S.	IMPERIAL	METRIC
2 tbs	1 fl oz	30 ml
3 tbs	1 1/2 fl oz	45 ml
1/4 cup	2 fl oz	60 ml
1/3 cup	2 1/2 fl oz	75 ml
1/3 cup + 1 tbs	3 fl oz	90 ml
1/3 cup + 2 tbs	3 1/2 fl oz	100 ml
1/2 cup	4 fl oz	125 ml
2/3 cup	5 fl oz	150 ml
3/4 cup	6 fl oz	175 ml
3/4 cup + 2 tbs	7 fl oz	200 ml
1 cup	8 fl oz	250 ml
1 cup + 2 tbs	9 fl oz	275 ml
1 1/4 cups	10 fl oz	300 ml
1 1/3 cups	11 fl oz	325 ml
1 1/2 cups	12 fl oz	350 ml
1 2/3 cups	13 fl oz	375 ml
1 3/4 cups	14 fl oz	400 ml
1 3/4 cups + 2 tbs	15 fl oz	450 ml
2 cups (1 pint)	16 fl oz	500 ml
2 1/2 cups	20 fl oz (1 pint)	600 ml
3 3/4 cups	1 1/2 pints	900 ml
4 cups	1 3/4 pints	1 liter

APPROXIMATE EQUIVALENTS

1 stick butter = 8 tbs = 4 oz = 1/2 cup = 115 g

1 cup all-purpose presifted flour = 4.7 oz

1 cup granulated sugar = 8 oz = 220 g

1 cup (firmly packed) brown sugar = 6 oz = 220g to 230 g

1 cup confectioners' sugar = 4 1/2 oz = 115 g

1 cup honey or syrup = 12 oz

1 cup grated cheese = 4 oz

1 cup dried beans = 6 oz

1 large egg = about 2 oz or about 3 tbs

1 egg yolk = about 1 tbs

1 egg white = about 2 tbs

INDEX

Graham crackers, in s'mores, 262–64
Grapefruit fizz, 73
Gravy:
  Portland *poutine*, 11
  sausage, and waffles, 45
  Taiwanese pork sauce, 122
Green beans, in *ejotes* and egg tacos, 86–88
Greens:
  eggs and, 74–75
  with turkey necks, 113
Grilled cheese:
  cheeseasaurus, 172
  cheeseburger, 198–99
  mac and cheese sandwiches, 170–71
The Grilled Cheese Grill (Portland, Oreg.), 198
The Grilled Cheese Truck (Venice, Calif.), 20, 169–70
Grill 'Em All (Los Angeles, Calif.), 200
Guacamole:
  salsa verde, 83
  sauce, 193
El Güero Canelo (Tucson, Ariz.), 189, 190–92
Güero chiles, in *toritos*, 134–35

H

Habanero mint sauce, 168
Halal food, 118
Ham:
  croque monsieur "tacos," 52–53
  cubano sandwiches, 158–59
Ham croquetas, 21
Harissa, Fliphappy, 63
Harper, Andy, 2
Haute Texan Tacos (Houston, Tex.), 227
Hawaiian flavors: Spam *musubi*, 102–3
Hearst, Michael, 272
Heavy Table, The (Sturdevant), 269
High Noon Quesadillas, 241–43
Hoagies:
  falafel and egg, 92–94
  scrapple, egg, and provolone, 89
Hoisin sauce, spicy, 239
Holy Cacao (Austin, Tex.), 259–64
Horchata, cheater's, 217
Hot dog embellishments:
  adzuki chili, 186
  basil aioli, 181–82
  crispy fried onions, 182
  fennel slaw, 179–80
  fire relish, 185
  garlic beet sauerkraut, 187
  guacamole sauce, 193
  jalapeño salsa, 192
  psychedelic relish, 185
  red onion in vinegar, 193
Hot dogs, 174–95
  Boston Speed's, 176–77
  California dogs, 181–82
  chicken dogs, Dante's, 194
  Dogtown Dogs, 178–80
  Meet Me in the Morning Dogs, 183–84

New York City–centric history of, 182
  Sonoran-style, 191–92
Hot sauce, Sriracha, 95
Hotteok (peanut rice pancakes), 58–59
Houston, Tex., 226–27
  commissaries in, 88
  Jarro Cafe, 224–25
  Melissa's Roasted Corn, 128–29
  Refresqueria Rio Verde, 247–48
  Tacos Mayra, 248
  taco trucks and buses in, 226–27, 235
  Taqueria Las Palmitas, 86–88
  El Ultimo Taco, 80–81, 83
El Huarache Loco (San Francisco, Calif.), 166
Huevos con chorizo breakfast burritos, 77
Huitlacoche, empanadas *de*, 24–25

I

Ice cream:
  olive oil and sea salt topping for, 273
  soft-serve, cheater, 271–73
  toasted curried coconut topping for, 271–72
  wasabi pea dust topping for, 272
India, street food in, 1
Indianapolis, Ind., Korean taco truck in, 208–9

In the World (Dara), 137
Italian flavors:
  chickpea and delicata sandwiches, 149–51
  olive oil and sea salt topping, 273
  porchetta, 164–66

J

Jackson, Frank, 112
Jackson, Tenn., roadside barbecue stand in, 101
Jalapeño(s):
  pickled carrots and, 230
  salsa, 192
Jamaican flavors:
  meat patties, 32–33
  sloppy jerk chicken sandwiches, 161
  sloppy jerk pork sandwiches, 160–61
Jambalaya, roots, 138–39
Jamerica Restaurant (Madison, Wis.), 32–33, 133, 160–61
Jammy cookies, oatmeal, 254–55
Japanese flavors:
  chicken mugs, 114
  Thai chicken *karaage*, 108–9
  tuna *onigiri*, 124
  wasabi pea dust topping, 272
Jarro Cafe (Houston, Tex.), 224–25
Jazz Fest (New Orleans, La.), 37
Jerk:
  sloppy chicken sandwiches, 161